OXFORD STUDIES IN AFRICAN AFFAIRS

General Editors
JOHN D. HARGREAVES *and* GEORGE SHEPPERSON

LABOUR, RACE, AND COLONIAL RULE

THE COPPERBELT
FROM 1924 TO INDEPENDENCE

LABOUR, RACE, AND COLONIAL RULE

The Copperbelt from 1924 to Independence

BY

ELENA L. BERGER

CLARENDON PRESS · OXFORD

1974

Oxford University Press, Ely House, London, W.1

GLASGOW NEW YORK TORONTO MELBOURNE WELLINGTON
CAPE TOWN IBADAN NAIROBI DAR ES SALAAM LUSAKA ADDIS ABABA
DELHI BOMBAY CALCUTTA MADRAS KARACHI LAHORE DACCA
KUALA LUMPUR SINGAPORE HONG KONG TOKYO

ISBN 0 19 821690 4

© *Oxford University Press 1974*

*Printed in Great Britain by
Richard Clay (The Chaucer Press) Ltd
Bungay, Suffolk*

To my mother and father,
Kitty and Morris Plotnikoff

Preface

DURING the forty years from 1924 to 1964 in which Zambia was under colonial rule, the development of the mining industry on the Copperbelt brought rapid social change. A large labour force was required in a remote and almost uninhabited area of the country. The railway line and roads were extended, towns were built, and within a short time the Copperbelt became the centre of the territory's prosperity and of a highly profitable industry.

Progress created labour problems which commanded the attention of the mining companies and the Government. The labour force was divided in a manner resembling the industrial areas of South Africa. Migrant African workers were paid at relatively low rates, while a privileged group of Europeans protected its own position with strongly organized trade-unionism. European labour also made its opinions known through a powerful voice in settler politics. African workers, although less well organized, were capable of sporadic protests when their interests were at stake.

The most important labour questions on the Copperbelt concerned the place of black labour in relation to the established white labour force. Should African workers be settled near the mines, to become permanent urban residents? Could they be trained to take over 'white' jobs? By what standards and by what methods should their pay rates be determined? To a considerable extent the treatment of these issues reflected a specific colonial relation. The fact that copper is a strategic commodity, for which demand varies sharply in world markets, added another dimension to the evolution of policy. Fluctuating prices were outside the control of either the industry or the Government, and were liable to cause economic difficulties for any administration, colonial, or national.

The relationship between the mining companies and the colonial administration was an intricate one. The Government had overall responsibility, but the companies enjoyed a wide local discretion, and in industrial matters the Government found it convenient to respect the rights of management. Much of the material on which this study of Government and company policies is based was consulted at the Copper Industry Service Bureau in Kitwe, Zambia. The Bureau was

formerly the Chamber of Mines of Northern Rhodesia. I also examined provincial and secretariat records of the colonial administration which are held at the National Archives in Lusaka. A 'twenty
year rule' operated at the Archives, and I consulted files dated to
1947. As the records of the Copper Industry Service Bureau begin
during the Second World War and continue up to the present time,
these sources conveniently overlap. It was not possible to treat the
evolution of policy in the secretariat with the same detail for the
periods before and after 1947, but Copper Industry Service Bureau
records contained many references to the Government's attitude towards Copperbelt problems, from which an outline of official policy
in the later period can be drawn.

Throughout my research I benefited from the advice of Professor
J. A. Gallagher, who provided encouragement and criticism with a
fund of patience and good humour. I also appreciated the support of
the Warden and Fellows of Nuffield College, Oxford, and particularly
the assistance of Professor S. H. Frankel. The Fellows of Lady
Margaret Hall helped me to begin the research. The study was
financed by a Hayter Award, with a grant from the Administrators of
the Beit Fund for the collection of records in Africa.

In Zambia both the Anglo American Corporation and the Copper
Industry Service Bureau were more than generous with their assistance. I am indebted to Dennis Etheredge of the Anglo American
Corporation for his interest, and to Norreys Davis and F. Juretic of
the Copper Industry Service Bureau for the facilities they placed at
my disposal when I was working on the Bureau's records.

Many people with past and present experience of Copperbelt
affairs gave me interviews which supplemented the documentary
sources in a valuable way. I would like to take this opportunity of
thanking them all for the time they spared to comment, sometimes in
great detail, on events described in this book.

Dr. Trevor Coombe, Dr. David Mulford, and Peter Harries Jones
discussed the early outline of the study with me at length, and offered
invaluable guidance on the location of records. At a much later stage
D. A. H. Dady and Professor Jaap van Velsen read the manuscript
and provided helpful criticism.

The courtesy of the library staff at the National Archives of Zambia
deserves special mention. The staff of Rhodes House Library in
Oxford also provided willing assistance over a long period.

I was privileged to enjoy Jinny and Trevor Coombe's extensive hospitality in Lusaka and their friendship, together with that of Robert and Margaret Bates, is a happy memory of my stay in Zambia.

Henriette F. Berger joined me in the final checking of the text, and with her customary attention to detail saved me from several pitfalls. Any errors of fact or interpretation which remain are my responsibility entirely.

It is a pleasure to acknowledge the help and encouragement of members of my family, and above all the assistance of my husband Daniel in enabling me to finish this book.

E.L.B.

Baltimore, Md.
April 1973

Contents

List of Maps

Sources

THE prefix C.I.S.B. has been used in the footnotes to indicate material from the Copper Industry Service Bureau, Kitwe (formerly the Chamber of Mines of Northern Rhodesia). Material from the National Archives of Zambia is not specifically identified if the file number begins with an easily recognizable secretariat heading such as SEC/NAT (native affairs) or SEC/LAB (labour). The letters C.O. indicate Colonial Office files at the Public Record Office, London, unless an additional reference is made to the Foreign and Commonwealth Office Library in Great Smith Street, London.

Abbreviations

AMAX	American Metal Climax Inc.
A.M.U.	African Mineworkers' Union
A.N.C.	African National Congress
C.O.	Colonial Office
M.A.S.A.	Mines African Staff Association
M.I.F.	Miners' International Federation
M.O.S.S.A.	Mine Officials and Salaried Staff Association
M.W.U.	Mine Workers' Union
N.U.M.	National Union of Mineworkers
P.C.	Provincial Commissioner
RST	Rhodesian Selection Trust
T.U.C.	Trades Union Congress
U.N.I.P.	United National Independence Party
Z.A.N.C.	Zambia African National Congress

CHAPTER I

Introduction: The Copper Industry

WHEN the British Colonial Office took over the administration of Northern Rhodesia from the British South Africa Company in 1924 the potential of the country's copper deposits was unknown. The Company was glad to give up responsibility for the area, which could not pay its way. Although it was three times the size of Britain, in 1926 the population numbered only 5,581 Europeans and an estimated 1,199,000 Africans.[1] European farming was not prosperous, and the Africans' main source of money was the export of labour to neighbouring countries. There was a distinct prospect that the Protectorate would become that Gladstonian nightmare, a burden on the British Treasury.

Within a few years the situation changed unexpectedly. Rich copper deposits were found near the Congo border, the foundations of a major industry were laid, and a welcome source of revenues was provided for the country's administration. In 1938, after a visit to the mining area, the Acting Governor described:

. . . the experience (which to a first visitor is astonishing) of the suddenness with which one comes upon each of the mining towns. After a drive of some thirty miles through unbroken African bush you turn a corner, and there before you rise the chimney-stacks, cranes and factories familiar enough in any manufacturing town in England, but a strange and portentous intrusion into the uneventfulness of the African countryside.[2]

A British Cabinet Paper recorded the connection with England from another point of view: 'These mines may before long be the governing factor in the copper markets of the world, and their output will become essential to national defence in the event of war and of primary importance to the Empire's trade and manufacture in peace time.'[3]

[1] *Report of the Rhodesia–Nyasaland Royal Commission* (Cmd. 5949 of 1939), p. 3. (*The Bledisloe Commission Report*.) The term 'European' commonly applied to the white community in Central Africa includes white South Africans.

Estimates of the size of the African population were based on rough surveys and guesswork. The first census, taken in 1963, recorded 3,409,110 Africans and showed the official estimate of that time to be 35 per cent too low.

[2] *Legislative Council Debates*, 30, 21 May 1938, 18.

[3] C.O. 795/90/45104, part 3: Cabinet Paper 137, May 1937, on Closer Association between Southern Rhodesia, Northern Rhodesia, and Nyasaland.

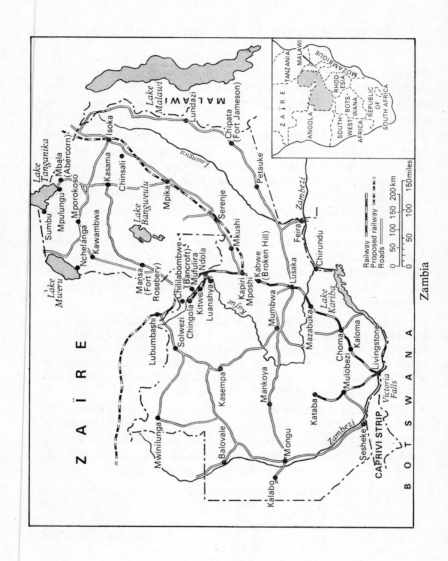

The mines, on which so much significance was now placed, had fallen within the circle of imperial interests by accident. Cecil Rhodes engineered the expansion of the British sphere of influence north of the Zambezi with little encouragement from the Government. He was spurred on by his Cape to Cairo dream, and by hopes of the discovery of a second Rand which would balance the development of the Transvaal politically and commercially.[1] His British South Africa Company, chartered in 1889, set about giving its northern operations a semblance of legitimacy through a series of treaties with African chiefs. In 1890 one of the Company's agents reached Katanga, already officially claimed by the Congo Free State, and tried unsuccessfully to secure a treaty with its ruler, Msiri. In the same year another agent

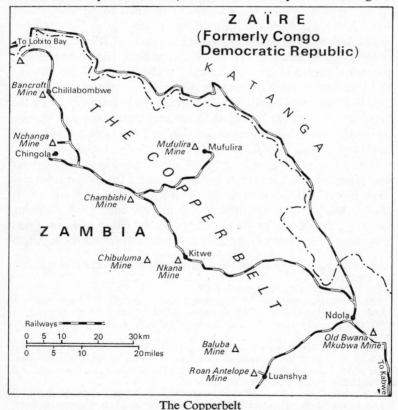

The Copperbelt

[1] R. Robinson and J. Gallagher, *Africa and the Victorians* (London, 1961), pp. 244–50.

Frank Lochner, signed a treaty with Lewanika, ruler of Barotseland, in which the Company undertook to defend his territory and in return gained exclusive mining rights in it.[1] The boundary between Belgian Katanga and British territory was roughly drawn by international agreement in 1894. When it was later found to bisect a great body of copper ore, the Company rested its claim to control mining development on the Northern Rhodesian side on the treaty with Lewanika— although its validity was doubtful.[2]

Africans had mined and smelted copper in the area long before Rhodes's interest was aroused.[3] A reference to the 'mines of Bembe' belonging to the ruler of the Congo appeared in 1591 in Fillipo Pigafetta's book, *A Report on the Kingdom of Congo*. European prospecting began in the 1890s, when a number of small copper-mines were found at the 'Hook' of the Kafue River. Under the auspices of companies formed by Edmund Davies, an associate of Rhodes, prospectors discovered lead and zinc in 1902 at Broken Hill (now Kabwe), and staked copper claims called Roan Antelope, Rietbok, and Bwana Mkubwa further north, in the area which was to become the Copperbelt. But Northern Rhodesia's prospects were overshadowed by the discovery of more easily treated 15 per cent copper ore in Katanga, and by the formation of the Belgian mining company Union Minière du Haut-Katanga in 1906.

The Copperbelt lay neglected until the 1920s, when rising copper prices induced Edmund Davis to look for more capital for his struggling Bwana Mkubwa mine. The American mining financier A. Chester Beatty[4] took an interest in it in 1920 through his holding company, Selection Trust Limited. In 1924 further assistance was provided by Sir Ernest Oppenheimer,[5] who had founded the Anglo

[1] L. H. Gann, *A History of Northern Rhodesia, Early Days to 1953* (London, 1964), pp. 58–64.

[2] R. Hall, *Zambia* (London, 1965), p. 71.

[3] The African copper trade is described in J. A. Bancroft, *Mining in Northern Rhodesia: a chronicle of mineral exploration and mining development*, prepared by T. D. Guernsey (London, 1952), ch. 1 and 2, and in K. Bradley, *Copper Venture* (London, 1952), ch. 1.

[4] Sir Alfred Chester Beatty, 1875–1968, Kt. 1956. In addition to his Copperbelt holdings A. Chester Beatty had extensive interests in the West African diamond trade which were organized through Sierra Leone Selection Trust Limited and Consolidated African Selection Trust Limited.

[5] Sir Ernest Oppenheimer, 1880–1957, Kt. 1921. Sir Ernest became chairman of De Beers, the South African diamond company, in 1929. He had important interests in the Rand gold-mining industry, and was instrumental in the development of the Orange Free State gold-fields.

American Corporation of South Africa in 1917. In a short while Beatty and Oppenheimer acquired the richest prizes of the Copperbelt for their respective mining groups. Beatty's Selection Trust incorporated the Roan Antelope and Mufulira mines in 1927 and 1930 respectively, while Oppenheimer's Anglo American Corporation developed the Nkana mine, forming the Rhokana Corporation Limited in 1931 to manage it. Anglo American also exploited the Nchanga deposits and, after many setbacks, incorporated Nchanga Consolidated Copper Mines Limited in 1937. The division of interests between Beatty and Oppenheimer was firmly established by 1928, when both reorganized their financial affairs. With backing from the American Metal Company of New York, Beatty formed the Rhodesian Selection Trust (RST) as a holding company for his diverse activities in Northern Rhodesia.[1] Later in the year the Anglo American Corporation grouped its various interests in the country under a new holding company called Rhodesian Anglo American Limited.[2]

Although RST had no shares in Rhodesian Anglo American and Anglo American had no direct holdings in RST, important financial links existed between the two groups, notably Anglo American's 32·3 per cent interest in RST's Mufulira mine. Rhodesian Anglo American also had a substantial holding in the British South Africa Company, which in turn had shares in various Copperbelt enterprises.

The financial control and management of the copper companies spanned three continents. During the depression in the 1930s the American Metal Company acquired a majority holding in the Rhodesian Selection Trust. Despite this the management of the RST group continued to be directed from London, and the American company took little part in the day-to-day conduct of its affairs.[3] The companies of the Anglo American group were under a more complicated system of control. The financial side of Rhodesian operations was arranged from London, but technical, buying, and other services were organized from the Johannesburg headquarters of the Anglo American Corporation of South Africa, and major decisions of policy were

---

[1] Bradley, p. 92.

[2] Sir Theodore Gregory, *Ernest Oppenheimer and the Economic Development of Southern Africa* (Cape Town, 1962), p. 399.

[3] As a result of a merger between the American Metal Company and Climax Molybdenum Company in 1957 to form American Metal Climax Inc. (AMAX) the majority holding in RST passed to the new company. In 1962, when Roan Antelope Copper Mines Ltd. was merged with RST, the share of AMAX in the enlarged company dropped to 43·5 per cent.

taken there.[1] The Rhodesian Anglo American and RST registered offices were situated in London until 1951 and 1953 respectively, when the former was moved to Kitwe on the Copperbelt and the latter to Lusaka. During the lifetime of the Federation of Rhodesia and Nyasaland both groups' head offices were in Salisbury, Southern Rhodesia. When the Federation disintegrated they were moved to Northern Rhodesia, where RST altered its name to Roan Selection Trust just after independence was granted in 1964. The two groups remained in control of the industry until 1 January 1970, when the Zambian Government took a 51 per cent stake in the mines and gave the companies contracts for a minimum period of ten years to manage the industry and arrange its copper sales.[2]

At the time of independence in 1964 total investment in the industry was variously estimated at between £300 million and £500 million, much of it provided by the companies themselves from retained profits.[3] Before the Second World War development costs came to about £25 million.[4] During the war progress was uneven, but when it ended an important period of expansion began, culminating during the 1950s in the opening of two new mines, Bancroft (Anglo American) and Chibuluma (RST), in the extension of Nkana and Mufulira, and in the establishment of highly profitable open-pit mining at Nchanga.

Financial journals often comment that the return on mining investments should be high in recognition of the wasting nature of the asset and the risks involved in development. In Northern Rhodesia these risks were illustrated by the closure of Mufulira in the depression and the flooding of Nchanga in 1931. Shareholders in Nchanga Consolidated Copper Mines Limited received no dividends for thirteen years, and the rate of return from Roan Antelope, Mufulira, and Rhokana was not particularly high. Up to 1941 the shareholders' total return had been about £17 million after tax, on investments of £25 million

---

[1] Gregory, pp. 339–400.

[2] In the complicated reorganization of the industry which followed the Zambian Government's decision to take a majority shareholding, the old mining companies ceased to exist as corporate entities. The Anglo American Group's copper mines became divisions of a new company called Nchanga Consolidated Copper Mines Ltd., while RST, in a similar manoeuvre, merged its mining operations into Roan Consolidated Mines.

[3] The lower figure is given in Hall, *Zambia*, p. 265. Publications of Zambian Anglo American Limited quote the higher figure.

[4] C.O. 795/118/45162: *Northern Rhodesia Copper Industry Excess Profits Tax.*

provided over fourteen years.[1] The uncertainties of mining investment were again revealed during the development boom of the 1950s. An effort to revive the old Kansanshi mine was halted in 1957 by flooding. The new Bancroft mine required expensive pumping equipment to remove water from its underground workings, and was forced to close temporarily in 1958 after a slump in copper prices. The first Bancroft shares were issued in 1953, but no dividends were paid until 1960. Development started on RST's Chibuluma mine in 1951, and shareholders received no dividends for twelve years.[2] Even long-established mines are not immune from disaster. In 1970 a cave-in at Mufulira, which brought production to a halt, killed eighty-nine men.

Obviously the industry would attract no investments at all if there was not another side to the picture. In the early 1950s the share-holders of the four established mines enjoyed generous returns on their capital, and the total sum paid out in dividends by all of the companies between June 1954 and June 1964 has been estimated at £259 million.[3] In the boom year of 1956 the net profits of Rhokana and Nchanga were about £16 million and £17 million, while Roan Antelope made over £8 million and Mufulira about £10·2 million. However, the slump which began the same year reduced the total profits of the four mines to about £15 million in 1958. An un-expected recovery occurred in 1959–60. The companies were strike-free for the first time in many years, while the United States mines suffered strikes lasting seven months. Nchanga's net profit was about £13 million, Rhokana made £11·5 million, and Mufulira and Roan Antelope £5·7 million and £4 million respectively. The figures de-clined slightly in each of the following years, and in 1964 Rhokana's net profits were £8·6 million and those of the RST mines totalled £4·7 million. Only Nchanga's had risen slightly, to £11·2 million.[4]

The growth of the industry has been remarkable. The first copper was produced at Roan Antelope in 1931, and at Nkana a year later. Despite many setbacks in the depression the Copperbelt was able to

[1] Anglo American Corporation, Confidential Joint Memorandum on the Companies Operating in Northern Rhodesia of the Anglo American Corporation Group and the Rhodesian Selection Trust, 11 July 1963, p. 7; 'African Advancement', by E. C. Bromwich, 5 Feb. 1962, p. 3; The Economist, 22 Mar. 1941, p. 370.
[2] Confidential Joint Memorandum, pp. 16–17.   [3] Hall, p. 265.
[4] Annual company reports published in The Economist. These approximate figures are quoted to give the trend of company profits, but they are not strictly comparable. Accounting methods differ, and the financial year in the Nchanga reports covers a different period from that of the other mines, ending on 31 Mar. instead of 30 June.

supply 9 per cent of world production during the Second World War, and had already overtaken the Katanga mines' output. By 1960 Copperbelt production exceeded that of Chile and accounted for 15 per cent of world production. Although American production was greater, most of it was reserved for domestic needs, and Northern Rhodesia became the world's largest exporter of copper.[1]

An industry of this potential in a territory as poor as Northern Rhodesia naturally dominated development from an early date. Many other industries, transport facilities, and power supplies were dependent on the mines. Even the Government itself relied heavily on them for revenues. This close relation was not frowned on by officials: administrators of such territories prayed for the windfall of a mineral discovery to help finance development or simply pay for current expenses. On one occasion during the 1930s Government revenues were so low that the Rhokana Corporation and the Roan Antelope Mine had to pay their income tax in advance.

The Government's dependence on the industry was confirmed after the war, when income tax paid by the copper companies rose from about 28 per cent of total revenues in 1947 to 57·5 per cent in 1952 (see Table 1).

TABLE 1

*Income Tax Paid by the Mining Companies**

	Total Revenues	Income Tax Paid by Copper Companies	Per cent of Revenues
1947	4,292,711	1,189,918	27·7
1948	6,318,677	2,841,900	44·9
1949	9,895,885	5,009,555	50·6
1950	11,889,033	5,699,329	47·9
1951	15,836,186	7,594,005	48·0
1952	26,064,540	14,987,615	57·5
1953	30,340,709	16,770,911	55·3

* Sources: The figures for total Government revenues are taken from the *Annual Reports by the Accountant-General*, and for copper mining companies, income tax payments from the *Mines Department Annual Reports*.

The companies were the source of an even higher percentage of Government revenues than their income tax payments indicate. In addition to these payments they incurred heavy customs duties on

[1] Gregory, p. 439; *Northern Rhodesia Chamber of Mines Year Book 1963* (Kitwe, 1964), p. 20.

imported supplies, provided employment for a large number of tax-payers, and were indirectly responsible for much of the tax paid by Rhodesia Railways and the British South Africa Company in the territory.

The establishment of the Federation of Rhodesia and Nyasaland coincided with the height of a boom in copper prices. Taxes directly or indirectly paid by the mining industry, including the taxes of the British South Africa Company and employees' income tax, accounted for the following percentage share of total Federal and territorial revenues:[1]

1954	42·9
1955	33·5
1956	36·9
1957	36·3
1958	22·0
1959	15·3
1960	24·3
1961	25·4
1962	22·1
1963	21·0

The mining industry did not spark the growth of many secondary industries, nor did it lead to improved prospects in the rural areas of the country. The benefits it might have brought were limited in part by the Government's narrow concept of development planning, which concentrated on the requirements of the money (or European) sector based on the line of rail.[2] Also, the Government did not obtain all of the revenues paid out by the companies.[3] Until the Anglo American and RST Groups changed their domicile from Britain to Northern Rhodesia in 1951 and 1953 respectively, they were taxed at the rate current in Britain and the two Governments shared the payments. This double taxation arrangement hampered the early development of the impoverished dependency.

---

[1] *Northern Rhodesia Chamber of Mines Year Book 1963*, Table 4, p. 23.

[2] R. E. Baldwin, *Economic Development and Export Growth*, pp. 144, 201; W. J. Barber, *The Economy of British Central Africa* (London, 1961), pp. 137–9.

[3] The government of Chile, with an economy also dependent on the copper industry, pursued a much more vigorous fiscal policy than Northern Rhodesia: of course, as an independent government, it was very differently placed. For an account of its relations with the Chilean mining industry see C. W. Reynolds, 'Development Problems of an Export Economy' in M. Mamalakis and C. W. Reynolds, *Essays on the Chilean Economy* (Homewood, Ill., 1965).

The companies' change of domicile did not benefit Northern Rhodesia for long. From 1953 the Federation of Rhodesia and Nyasaland collected revenues from the country, and for all but one year of its life Northern Rhodesia subsidized Southern Rhodesia and Nyasaland at an average annual rate of nearly £8 million. During the Federal period secondary industrial development was concentrated in the Salisbury area, although the Copperbelt might have provided a bigger market.[1] The mining companies contributed £20 million to the costs of the Kariba hydro-electric scheme, despite earlier hopes that the project would be built on the Kafue River in Northern Rhodesia.

In addition to these drains on the territory's resources the Government was denied another potential source of finance from royalties on mining operations. The British South Africa Company had acquired the mineral rights of a large part of the country through treaties made with African chiefs. These rights had been retained when the Company handed over the administration of the country to Britain in 1924, although their potential value was then unsuspected. In 1938 the Governor of the territory challenged them, but successive Colonial Secretaries, William Ormsby-Gore and Malcolm MacDonald, upheld the Company's position. The case against the Company rested on the fact that the Copperbelt mineral rights were derived from the treaty made in 1890 with Lewanika, whose authority did not extend to the area.

After the Second World War the elected members of the territory's Legislative Council launched another attack, and the British South Africa Company eventually signed an agreement in 1950 which gave one-fifth of the royalty payments to the territorial government. In return the Company's mineral rights were confirmed until 1986. The Company did not lose by the deal, for in the next decade the royalties soared to unexpected heights. From £12,781 in 1925 they had reached £300,000 a year by 1937 and over £400,000 just after the war. By the time the agreement was signed they had passed £2 million a year.[2] In the subsequent period, when royalties on the copper content of mined ore were payable according to a formula of 13·5 per cent of the average London Metal Exchange quotation per long ton, less £8, the following totals were reached:[3]

[1] *African Integration and Disintegration*, ed. A. Hazlewood (London, 1967), pp. 202–3, 212, 217.
[2] Hall, pp. 80–6, 139–44.
[3] *Northern Rhodesia Chamber of Mines Year Books*, 1955–63.

1955	£13,501,913
1956	£13,711,680
1957	£8,857,691
1958	£6,699,693
1959	£12,688,541
1960	£13,814,059
1961	£12,963,343
1962	£12,623,050
1963	£13,361,933

Until 1963 total payments to the Company were estimated at £160 million, or £82 million after tax.

In 1964 the African Government which received independence from Britain refused to countenance this drain on its revenues. According to an informed observer of Zambian affairs the final disposition of the mineral rights was almost as bizarre as the Company's original acquisition of them. At a state garden party in Lusaka on the day independence was granted the President of the British South Africa Company met the British Secretary of State for Commonwealth Relations, Arthur Bottomley, and after a discussion behind a tea-tent an agreement on compensation was reached. The Company accepted £4 million for the loss of its rights, £2 million each to be provided by the British and the Zambian Governments.[1]

Throughout the colonial period the taxation and royalty arrangements to which the industry was subject undoubtedly limited the benefits it might have provided for the country's development.

[1] Hall, pp. 230–4.

CHAPTER II

The Mine Labour Force

A SERIOUS shortage of African labour was predicted when the development of the Copperbelt began in 1926. The population density of the area was so low, averaging 2·2 persons per square mile, that no local labour was available.[1] A tradition of migrant labour existed in several parts of the country, but the new mines had to compete with long-established labour routes. The Broken Hill lead and zinc mine had been in operation since 1904. Labour recruiters from Southern Rhodesia had been active north of the Zambezi from the turn of the century, when slave raiders were still travelling from the west coast into Barotseland.[2] In 1928 the total number of Northern Rhodesians employed in Southern Rhodesia was 21,334, and recruitment that year was more than 4,000 men.[3] Recruiting for the Katanga mines had opened in the north of the territory in 1911, and ten years later Northern Rhodesians accounted for some 56 per cent (about 6,000 men) of the Union Minière labour force. Some 10,500 Northern Rhodesian workers were estimated to be in Katanga in 1929, in which year about 4,000 of them were recruited.[4] A further 46,000 workers were in employment in Northern Rhodesia itself, excluding the mines.[5]

A report prepared by Rhodesian Anglo American in 1929 concluded that 'The question of native labour shortage will have to be met by mechanization. This policy is, of course, all to the good from every aspect.'[6] Two years later the depression produced a plentiful supply of labour, willing to work for wage rates lower than those

[1] J. Merle Davis, *Modern Industry and the African* (London, 1933), pp. 33–4.
[2] *Colonial Office Confidential Prints*, African (South) No. 659: Milner to Chamberlain, 12 Mar. 1901 (p. 119); Colin Harding, Acting Administrator, North-West Rhodesia to Administrator, Rhodesia, n.d., 1901 (p. 186).
[3] *Annual Report Upon Native Affairs 1931*, pp. 30–1.
[4] *Annual Report Upon Native Affairs 1929*, pp. 15–16.
[5] A. Pim and S. Milligan, *Report of the Commission Appointed to Enquire into the Financial and Economic Position of Northern Rhodesia* (Colonial No. 145 of 1938), p. 134 (The *Pim Report*).
[6] Rhodesian Anglo American Limited, *Mining Developments in Northern Rhodesia*, 1929, p. 63.

previously offered, and the thought of mechanizing operations to a high degree was dropped.

The mines at first secured the major part of their labour force by recruiting in distant regions, usually east of the Fort Rosebery area favoured by Congo recruiters, and by offering contracts for 180 days' work. In 1930 they joined together to form a recruiting organization, the Native Labour Association, but the high level of unemployment caused by the depression soon made it unnecessary. At this time the mines did not manage to attract many experienced workers. Raw recruits were unaccustomed to most of the tasks assigned to them, and underground work was particularly disliked. It was not uncommon 'to find the night shift gang standing dumbly defiant before a distracted European miner who was doing his best to get them to go down'. If the supervisor was too persistent 'the following day most of them had deserted and completely vanished'.[1] The Roan Antelope mine suffered an additional difficulty, the workers' fear of a mysterious spirit, a snake known as 'Sanguni' who was believed to live in the Luanshya river. The managements' efforts to exorcise the spirit with the aid of tribal dignitaries had no effect, but they inadvertently solved the problem by destroying the snake's lair when a section of the river was diverted as part of the malaria control programme.[2] Despite various problems the mines managed to increase their labour force substantially each year as construction work progressed. Early in 1927 there were about 8,500 workers on all the mines and concessions in the territory. At the end of 1928 the figure had risen to 16,073; to 22,341 at the end of 1929; to 29,689 at the end of 1930; and to a peak of 31,941 in September 1930.[3]

At first the mines imported experienced Nyasa workers through a Southern Rhodesian recruiting agency.[4] During the depression they had a wider choice of local labour and its quality rapidly improved. A random survey of forty-two workers made at Nkana about 1937 showed that thirty of the men had left home to find jobs more than seventeen years earlier. Only fifteen had worked in Northern Rhodesia alone. Eighteen of the others had worked in Southern Rhodesia, fourteen in the Congo, and five in South Africa or Tanganyika.[5] An expert on colonial labour policy observed that the extent to which the

---

[1] F. Spearpoint, 'The African Native and the Rhodesian Copper Mines', *Supplement to the Journal of the Royal African Society*, July 1937, vol. xxxvi, no. cxliv, p. 3.
[2] Spearpoint, pp. 5–7.   [3] Merle Davis, p. 151.   [4] Spearpoint, pp. 8–9.
[5] *Pim Report*, p. 46.

African worker travelled and compared conditions of employment was not generally realized.[1]

Only rough estimates existed of the size of the tribes from which Northern Rhodesian workers were drawn, although impressively precise figures appeared on Government records. The most important tribes in the north of the country were the Bemba, thought to number about 108,565 by the Government officers in 1929, the Bisa (49,039), and the Lunda (60,761). In the north-east the Senga (62,394), the Chewa (75,058), and the Ngoni (51,004) were prominent. The Lala (40,880) and the Lamba (23,776) lived in the central regions; the Kaonde (35,397), Lovale (32,672), and Lozi (55,250) in the south-west, together with a branch of the Lunda; and the Ila (21,485) and the Tonga (94,545) in the south.[2] The mine labour force was mainly drawn from the northern half of the territory. An anthropologist who worked there between 1930 and 1934 described the reasons for the steady labour flow from the Bemba and Bisa regions:

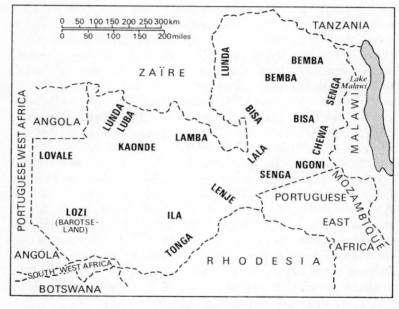

Main Tribes

[1] G. St. J. Orde Browne, *The African Labourer* (London, 1933), p. 120.
[2] *Annual Report Upon Native Affairs 1929*, Appendix D, p. 31.

As regards its present economic position Bembaland must be regarded as a labour reserve. No economic crop has been found for this people owing to the poverty of the soil and the prohibitive cost of transport either to Abercorn, at the base of Lake Tanganyika, or to Broken Hill, the nearest station on the railway line. For the same reasons white settlement practically does not exist, except in the region round Abercorn. Thus wage-earning possibilities are scanty for the natives of this area, and to pay their Government tax, now 7s. 6d. a year, and to purchase the European goods to which they have become accustomed, large numbers of the adult men of the tribe —from 40 to 60 per cent—are obliged to leave the territory annually to look for work, mostly in the copper mines of Northern Rhodesia, but also in the Katanga mines, Southern Rhodesia, and even South Africa. It is rare to find a man who has never left his country to work abroad, and the majority migrate to and fro between the mines and the villages and only finally settle in their home districts in their old age.[1]

Many workers walked hundreds of miles through the bush to labour centres, only to find themselves in the large pool of unemployed that persisted during the depression.

After the northern areas the region providing the largest labour contingent was Barotseland, in the south-west. A few hundred workers from the Eastern and Central Provinces were employed at each mine, but the Southern Province was barely represented. Nyasa workers predominated among the workers drawn from neighbouring territories (see Table 2).

TABLE 2

Africans Employed at the Copper Mines, April 1937*

	Nkana	Roan Antelope	Mufulira
Northern Province	3,319	2,432	3,001
Eastern Province	497	952	304
Central Province	668	934	383
Barotse Province	1,398	946	620
Southern Province	88	192	51
Aliens			
Nyasaland	357	515	95
Tanganyika Territory	42	19	33
Congo	27	16	13
Port. East Africa	41	37	6
Port. West Africa	40	44	17
Other Territories	18	20	6
Total	6,495	6,107	4,529

* Source: *Pim Report*, Appendix VI, p. 362.

[1] Audrey Richards, *Land, Labour and Diet in Northern Rhodesia* (London, 1939), pp. 22–3.

A further source of labour became important after the Second World War. Nyakusa workers from Tanganyika, who were often employed on the hard task of clearing ore underground, came to the mines in such numbers that they became the largest tribal group after the Bemba.[1]

Although African wages, in real terms, probably did not increase much during the 1930s and 1940s, the difference between urban and rural incomes provided a substantial incentive for migration. Just after the Second World War annual village income, including the estimated value of subsistence farming, was thought to be about £4. 16s. per head, while the average income for a person in town was calculated as £16. 17s.[2]

Bustling towns soon grew up at each of the mines. At Nkana and Roan Antelope they were called Kitwe and Luanshya respectively. The town at Nchanga was named Chingola, and the one at Mufulira was called after the mine. Population estimates show the rapid expansion of these urban areas beside the mines (see Table 3).

TABLE 3

	African Population*		European Population†	
	1944	1963	1946	1961
Ndola	11,501	76,800	1,175	9,250
Kitwe	25,836	101,570	2,951	12,460
Luanshya	27,177	66,160	2,314	5,280
Mufulira	17,925	69,310	2,146	6,740
Chingola	7,496	50,690	1,163	5,580
Bancroft (now Chililabombwe)	—	27,770	—	2,330

* W. J. Busschau, *Report on the Development of Secondary Industries in Northern Rhodesia* (Lusaka, 1945), p. 22; *Annual Report of the Department of Labour 1963*, p. 81.

† George Kay, *A Social Geography of Zambia* (London, 1967), p. 35.

For white workers the opening up of the Copperbelt was a boom period. Mining experts were brought from America, skilled men were imported from there and from Britain, Yugoslav timbermen were engaged to help line the shafts, and many workers were recruited in the Transvaal.[3] Before the opening of the mines the main fields of employment for Europeans had been the Public Service and farming,

[1] A. L. Epstein, *Politics in an Urban African Community* (Manchester, 1958), p. 8.
[2] Baldwin, *Economic Development and Export Growth*, pp. 85–7; Phyllis Deane, *Colonial Social Accounting* (Cambridge, 1953), p. 29.
[3] Gann, *History*, p. 209.

but by 1931 mining accounted for 35·1 per cent of the European work force, compared with 41·1 per cent for Public Service and only 7·3 per cent for agriculture.[1]

These white mine-workers were attracted to what was then a remote region of Africa by high rates of pay, which were necessary as an inducement to work in a frontier area with no amenities and considerable health risks. (One of the first tasks facing the mines was the need to control malaria by draining near-by swamps.) In time conditions on the Copperbelt improved, but the high pay rates remained. The mines provided European workers with well-designed houses at a nominal rent, excellent medical services, and a good range of amenities and leisure activities.

African workers were provided with rations and simple housing, in barracks if they were single, or in small thatched or iron-roofed family huts. At the RST mines trees had been left standing to provide some shade in the dusty compounds, and at Roan Antelope workers were encouraged to fence in small gardens and build their own kitchens. The general appearance of the compounds was austere, with monotonous rows of huts stretching over a large area, but to people from distant villages they had some of the glamour and excitement of life in a big city. The beer halls, surrounded by small thatched kiosks, were busy social centres, and dancing and football were popular at weekends. The cinema had a big following, especially for cowboy films. Local markets, often overpriced, sold food and small household items. Many workers were saving for more expensive purchases—clothes, blankets, sewing-machines, and bicycles. The compounds had adequate medical services, but the provision for education was minimal, and hundreds of children living there had no schooling. The attraction of the new urban areas was so great that many families had a relative or unemployed friend staying with them. The authorities were unsure of the exact number of these 'loafers', who placed a considerable strain on the limited accommodation and rations of their hosts.

Africans coming to the towns had to obtain *chitupas*, identity cards on which employers engaging a worker for more than forty-eight hours entered details of the job, and later of the man's discharge. This procedure was full of loopholes, as there was no central registry or foolproof method of identification, and nothing to stop a man acquiring several *chitupas* under different names. The pass laws in Southern

[1] P. Deane, p. 20.

Rhodesia, where Africans had to carry registration certificates together with passes giving permission to work in an urban area, were much more onerous. In Northern Rhodesia the Government had neither the men nor the money to enforce its own regulations.

Men applying for work at the mines were given a thorough medical screening and some basic training for the work to which they had been assigned. Some were sent underground, where the ore was blasted from the rock face, broken into small pieces, and moved to the surface. Others were employed in the various processes by which the ore was purified at the concentrator plant, at the smelter and in the refinery. They were paid by the ticket system which had been used in the territory from an early date to provide a simple form of contract for Africans unused to a working week. Men contracted to work for thirty days out of a total of forty, and the employer marked the completion of each day's work on a ticket. It normally took thirty-five or thirty-six days, including one day off per week, to complete a ticket, and about 10·5 tickets could be completed in a year. Wage levels were substantially higher than those elsewhere in the country. In 1935, when the average monthly wage at the mines was 23s. 6d., workers on the railway received 13s. 6d., Zambezi Saw Mills in the south of the country paid 12s. 6d., and farm labour was worth 5s. to 10s. a month.[1] The difference in wage rates caused a steady drift of workers to the mining area. The experience of working at the mines and living in the compounds created new standards and habits which replaced or supplemented tribal customs. Africans adapted to urban life with speed, taking Government and employers alike by surprise, and by the time official notice was taken of the situation a new African way of life had developed on the Copperbelt.

[1] *Annual Report Upon Native Affairs 1935*, p. 8.

CHAPTER III

Government in the Depression

IN the 1930s the colonial rulers of Northern Rhodesia were often accused of an apparent lack of interest in the African labour force at the copper-mines. In 1932 J. Merle Davis, who was preparing an account of the problems of industrial development on the Copperbelt, was surprised to find no definite policy or Government programme on the subject.[1] African strikes at the mines in 1935 and 1940, in which troops fired on crowds of workers, brought strong criticism from London and from local sources about the Administration's handling of labour affairs. In 1938 an official investigation of labour conditions by Major Granville Orde Browne, who was about to become an adviser to the Secretary of State for the Colonies, found that problems in this field had been neglected.[2] An inquiry into the Protectorate's financial position by Sir Alan Pim claimed that there were serious defects in the administration of the Copperbelt 'and they arise in the main from the absence of any definite policy with regard to labour'.[3]

Despite these criticisms, a study of the general issues faced by the Government at this early period shows that its attitude was not one of wilful neglect. Rather, the available options were limited, and a situation was developing which was at least partly outside its control. If the Administration's general attitude towards labour problems seemed negative, this reflected an unusually daunting set of circumstances, in which judgement was often compromised by the unquestioning acceptance of current theories of Indirect Rule, native taxation, and rural economic development.

The Administration's attitude towards labour questions was strongly influenced by its financial difficulties. The Colonial Office had taken over a country three times the size of Britain, and

---

[1] Merle Davis Papers, World Council of Churches: J. Merle Davis to Dr. John R. Mott, 14 Dec. 1932.

[2] G. St. J. Orde Browne, *Labour Conditions in Northern Rhodesia* (Colonial No. 150 of 1938), p. 4. (The *Orde Browne Report*.)

[3] *Pim Report*, p. 47.

administered it for only £340,327 in 1924–5.[1] The small outlay, and the fact that budgets were expected to balance with minimal aid from the British Treasury, were the key to colonial rule.

The territory had little hope of economic progress until the international mining groups began to open up the Copperbelt, providing employment for thousands in the initial construction boom from 1928 to 1930, and swelling Government revenues from tax and customs duties. In 1928–9 Northern Rhodesia's revenue exceeded expenditure for the first time, and a modest surplus of £16,438 was recorded from the Government's income of £541,606. When the surpluses for the next two years rose to £117,761 and £125,268 the British Treasury confidently relinquished direct control of the country's financial arrangements.[2] Later that same year, 1931, the depression hit the mining industry and spread to the railways, commerce, and farming, ruining the short-lived prosperity.

When the international price of copper slipped from 24 cents per pound in 1929 to 6¼ cents at the end of 1931, the mining companies tried to cut their operating losses.[3] The Bwana Mkubwa mine, plagued by technical troubles, was shut down in February 1931. The Broken Hill zinc mine was closed in July, followed by the Chambishi copper mine in August, the Nchanga mine in September, and Mufulira, which was just about to go into production, in December. In the same year construction work ended at the Roan Antelope mine in May and at Nkana in December, creating further unemployment. A development programme at the Kansanshi copper-mine ended in 1932. The total European population of the territory dropped from an estimated 13,305 at the end of 1931 to about 10,553 a year later, mainly through the emigration of unemployed miners, and only about a thousand white workers were left on the Copperbelt.[4] The number of African mine employees, which had reached a peak of 31,941 in September 1930 during the construction boom, dropped to 19,313 in September of the following year, and to 6,677 at the end of 1932.[5]

Rising unemployment in the white community severely taxed the Administration's resources. Many European miners had been dis-

---

[1] *Pim Report*, p. 85.

[2] *Pim Report*, p. 85.

[3] Gann, *History*, p. 251.

[4] R. R. Kuczynski, *Demographic Survey of the British Colonial Empire* (London, 1949), p. 421.

[5] Merle Davis, p. 151; *Annual Report Upon Native Affairs 1932*, p. 26.

charged at one day's notice, and although some were given their fares home by employers many others had to be repatriated by the Government. Rations were issued to several hundred destitute Europeans, attempts were made to find work for some of them, and more than 750 men, women, and children were returned to their countries of origin at Government expense.[1] According to the Secretary for Native Affairs, the African side of the unemployment problem gave little cause for anxiety:

> The requirements of the natives of this territory are not very great. . . . Natives are fortunate in that they have more land than they can make use of for agricultural purposes. . . . Unemployed natives, if they belong to Northern Rhodesia, can return to their homes and work for their friends and relatives, who will feed them, or their family clan will look after them until they can produce crops of their own.[2]

Unfortunately the report of his own department for the following year showed that the depression had coincided with other difficulties in many of the villages: drought, crop failure, a plague of locusts, shortage of food in some areas, and the cattle trade at a standstill.[3] Certain workers who had been away from the villages in wage employment for a long time felt so out of touch that they refused to return, while other men continued to flock from the villages to the towns in the vain hope of finding work.

The Government's deficit in 1932–3 was £177,041, and despite stern measures to balance the budget financial recovery was not assured until 1938.[4] The Administration was doubly hit by the loss of revenues and by the sudden scourge of unemployment in a country accustomed to a scarcity of labour. A Finance Commission appointed by the Governor in 1932 recommended reductions in staff and departmental programmes,[5] although it was later decided to continue with the building of a new capital at Lusaka in the hope that the project might absorb some of the unemployed. The work of technical

---

[1] Gann, *History*, pp. 254–5; Kuczynski, p. 420, f.n. 3.

[2] *Legislative Council Debates*, 16, 15 Feb. 1932, 146–7.

[3] *Annual Report Upon Native Affairs 1933*, pp. 1, 22.

[4] *Pim Report*, p. 85. The above deficit was for the financial year from 1 Apr. 1932 to 31 Mar. 1933. The financial year was then changed to correspond to the calendar year, and the deficit for the remaining nine months of 1933 was £61,990. In 1934 there was a deficit of £19,565, followed in 1935–7 by surpluses of £27,055, £5,838, and £2,000 respectively.

[5] *Report of the Finance Commission* (Livingstone, 1932), pp. 15–18, 28.

departments was ruthlessly cut back and the number of departmental officials was pruned from 685 in 1932 to 516 two years later.[1]

The Government, overwhelmed by financial deficits and the unemployment situation, became convinced that the recession was a long-term problem: but in fact recovery on the mines was remarkably quick. In 1932 only the Nkana and Roan Antelope mines were producing ore. Copper prices were disastrously low, and the general manager of the Roan Antelope mine wrote later that though the company met its payroll regularly 'it was a pretty near thing'.[2] By 1935 the situation had improved sufficiently for this company to pay its first dividend. Work had been resumed at Mufulira in 1933, and after the plant went into operation in October that year capacity was increased and a smelter built, which was ready for use in January 1937. Ernest Oppenheimer was not willing to let the Rhodesian Selection Trust's expansion pass unchallenged, and the Anglo American Corporation decided to resume the development of the Nchanga mine.[3]

Despite the companies' ambitious plans for improving their properties the Administration remained uneasy about the general financial situation of the territory. Plans for expanding Government services had been halted in 1932 on the recommendation of the Finance Commission. In 1934 the new Governor, Sir Hubert Young,[4] committed the country to an ultra-conservative financial policy designed to build up a reserve of £400,000, equal to half of a normal year's revenue, together with a working balance of £100,000, as a guard against a repetition of the budgetary disasters of the previous two years.[5] By 1939 the estimate of a desirable reserve fund had risen to £900,000.[6] This policy precluded expenditure on the expansion of social services, and the education, medical and agriculture departments carried on with skeleton staffs and minimal budgets.

Planning efforts were concentrated on avoiding the financial strictures of a future slump. Experience of the depression generated a

[1] *Pim Report*, p. 88.
[2] Bradley, p. 97.
[3] Gregory, pp. 442–5.
[4] Major Sir Hubert Winthrop Young, 1885–1950. Indian Army, 1908; War Service in the Middle East, 1915–18; Foreign Office, Middle East Department, 1919–21; Colonial Secretary, Gibraltar, 1927–9; Counsellor to High Commissioner for Iraq, 1929–32; Governor, Nyasaland, 1932–4; Governor, Northern Rhodesia, 1934–8; Governor, Trinidad and Tobago, 1938–42.
[5] *Legislative Council Debates*, 23, 1 Dec. 1934, 6.
[6] *Legislative Council Debates*, 31, 3 Dec. 1938, 16.

philosophy of penny-pinching and near despair among the officials of the secretariat. The Governor himself informed the elected members of the Legislative Council in 1936 that the country was on the verge of bankruptcy.[1] Soon afterwards the Government and the Colonial Office arranged for Sir Alan Pim and a colleague to conduct an investigation into the territory's finances with a view to reducing the costs of administration still further; but the Commissioners were so shocked by the limited provision for Government services that they felt obliged to recommend a number of important increases in expenditure instead.[2]

It might be thought that the revival of the mining industry would have dispelled the Government's doubts about the country's future. Instead, while the mining groups invested further large sums in their properties and townships, the Government continued to economize, and a senior Colonial Office adviser who reviewed the situation in 1938 observed that 'mine management has been compelled to undertake duties and responsibilities which should scarcely come within its sphere.'[3] On another occasion he described the relations of the administration and the companies less elegantly as that of 'a terrier pursuing a motor-car'.[4] Not surprisingly, he also saw 'a certain lack of mutual comprehension in the relations between the industry and the Administration . . . there is a perceptible air of suspicion in the transaction of business, which is unfortunate'.[5]

The Government's caution derived from an appreciation of the speculative nature of mining in Southern Africa, which at that time had had a few rich prizes but also enjoyed a record of early bonanzas followed by quick collapse. Its past history was one of insecurity, the future outlook was uncertain, and if financiers ploughed large capital investments into mining it was more in the hope of reaping a reasonably fast profit than of establishing a permanent industry, for no one knew how long rich ores or favourable conditions might last. The risk of mining investment made optimists and gamblers of international financiers such as Ernest Oppenheimer and A. Chester

---

[1] S. Gore-Browne, 'Legislative Council in Northern Rhodesia Twenty Years Ago', *Northern Rhodesian Journal*, vol. ii, no. 4 (1954), p. 41.

[2] *Pim Report*, pp. 334–5.

[3] *Orde Browne Report*, p. 5.

[4] Foreign and Commonwealth Office Library, record of oral evidence heard by the Bledisloe Commission: evidence of Major G. St. J. Orde Browne, Salisbury, 17 May 1938.

[5] *Orde Browne Report*, p. 5.

Beatty, although improved scientific techniques of prospecting had begun to lessen the odds against them.[1]

Government officials were neither natural gamblers nor born optimists. It was known that in South Africa, where the mining industry was well developed, the low-grade Rand mines had lurched from crisis to crisis over rising production costs; the Government Mining Engineer had made a depressing calculation in 1929 that the future life of the goldmines was only twenty years; and the Kimberley diamond-mines had been forced to close in 1932, a warning of the fragility of profits drawn from erratic world markets.[2] Against this chequered recent history of a more advanced mining industry, the Northern Rhodesian Government had some grounds for caution.[3] Its policies hinged on the realization that the recovery of the mines might well be temporary, and on the expectation of another depression. Even in the 1940s it was generally held by both the Government and the mining companies that the wartime boom in copper had merely postponed the expected slump, which would come inevitably with peace. In African colonies British administrators traditionally looked to agriculture as the basis for secure economic growth, but here again the Government found no grounds for optimism. Only in the Southern Province were European and African farmers prosperous. Officials saw little future for tobacco growing in the Fort Jameson district, and in the absence of funds for the development of the African Reserves subsistence farming declined in many areas.

The economic outlook during the 1930s was bleak. There was a need for forceful, imaginative policies, but the Government's insolvency placed initiative out of reach. Nowhere was this seen more clearly than in the ordinary conduct of business, which was sorely handicapped by the shortage of staff and resulting makeshift admini-

---

[1] Dr. J. Austen Bancroft, consulting geologist to the Anglo American Corporation, records that when Ernest Oppenheimer visited him at the site of the Nkana mine in January 1929 he could not show extensive drilling results because of delayed delivery of equipment. However he gave his opinion that the site was a very rich one, and the following morning Ernest Oppenheimer 'laughingly said, "You had better live up to what you told me yesterday as I arranged to put up a million pounds this morning".' J. A. Bancroft, *Mining in Northern Rhodesia* (London, 1961), p. 157.

[2] R. Horwitz, *The Political Economy of South Africa* (London, 1967), pp. 177, 222.

[3] The Colonial Office shared these doubts. Its Economic Adviser, Sir John Campbell, turned to the American copper-mining industry for comparison, but he found it impossible to try to predict future trends in the international market for copper. C.O. 795/72/25680: minute by Sir J. Campbell, 16 Jan. 1935.

strative arrangements. In some departments, including the Provincial Administration, the establishment was lower at times in the 1930s than it had been when the Colonial Office took responsibility for the territory in 1924.[1] At the provincial level frequent changes of officials prevented continuity of local government, and a member of the Legislative Council, Col. Stewart Gore-Browne, gave a depressing account of the situation:

> In the Province in which I live we have had five Provincial Commissioners in the last two years. I should need a ready reckoner to count the number of District Officers in the two districts in which I am concerned, and the result has been bewilderment, either a perpetually changing policy or no policy at all. . . . One point alone: I do not know how long it is since we had a District Commissioner in my part of the world who could talk the local native language.[2]

Similar difficulties were found at the highest levels of government where policy was made and directed. The Bledisloe Commission described the extraordinary state of affairs in 1938, when the shortage of senior officers was particularly acute:

> Upon our arrival at Lusaka for the purpose of taking evidence, we found that in many cases the chief executive offices of the Government were temporarily filled by acting officers. The Governor had left the Protectorate in March, 1938, to take up appointment as Governor of Trinidad, and his successor did not arrive until after we left Africa. The Chief Secretary to the Government, who was administering the Government in the meantime, had been transferred to Northern Rhodesia as recently as November, 1937. The office of Chief Secretary was temporarily occupied by the Financial Secretary, who had himself been transferred from Nyasaland only a few months before our arrival. His duties as Financial Secretary were in turn being performed by one of the Secretariat officers. The Principal Assistant Chief Secretary had also left on transfer to another post, and the Senior Provincial Commissioner was carrying out his duties. The Attorney-General had only recently been transferred to Northern Rhodesia. In addition, the Director of Agriculture, the Commissioner of Police and the Solicitor-General were absent on leave.[3]

A member of the Legislative Council wryly commented that the only parallel he could think of was planned for 5 November 1605.[4] Under

---

[1] *Pim Report*, p. 100.
[2] *Legislative Council Debates*, 25, 2 Dec. 1935, 204–5.
[3] *Bledisloe Commission Report*, p. 161.
[4] Evidence to the Bledisloe Commission: Col. S. Gore-Browne, Broken Hill, 15 July 1938.

such circumstances, it was a wonder that government was carried on at all. Northern Rhodesia, which had seemed a backwater of imperialism in 1924, seemed even more so after the depression. The Administration was in a permanent state of crisis caused by poor revenues and shortage of staff, and its response to problems was soon conditioned: 'how much?' and 'how many men?' were the ruling considerations.

THE ADMINISTRATION AND THE MINES

The prolonged policy of retrenchment ended a promising early interest in labour questions. Sir James Maxwell, the second Governor, had a ready appreciation of the problems created by the development of the Copperbelt.[1] With the support of the annual Provincial Commissioners' conference a plan for the creation of a labour sub-department within the Department of Native Affairs was drawn up in 1930.[2] Although the staff was to consist initially of only a Labour Commissioner and two labour officers, one each for the Copperbelt and for the southern farming area around Mazabuka,[3] Maxwell expected it

to study questions of supply and demand; devise means whereby waste of labour may be avoided; report on and to make recommendations on recruiting; study the effect on health and prepare vital statistics; study the effect of labour on tribal life; collect information with regard to wages; inspect and report, collect, collate and analyse statistics; study and advise on proposed legislation; keep in touch with labour developments and legislation in other territories; compile an annual report giving information with regard to native labour.[4]

By April 1931 these ambitious aims had been abandoned[5] and the following year at a Colonial Office conference attended by his successor, Sir Ronald Storrs, Maxwell explained that in view of the recession a labour department would not be needed in the foreseeable future.[6]

---

[1] Sir James Crawford Maxwell, 1869–1932. Colonial Secretary, Sierra Leone, 1920–2; Gold Coast, 1922–7; Governor, Northern Rhodesia, 1927–32.

[2] SEC/LAB/35, vol. i: Extract from Minutes of Provincial Commissioners' Conference 1929, p. 71, and minute on the formation of a Labour Department by J. W. Sharratt Horne, 18 Aug. 1930.

[3] Minute, J. W. Sharratt Horne, 18 Aug. 1930.

[4] Legislative Council Debates, 12, 2 Dec. 1930, 151.

[5] SEC/LAB/35, vol. i: J. C. Maxwell to Lord Passfield, Secretary of State for the Colonies, 8 Apr. 1931.

[6] National Archives of Zambia, B1/4/EA/1: Note of a discussion held at the Colonial Office on 28 Oct. 1932.

Despite the heavy concentration of workers on the Copperbelt at the height of the construction boom, until 1931 the administration of the area was conducted from Ndola, some twenty miles from the nearest mine. Although Government stations were opened at the four mine settlements in 1931, the appointments at Nchanga and Mufulira were withdrawn the following year during the depression. Officers were not reassigned to Mufulira until late in 1934, and to Nchanga several years after that.

District Officers posted to the Copperbelt found it difficult to play a strong part in labour affairs or even to assume the traditional paternal role of a rural District Officer in relation to the African population. They supervised Africans living in small settlements outside the mines, but they had little to do with the thousands of labourers housed in mine compounds under the firm control of the companies' compound managers, who were responsible for the hiring, welfare, and discipline of African workers. The organization of compound life varied according to the theories current at each mine, but one principle common to all was that raw recruits could only understand a simple pyramid of command, and therefore no authority should seem to challenge that of the compound manager.

District Officers respected this convention, as did the higher officers of the Administration. Although the compounds were on private property, under the Employment of Natives Ordinance District Officers had a legal right of entry. In practice an officer usually informed the compound manager of his intended visit and was accompanied by the manager on his tour. Even if this custom had not restricted officers' contacts with African mine-workers, other circumstances prevented it. Government officials on the Copperbelt were burdened by a weight of paperwork, judicial cases, and interviews concerning the grievances of the European population. The District Officer at Nkana found he needed two days a week to attend to civil court cases, two days for criminal cases, and often a fifth day for inquests and other matters requiring the presence of a magistrate.[1] Inevitably compound managers usurped some of the judicial functions given to District Officers under the Employment of Natives Ordinance, and most minor breaches of discipline by Africans on the mines were dealt with summarily in the compound by deductions

[1] National Archives of Zambia, Evidence to the Commission appointed to inquire into the disturbances in the Copperbelt of Northern Rhodesia (the Russell Commission), 1935, vol. i, p. 437: Alexander Williams, District Officer, Nkana.

from efficiency bonuses or, at least on one mine, by corporal punish-ment.[1]

Although serious cases might be sent to the District Officer, this further weakened his traditionally paternal role: Charles Dundas, Chief Secretary from 1934, deplored the fact that in the industrial area officers came in contact with Africans 'almost only in the guise of public authority and power—that is as the avenging magistrate and the Tax Collector'. He felt that the position had arisen partly out of deference to the mine managements, and because of the tradition in Africa for the white man's servants to be more or less entirely under their master's control. However much this might be generally desir-able, Dundas thought that the old custom was hardly applicable to the Copperbelt.[2]

The inadequacy of the Government's administration of the Copper-belt was suddenly exposed in 1935 when, during a disturbance at the Roan Antelope mine, troops opened fire on a disorderly crowd and six Africans were killed. The unrest was caused by a Government decision to increase taxation from 12s. 6d. to 15s. on the Copperbelt, where mine wages were among the highest in the territory, while reducing the tax rate in the countryside where the depression had cut the amount of money in circulation. At Mufulira the District Officer and the compound manager had planned that an announcement of the changes should be made through representatives of the tribes working at the mine; but an African policeman anticipated this by running through the compound shouting news of the tax increase. The African strike which followed on 22–3 May spread to Nkana on 27 May and to Roan Antelope on 29–30 May.

Little is known about African leaders on the Copperbelt at this time, but the case of Henry Chibangwa gives some insight into the accumulated discontent behind the strike. Henry Chibangwa, a Bemba clerk and interpreter at Luanshya, formed an association of Bemba workers around 1933. They collected £5 to send him down to Livingstone to protest about unemployment and wage reductions caused by the depression. One account says that Chibangwa saw the Secretary for Native Affairs in Livingstone, and told him, 'I have been without a post for eighteen months. People like me can't go

[1] *Report of the Commission appointed to enquire into the disturbances on the Copperbelt of Northern Rhodesia* (London, 1935), Cmd. 5009, pp. 16–17. (The *Russell Commission Report*.)

[2] Evidence to the Russell Commission, vol. i, p. 57: Charles Dundas, Chief Secretary.

home. We have settled in the towns, adopted European ways and no longer know village life.' Despite this plea he was advised to return to his home village in the north, at Mporokoso.[1] Another account has it that Chibangwa was told in Livingstone that the Governor would hear his grievances on a forthcoming visit to Luanshya, but when officials discovered that he had been deported from Southern Rhodesia for causing unrest there his complaints were ignored. Chibangwa, who was a member of the Watch Tower movement, now began preaching that he had powers superior to those of the Government's administrative officers, and that Africans must get back their wages which had been cut in the depression. He later moved to Mufulira but came back occasionally to preach at Luanshya, where he was spreading the word that the war of Armageddon was coming, two days before the 1935 strike at the Roan Antelope mine.[2]

The recently appointed Governor, Sir Hubert Young, faced inquiries about the disturbances from the Colonial Office and criticism from a hostile combination of mine management officials, missionaries, and elected members of the Legislative Council. The local opposition was indignant to find that the three commissioners appointed to inquire into the shooting included the Chief Secretary and the Secretary for Native Affairs. Protests of Government bias resulted in the addition of a leading missionary to the Commission, while Sir Alison Russell, a former Chief Justice of Tanganyika, was sent out from Britain to act as its chairman.

The Commission pointed out in its report that insufficient contacts between Copperbelt District Officers and the African population had contributed to the disorderly manner in which the tax announcement was made.[3] The Governor, Sir Hubert Young, was well aware of the truth of this criticism, but felt that financial considerations must be borne in mind: because of the reduction in staff during the depression any expansion of administrative arrangements on the Copperbelt would be made at the expense of the rural areas. In any case he felt that the need to increase the size of the police force, which consisted of only fifty-six Europeans and 437 Africans for the whole territory, had first consideration. The addition to the force of nine Europeans and ninety-six Africans would permit full station complements to be

---

[1] Gann, *History*, p. 254.
[2] Evidence to the Russell Commission, 1935, vol. ii, pp. 753 ff., Sam Kawinga Kamchacha Mwase; vol. ii, p. 757, Eliti Tuli Phili.
[3] *Russell Commission Report*, pp. 40–1.

posted to the Copperbelt.[1] The Secretary of State's reluctant permission for the increase was secured, although the Colonial Office was now concerned about priorities in distribution of the Protectorate's uncertain income.[2] Otherwise Copperbelt administration was not decisively strengthened. Extra European clerks and an additional magistrate were appointed to relieve the District Officers at Nkana and Mufulira of desk work and legal duties so that they could spend more time on the affairs of the African population[3]; but Young was hesitant about the extent to which they could interest themselves in the affairs of the mines' African workers without appearing to undermine the authority of the compound managers. The Provincial Commissioner at Ndola felt that friction with the mines would be inevitable if District Officers established themselves in a stronger position.[4]

Although improvements in local administration were limited, Young's awareness of the need to investigate current social changes led eventually to the establishment of the Rhodes–Livingstone Institute, which undertook research on the Africans' way of life. He also took an important initiative to foster better contacts between the Administration and the copper industry. In the past, not only had there been a lack of machinery for a regular exchange of views on matters of mutual interest, but, as the Provincial Commissioner for the Central Province bluntly pointed out, the officers posted to mine stations lacked experience of important negotiations: 'It is placing a junior District Officer in a very difficult position to expect him to hold his own with men of such wide experience [the mine managers]. While the present holders of these offices have carried out their duties extremely efficiently I cannot help feeling that Government has been running risks.'[5] Before the Russell Commission made its report Young announced the formation of a Native Industrial Labour Advisory Board on which the mine managers and other parties con-

[1] Legislative Council Debates, 25, 21 Nov. 1935, 182.
[2] SEC/LAB/69: J. H. Thomas, Secretary of State, to Sir Hubert Young, 3 Jan. 1936.
[3] SEC/LAB/69: Sir Hubert Young to Malcolm MacDonald, Secretary of State, 23 Oct. 1935; SEC/NAT/5: T. F. Sandford, P. C. Central Province to Chief Secretary, 22 Aug. 1935 and 4 Sept. 1935.
[4] SEC/LAB/69: Sir Hubert Young to Malcolm MacDonald, Secretary of State, 23 Oct. 1935; SEC/NAT/5: E. B. H. Goodall, P. C. Central Province to Chief Secretary, 20 July 1935.
[5] SEC/NAT/5: T. F. Sandford, P.C. Central Province to Chief Secretary, 22 Aug. 1935.

cerned with African labour in industry would sit.[1] The Provincial Commissioner for the Central Province (which then included the Copperbelt), the District Commissioner, Ndola, the Assistant Chief Secretary for Native Affairs and the Director of Medical Services were to represent the Government and safeguard African interests. Young felt that for too long the compound managers had been regarded as solely responsible for Africans at the mines, and he was now anxious to examine the problems raised by the great concentration of labour there.[2]

A CHANGE OF POLICY

The question of African settlement on the Copperbelt was, in the opinion of Sir Hubert Young, one of the 'foremost and most urgent problems of the Territory'.[3] The considerations involved in encouraging a migrant labour force or a stable one were closely linked to the degree of skill required from the African worker, but in Young's time the late establishment of the copper-mines and the dampening effect of the slump on their progress had delayed an assessment of this issue.

Before the effects of the depression became apparent, however, the development of the Copperbelt had seemed to earlier administrators and to some far-sighted company officials to present a choice between the labour policies of the South African mining industry, and those of the Union Minière du Haut-Katanga in the Belgian Congo.

The South African mines were forced by political circumstances to make inefficient use of their African labour. They depended on migrant workers, and housed single men in barracks for a contract period of ten to twelve months. In 1930 married quarters were provided for only 1,474 specially skilled African workers out of a labour force of some 200,000 men at the Rand gold-mines.[4] The system of returning the majority of African workers to their tribal homes and

---

[1] The unofficial members were the General Managers of the Broken Hill, Roan Antelope and Mufulira mines, of the Rhokana Corporation and the Native Labour Association, together with the District Engineer of Rhodesia Railways, the Ndola Secretary of the British South Africa Company, and Lt.-Col. the Hon. S. Gore-Browne, member of the Legislative Council for the Northern electoral area, which included Broken Hill.

[2] *Chairman's Report of Meetings of the Native Industrial Labour Advisory Board held at Ndola on November 7th and 8th, 1935* (Lusaka, 1935), p. 2.

[3] SEC/LAB/33: Sir Hubert Young to Secretary of State, 29 Aug. 1935; also SEC/LAB/177: Sir Hubert Young to Chief Secretary, 25 Aug. 1935.

[4] S. T. Van Der Horst, *Native Labour in South Africa* (London, 1942), p. 186.

families for long spells between contracts was very wasteful in terms of training an efficient labour force, but it was enforced by legal and customary colour-bar restrictions which required the use of white workers in semi-skilled jobs. The South African Government exerted strong pressure to inhibit the growth of a permanent African mine labour force.

On the Katanga mines a very different policy had been pursued with the support of the administration, which was anxious to limit labour migration because of its adverse effects on tribal society. Union Minière, keen to reduce the heavy costs of recruiting labour, adopted a policy of establishing a settled African work force at the mines. The existing six-month and one-year contracts were gradually replaced by three-year contracts, which covered 98 per cent of the labour force by 1931.[1] Union Minière officials believed that three years was the time needed to loosen the bonds tying an African worker to his home district and enable him to adapt to work in an industrial environment.[2] To reinforce this, family life was encouraged and the company even advanced money for a bride price to unmarried workers. Extensive welfare facilities were provided, and education was carefully designed for the company's needs, with an emphasis on discipline and manual work. This integrated system of domestic life, education, and industrial training in furtherance of company aims was strengthened by the colonial administration's attitude towards European settlement. No franchise had been granted to Europeans, and the limited opportunities for political pressure favoured the gradual advance of Africans in semi-skilled work, enabling companies to insist that the training of Africans in industrial skills was a normal duty of European employees.

In their early organization of labour the mines had hoped to avoid the South African system,[3] and the Governor, Sir James Maxwell, had been equally bold. In 1930 he told a meeting of the African Society in London that fears of the detribalization of African workers on the Copperbelt were misplaced: regular work had a beneficial effect on character, and better homes, food, and medical attention were provided. He hoped that Africans returning to the villages

[1] Dr. L. Mottoulle, *Politique Sociale de l'Union Minière* . . ., Institut Royal Colonial Belge (Brussels, 1946), p. 53.

[2] Ibid., p. 17.

[3] Gregory, p. 473; Harry Oppenheimer, 'Sir Ernest Oppenheimer: a portrait by his son', *Optima*, Sept. 1967, p. 98.

would be thoroughly discontented with conditions there, 'inclined to kick against them and perhaps to discard their old tribal system altogether'.[1] Maxwell was conscious of strong political pressures in Northern Rhodesia towards conformity with the native policies of South Africa, but he wanted to resist them, and felt that 'his government had entered a road leading in the opposite direction to that which the Union is following . . .'[2]

At the end of 1933 Maxwell's successor, Sir Ronald Storrs,[3] discussed the settlement of the African labour force at the mines with Sir Auckland Geddes, chairman of the Rhokana Corporation, in the presence of senior administrative officers. Geddes was perturbed by the poor provision for married quarters at Nkana and had been told by the compound manager, William Scrivener, that he believed the Government was opposed to permanent settlement at the mines because of the problems of detribalization. The Chief Secretary promptly contradicted this, and said that it had always been accepted that mining development would result in a certain degree of detribalization of African labour. The Secretary for Native Affairs said that he had always understood that there must be a settled population round the mines. Storrs himself announced that no declaration against a settled labour force on the Copperbelt had been made in his time, nor had he seen any evidence that one had been made previously.[4]

Probably none of the parties intended that the entire mine work force should be permanently settled on the Copperbelt, but there seems to have been general agreement that African workers ought to be encouraged to bring their families, work continuously for long periods, and enjoy improved housing and other amenities. The discussion proved largely theoretical, since the general manager at Nkana continued to encourage a regular high turnover of labour.[5] However the Roan Antelope and Mufulira managements favoured a

[1] Sir James Crawford Maxwell, 'Some Aspects of Native Policy in Northern Rhodesia', *Journal of the African Society*, vol. xxix, no. cxvii, Oct. 1930, p. 473.

[2] Merle Davis Papers, World Council of Churches: J. Merle Davis to Dr. John R. Mott, 24 Dec. 1931.

[3] Sir Ronald Storrs, 1881–1955. Service in Egypt and the Middle East, from 1904; Governor of Jerusalem, 1917–26; Governor of Cyprus, 1926–32; Governor of Northern Rhodesia, 1932–4.

[4] National Archives of Zambia, B1/4/LAB/2: Notes of a meeting held in the office of His Excellency the Governor, 13 Dec. 1933.

[5] *Chairman's Report . . . Native Industrial Labour Advisory Board . . . November 7th and 8th and December 16th and 17th, 1935*, p. 5.

more stable working force, and at Roan Antelope in particular improved married quarters were provided.

Two years later, under a new Governor, the Administration was much less assured about its position. Sir Ronald Storrs's tenure of office had been cut short by illness, and Sir Hubert Young, the Governor of Nyasaland, was transferred to succeed him in 1934 at a critical time for the country. The effects of the depression on revenue seemed more ominous than ever, and the costs of administration were pared to a fine degree. Less than a year after Young's arrival the disturbances at the mines forced a reappraisal of the Copperbelt labour situation in which questions of security, public order, and unemployment were prominent.

The Commission investigating the 1935 riots pointed to the high level of unemployment on the Copperbelt as a contributory cause of the unrest.[1] The Administration felt that unemployment was tolerable provided men had the option of returning to their tribal homes. In this respect Union Minière's experience had provided a warning of the pitfalls of stabilization. During the depression the Katanga company reduced its African labour force from 17,257 in 1929 to only 3,758 in July 1932, and because the labour stabilization policy had only recently been introduced it was still possible to disperse the workers to their home villages. But already children had been born to parents themselves raised in Union Minière compounds, 'the forerunners of an industrial population with the strength of those who have been brought up to the activities of an industrial life, but with the weakness of those who have no alternative open to them'.[2] Not only the Government but the Northern Rhodesian copper companies became cautious about committing themselves to settlement on the Congo pattern, both from fear of another slump and from doubts about the long-term life of the mines. Sir Auckland Geddes, when pressed by Storrs in 1935 about the prospects for permanent employment for Africans at the mines, had replied that 'they could not give a guarantee for an indefinite future'.[3] As in South Africa, it became popular to argue that mining was a temporary industry, and that it was bad policy to allow a primitive people to specialize in it. The argument was not extended to white workers, nor was it admitted

[1] *Russell Commission Report*, pp. 39–40.
[2] Merle Davis, p. 176.
[3] National Archives of Zambia, B1/4/LAB/2: Notes of a meeting . . . 13 Dec. 1933.

that migrant labour might become as dependent on mining for an income as a settled industrial population.[1]

By 1935 Storrs's policy had already fallen from favour, and the Chief Secretary, Charles Dundas, was one of the few members of the Administration who still supported it. Unlike many of his contemporaries Dundas felt that the copper-mines must be regarded as a permanent industry, and that the companies' method of housing labour in compounds under strict discipline should be supplemented by a village system for skilled workers, under the general supervision of the District Administration rather than a compound manager. Dundas was a strong supporter of Indirect Rule, but he also believed that men who had spent long periods working at the mines were misfits in tribal society, and should be settled near their place of work.[2] Sir Hubert Young had strong reservations about committing the Government to such a policy. He was willing to approve the permanent settlement of a small number of Africans on the Copperbelt, provided the majority were repatriated to their home villages at regular intervals.[3] By 1937 the repatriation of workers every two years was an accepted Government aim. Young's overriding concern was the integrity of Indirect Rule, not the requirements of industrial development.

The Administration had very little direct knowledge of the organization of the mining industry. As the Russell Commission of Enquiry discovered in 1935, the few Government officers on the Copperbelt were fully occupied with paper-work and judicial duties, and had little time for the problems of African labour. The Government's closest experience of these problems was in the tribal village, at the rural origins of the migrant labour system. Consequently Sir Hubert Young's labour policy gained its impetus not from the policies of Katanga or South Africa, but from Nyasaland. In 1936, two years after he was transferred to Northern Rhodesia, Nyasaland's *Report on Emigrant Labour* was published, revealing extensive damage to tribal society through the absence of a high proportion of adult men at distant labour centres.[4] Young was aware that its findings were

[1] Van Der Horst, p. 190.

[2] SEC/LAB/177: Charles Dundas to Sir Hubert Young, 23 Aug. 1935.

[3] SEC/LAB/177: Sir Hubert Young to Charles Dundas, 25 Aug. 1935; *Chairman's Report . . . Native Industrial Advisory Board . . . November 7th and 8th and December 16th and 17th, 1935*, p. 3; SEC/LAB/67: Sir Hubert Young to Malcolm MacDonald, Secretary of State, 23 Oct. 1935.

[4] *Report of the Committee appointed . . . to enquire into Emigrant Labour*, Zomba, 1936.

applicable to his new territory, and to the development of Indirect Rule there. Despite the fact that the International Labour Office was currently in favour of ending the recruitment of native labour,[1] his Administration agreed with the Nyasaland *Report* that the only way to protect tribal society and control migrant labour was to promote the recruitment of labour under contract, as by this means the regular return of indentured workers to their tribal villages could be ensured.

To some Colonial Office officials deeply concerned about the policy of Indirect Rule, Sir Hubert Young's interpretation of it was open to sharp criticism. The head of the Tanganyika Department once minuted that Young's period as Governor of Nyasaland had put the clock back in that country for a generation.[2] Nevertheless, criticism was mainly levelled at his 'rather dictatorial temperament', at his theories on limiting the financial independence of Native Authorities, and at his plans to allow Europeans to settle on land previously reserved for Africans.[3] His labour policy for the Copperbelt received no adverse comment from the Secretary of State, who advised him in 1935 that a decision on stabilization at the mines must be based on local experience, and offered no further comment apart from stressing the need to make a thorough investigation of the question.[4]

Young and his Senior Provincial Commissioner, Thomas Sandford, believed that migrant labour would not only preserve tribal society but would literally enrich it. In an ideal application of Indirect Rule native agriculture should have supported a stable tribal society, but most of the African Reserves in Northern Rhodesia were so poor, and the Administration's exchequer so depleted, that the best hope for any economic progress in those areas seemed to lie in the circulation of wages earned at the mines and elsewhere. Government representatives put this view to a Native Industrial Labour Advisory Board meeting in February 1937: 'A more rapid turnover of persons visiting the Mines would enable money to circulate more freely in rural areas and by its educative effect would tend to raise the level of the village,

[1] SEC/LAB/5: Circular Despatch from P. Cunliffe-Lister, Secretary of State for the Colonies, 20 July 1934.

[2] C.O. 795/78/45120: Minute by J. A. Calder, head of the Tanganyika Department, 21 Oct. 1935.

[3] C.O. 795/78/45117: Minute by Sir John Cambell, Economic and Financial Adviser to the Colonial Office, 23 Dec. 1935; and file 45120: Minute by W. C. Bottomley, Assistant Under-Secretary of State, 22 Oct. 1935.

[4] C.O. 795/76/45083, pt. 2: J. H. Thomas, Secretary of State, to Sir Hubert Young, 24 Dec. 1935.

and the inequality between conditions in the industrial areas and the villages would be less apparent.'[1]

In November 1938, when no progress had been made in persuading the mines to take up recruiting or to withhold a proportion of pay until workers returned to their villages, another Government speaker warned the Board 'that perhaps the tremendous lack of cash which prevailed in the outside areas was not appreciated by all members' and described the impossibility of improving conditions until money could be circulated in the backward areas.[2] Despite these pleas the mines remained adamantly against deferred pay, although they agreed to provide facilities for voluntary payments to be sent to workers' families in the country.

An important reason for the Government's concern about the adequate circulation of money in the rural areas was its vested interest in the collection of native tax. In many respects tax collection was the *raison d'être* of the Provincial Administration: the organization of touring and the work of junior officers centred on the twin duties of tax collection and the upkeep of tax registers. Officers were inclined to transfer to the African population the sentiment held in the Administration itself, that 'among the middle-aged and elderly natives particularly, the paying of tax is still considered as a very real rendering of tribute to Government'.[3] Career-conscious District Officers felt that a high rate of tax collection was proof of their efficiency.

Tax collection was such a fundamental aspect of administration that its effect on labour policy was rarely considered in depth, despite a stern warning from Lord Passfield in 1930: 'I may remind you that it is contrary to the policy of His Majesty's Government that any taxation levied upon the natives should be such that, in its results, it obliges them to labour for wages as the only practicable means of obtaining the money to pay their taxes.'[4] The Colonial Secretary's instructions were not followed. There were no markets for native produce in many areas, and native tax was an important source of revenue. When collection dropped from £148,000 in 1931–2 to £104,000 in 1933, the Government, anxious to secure every penny of

[1] SEC/LAB/34, vol. i: Chairman's Report of the Native Industrial Labour Advisory Board held at Ndola on 11 and 12 Feb. 1937, p. 7.

[2] SEC/LAB/34, vol. ii: Native Industrial Labour Advisory Board, Meeting held at Ndola on 14 Nov. 1938, pp. 16–17.

[3] SEC/LAB/21: Report on Emigrant Labour, District Commissioner, Sesheke, 1937, p. 8.

[4] National Archives of Zambia, ZA 1/9: Lord Passfield to Sir James Maxwell, 7 Feb. 1930.

revenue it could, encouraged any opportunity at home and abroad for Africans to find work.[1] The reductions in the tax rate during the 1930s were not made to relieve the African population from the obligation of seeking work, but merely acknowledged that tax arrears had reached an impossible level.[2] Nor were the reductions realistic in view of the extreme poverty of some parts of the territory. In 1935 the lowest tax rates, which were 10s. in North-Eastern Rhodesia, 12s. 6d. in North-Western Rhodesia, and 7s. 6d. in Balovale, were reduced to 7s. 6d. in almost all rural areas. In 1938 it was agreed that this minimum rate should be lowered to 6s., which the Provincial Commissioners' Conference felt could be met throughout the country. The previous year the District Officers' Conference had thought 3s. was the highest tax rate all natives could pay, while the *Pim Report* stated that if the traditional criterion of equating taxation to one month's income was to be maintained, the rate in the poorest areas should not be more than 6d. or 1s.[3]

While many Africans would have travelled in search of work without the pressure of taxation, the high tax rates increased their numbers. The District Commissioner in Balovale, a particularly poor area, summed up the effects of tax policy in many such places: 'The problem in this district is not how to stop emigration but how to increase it and at the same time control it.'[4] This remark was made during an investigation of the effects of labour migration on tribal society which was begun in 1936, after the publication of the Nyasaland *Report* had drawn attention to its damaging effect on village life. Three of the six Northern Rhodesian Provinces, Eastern, Northern, and Barotse, reported a high incidence of emigrant labour. Although it was difficult to judge it exactly the Provincial Commissioners estimated that over 50 per cent of the adult men were absent in the first two regions, and over 40 per cent in Barotseland.[5]

The Administration considered that these levels of emigration were dangerous, but that it would be impossible to end labour migration where it was so long established, and indeed serving a useful purpose

[1] *Pim Report*, p. 112.
[2] By the end of 1933 the tax arrears for the previous four years amounted to £152,000 (loc. cit.).
[3] *Pim Report*, pp. 111–18; *Legislative Council Debates*, 31, 3 Dec. 1938, 9.
[4] SEC/LAB/21: Report by District Commissioner, Balovale, n.d.
[5] SEC/LAB/17: Summary of reports on emigrant labour, Northern Province, by R. S. Hudson, 12 Aug. 1937; SEC/LAB/18: Summary of views on emigrant labour, Eastern Province, unsigned, May 1937; SEC/LAB/21: Report by the Provincial Commissioner, Barotse Province, 26 Apr. 1937.

in bringing money to villages with no other means of earning it. The answer to the problem seemed to lie in control of emigration by ensuring the regular return of workers, together with a proportion of their wages, to their home districts. But for effective action the cooperation of employers was necessary, and employers were unwilling to do anything which might restrict supplies of labour when they were unusually plentiful, or have an unsettling effect on compound discipline.

The Government thought that emigration could be more easily controlled if the companies restored recruiting in the rural areas, to remove the incentive which was drawing Africans to the Copperbelt in inconveniently large numbers.[1] The companies steadily opposed the idea, for the maintenance of a recruiting organization was expensive and a good supply of labour could be obtained from the pool of unemployed men drifting around the Copperbelt. At the Nkana mine alone in 1935 over 20,000 men applied for work, of whom only 6,723 were accepted. At Roan Antelope and Mufulira, where workers were encouraged to stay for longer periods and turnover was consequently lower, the managements had an even wider choice.[2] In face of the opposition of the mining companies the effort to re-establish recruiting came to nothing. In practice the companies pursued an equivocal course, for although they did not wish to commit themselves to a formal policy of long-term settlement with all the responsibilities it might involve, they did not like a policy of restricted short-term engagements which also threw new administrative obligations on them. They preferred a fluid and uncontrolled situation, in which workers could be recruited at the compound gate, and satisfactory employees retained for longer than two years if necessary.

In addition to efforts to influence employers the Administration tried to induce neighbouring governments to enforce its policy for migrant Northern Rhodesian workers in their territories. Because of the lack of opportunities for local employment, Africans had turned increasingly to time-honoured labour routes into neighbouring territories. The number in Southern Rhodesia reached 34,212 by 1936 after dropping during the slump to 8,518 in 1933, while in Tanganyika

---

[1] SEC/LAB/34, vol. i: Chairman's Report ... Native Industrial Labour Advisory Board ... 11th and 12th Feb. 1937, pp. 7–8.
[2] SEC/LAB/34, vol. i: *Report of the Sub-Committee of the Native Industrial Labour Advisory Board on Administrative Control of Industrial Population* (Lusaka, 1936), p. 4.

Territory it rose from 2,500 in 1928 to about 15,000 in 1936.[1] The Administration combined concern for the integrity of tribal life with encouragement of this flow of labour to other countries, anxious only to ensure the return of workers to the villages at regular intervals. It tried to secure their repatriation in the unsatisfactory Salisbury Agreement signed with Nyasaland and Southern Rhodesia in 1936, without success. The Agreement acknowledged Southern Rhodesia's prior claim over that of South Africa to northern labour, and in return Southern Rhodesia recognized that it was desirable that Northern Rhodesia and Nyasaland workers should return home every two years. But the two northern governments were bound only to hold talks with Southern Rhodesia before entering into labour agreements with South Africa, and in turn Southern Rhodesia did little to implement the clause on repatriation except in the case of recruited labour.[2] Efforts by the Northern Rhodesia Government to secure an effective agreement with Tanganyika Territory failed completely,[3] and only in its dealings with the Witwatersrand Native Labour Bureau, which in 1936 resumed northern operations, did the Administration receive satisfaction about the repatriation of workers.[4]

For various reasons, in the mid-1930s, the Government committed itself firmly to a migrant labour system. This system had been long established in Central Africa, and could not be easily turned aside. But the Government deliberately encouraged it, expanded it through the pressures of taxation, and rejected the opportunity which arose in one part of the country, on the Copperbelt, to foster a settled African labour force. The justification given for a migrant labour policy was that migration could be controlled: workers could be withdrawn from their villages for two years with a minimum of disruption to tribal life. But the Government lacked the administrative machinery to enforce such a plan, and tried in vain to persuade local employers and foreign governments to support it, for it was clearly against their interests.

The Government's policy on migrant labour was formed by the economic pressures of the depression and from consideration of

---

[1] *Orde Browne Report*, p. 13.

[2] SEC/LAB/12: George Howe, Acting Labour Commissioner to Chief Secretary, 1 Sept. 1939.

[3] SEC/LAB/34, vol. iii: Governor to the Secretary of State, Malcolm MacDonald, 9 Aug. 1938; SEC/LAB/9: W. E. H. Scupham for Chief Secretary, Tanganyika Territory to Chief Secretary, Northern Rhodesia, 12 July 1940.

[4] *Annual Report, Native Affairs, 1936*, pp. 7, 34, 90.

native policy in a rural rather than an industrial context. Lack of faith in the future of the copper industry, fear of the expenses of large-scale urban administration, devotion to Indirect Rule, and a wish to circulate money in the remote and poor country districts away from the line of rail led the Government to discourage the creation of a large class of settled workers. This policy also helped officials to ignore what they did not want to see, that a growing number of Africans was already taking up long-term residence on the Copperbelt. If the Government's outlook was tailored to its meagre financial resources, it also fitted the political situation in the territory. A migrant labour policy was not likely to encourage the acquisition of industrial skills by African workers, a prospect that was already causing alarm in the white community.

CHAPTER IV

The Industrial Colour Bar

NORTHERN RHODESIA was by custom and practice a 'colour-bar' country in the tradition of its southern neighbours. The African's home was considered to be in the isolated villages, and his presence in the towns along the line of rail was tolerated only out of fear of a labour shortage. The normal relation of white and black was that of master and servant, a circumstance which froze the position of the African in mixed society. The colonial system afforded him little protection, for the Government's wary concern for employers' rights often neutralized its duties of trusteeship. A Colonial Office spokesman admitted in 1935: 'As far as private employers were concerned there was no coercion to prevent them from discriminating against natives.'[1] The roots of the colour bar were embedded in the foundations of white colonial society. When the sums allocated for the education of the territory's European and African children were £5 and 8*d*. per head respectively,[2] there was little prospect of the emergence of an African élite familiar with European customs. The official Police Reports contained a section entitled *Black Peril* where offences of 'indecent curiosity' against European women were faithfully counted. The third Governor, Sir Ronald Storrs, complained that it was considered unacceptable for a white man to shake the hand of any African except the Litunga of Barotseland.[3] His successor, Sir Hubert Young, thought that 'the colour bar theory is held more rabidly by a section of the white population on the railway-line and in the Copper-belt of Northern Rhodesia than it is by the Government of Southern Rhodesia'.[4]

The natural bent of the European electorate towards union with

[1] Edinburgh House Library: Colonial Office, Advisory Committee on Education in the Colonies, report of meeting of Northern Rhodesia and Nyasaland sub-committee, 9 Oct. 1935.

[2] *Bledisloe Report*, p. 83. These figures are for 1938.

[3] Gann, *History*, p. 282, fn. 2.

[4] SEC/E/33: Sir Hubert Young to Sir John Shuckburgh, 27 Feb. 1936, cited by Trevor Coombe in 'The Origin of Secondary Education in Zambia', Part II, *African Social Research*, No. 4 (Dec. 1967). p. 289.

Southern Rhodesia was usually presented as a constitutional issue, but its underlying impetus came from a desire to secure the system of race relations which the electorate held desirable.[1] When Lord Passfield issued his Memorandum on native paramountcy in 1930 there was such an uproar in the Protectorate that within four years Sir Hubert Young interpreted the doctrine as meaning 'no less than that the interests of the non-native minority must not be subordinated to those of the native majority'.[2] The campaign to secure European predominance was waged on a double front: the demand for amalgamation with Southern Rhodesia was accompanied by a demand for a greater share in territorial government as an insurance against the postponement of union with Southern Rhodesia. Sir Hubert Young was sympathetic to the settlers' position, and after the 1938 election the official and the unofficial membership of the Legislative Council, which had been in a proportion of nine to seven, were made equal with eight members each.[3] This was a substantial advance for the unofficials (elected and nominated members) and placed the Governor in a difficult position, since, when they presented a united front on controversial issues, he was forced to use his casting vote. But it did not satisfy the unofficial members. The Bledisloe Commission's rejection of immediate steps towards closer union with Southern Rhodesia provoked fresh demands in 1939 for an unofficial majority in the Legislative Council. The new Governor, Sir John Maybin,[4] was prepared to give way, but the Colonial Office persuaded him that such a move would result in an unsound constitutional arrangement.[5]

As pressure from the electorate grew, the development of policy centred increasingly on the *de facto* existence of a colour bar in Northern Rhodesia and the *de jure* absence of it. The former was created by the recognized political community while the latter, imposed from the Colonial Office, had little support from the voting public. Tensions were inevitable as the social colour bar was extended to the field of employment, and a commentary on the resulting problems formed an important part of the report of the Bledisloe Com-

---

[1] J. W. Davidson, *The Northern Rhodesian Legislative Council* (London, 1948), p. 105.

[2] Ibid., p. 72.

[3] Ibid., p. 23.

[4] Sir John Alexander Maybin, 1889–1941. Chief Secretary, Nigeria, 1934–8; Governor of Northern Rhodesia, 1938–41.

[5] SEC/NAT/92: Sir John Maybin to Lord Lloyd, Secretary of State, 21 Jan. 1941.

mission, published in 1939, which examined the prospects for closer union between Northern Rhodesia, Southern Rhodesia and Nyasaland. This report saw a possibility of union at a distant unspecified date, but rejected immediate action because of the incompatibility of Southern Rhodesia's native policy with that of the Colonial Office territories. The significant difference of outlook concerned opportunities for African progress in employment: the Colonial Office had laid down that Africans must be encouraged to work in any position for which they were fit, while the Southern Rhodesian Land Apportionment Act of 1930 divided the country into native and European areas, only the first of which provided the African with opportunities for advancement. This was later defined by the Prime Minister, Godfrey Huggins,[1] as a policy of Parallel Development:

> Every step of the industrial and social pyramid must be open to him, excepting only—and always—the very top. . . . The native may be his own lawyer, doctor, builder, journalist or priest, and he must be protected from white competition in his own area. In the European areas the black man will be welcomed, when, tempted by wages, he offers his services as a labourer; but it will be on the understanding that there he shall merely assist, and not compete with, the white man.[2]

The Commission noted the uniformly hostile attitude of African witnesses in Northern Rhodesia and Nyasaland to Southern Rhodesian policy, and felt that if it were applied in these territories

> the exclusion of Africans from clerical posts in the central Government offices would seriously affect the prospects of advancement now open to natives. . . . The maintenance of these prospects is valued not only by those natives who may hope to secure remunerative employment in the Government service, but also generally as a recognition of the principle that more responsible work is not permanently beyond the capacity of the native.[3]

In theory there were important differences between Southern Rhodesia's policy of Parallel Development and the Colonial Office policy of unlimited opportunity which was applied to Northern Rhodesia. In practice, however, there were disconcerting similarities. In 1939 the Executive Council of the Northern Rhodesia Government

[1] Godfrey Huggins, 1883–1971. Cr. 1st Viscount Malvern 1955. Prime Minister, Southern Rhodesia, 1933–53; Minister of Native Affairs, Southern Rhodesia, 1933–49; of Defence, 1948–56; Prime Minister, Federation of Rhodesia and Nyasaland, 1953–6.
[2] *Bledisloe Report*, p. 170.
[3] *Bledisloe Report*, p. 163.

passed a resolution endorsing the territory's recognized policy 'that in principle every avenue of employment should be open to the native though it was recognized that the training of natives by this Government was directed towards their return to their Reserves to raise the standard of living therein'.[1] The Government's policy of encouraging migration of labour to secure the circulation of money and skills in the rural areas, and its anxiety about congregations of Africans at the towns in the event of widespread unemployment, reflected a feeling that the African's natural home was the country village. Indirect Rule underlined this attitude: the proper form of government for Africans was tribal, their proper home was in the Reserves, and sojourns in town, though desirable to secure the labour supply, must surely be temporary.

This official view was encouraged by an important section of European opinion. From 1930, when Lord Passfield's Memorandum on native paramountcy created a major political storm in the territory, many Europeans had been suspicious of Government attempts to promote African interests. In certain sectors of the economy European workers had succeeded in blocking African progress entirely. On Rhodesia Railways, a private company operating passenger and freight services throughout Northern and Southern Rhodesia, a colour bar was firmly established as a result of the activities of the European Railway Workers' Union, founded in 1916. The company's headquarters were at Bulawayo, and the Southern Rhodesian policy that Europeans be used for all skilled and semi-skilled work was followed in the company's operations in both territories.[2] Sir Hubert Young, appearing before the Bledisloe Commission, explained that:

As I have pointed out to the Colonial Office and the Advisory Committee, it is all very well in principle to say that a native should be trained up to any point, but supposing I started a school to train natives to drive railway engines the only effect would be a strike on the railways until the scheme was abolished. You have to temper theoretical principles and face facts. . . . The railway communities are very strong.[3]

The building industry also had a restrictive labour policy, and even

---

[1] SEC/NAT/92: Extract from Executive Council Minutes, 16 June 1939.
[2] In evidence to the Bledisloe Commission a representative of Rhodesia Railways said that policy was to a certain extent dictated by white labour, but this was not a matter of race: it was a question of training and of difficulties with European labour. (Evidence of Sir Henry Chapman, Bulawayo, 7 June 1938.)
[3] Private evidence of Sir Hubert Young to the Bledisloe Commission, London, 6 Apr. 1938.

the Government subscribed to it when handing out its early building contracts. These contained a clause stipulating that 50 per cent of the artisans employed by the contractor had to be European. In 1932 the Building Artisans Trade Union demanded a 'hundred per cent white labour' clause, but the Government rejected the proposal the following year, and the original restrictive clause was dropped from Government contracts in 1936.[1]

The restrictions in Government building contracts had been subject to sharp criticism in 1930 from the Colonial Office Advisory Committee on Education, which took a conscientious interest in the opportunities available to Africans after the completion of vocational training courses. Committee members questioned the fact that the building of the new capital, Lusaka, was contracted out by Government on such terms. They were informed by a representative of the Colonial Office that the Governor wanted natives to obtain technical education and they would find no colour bar in Government employment, but the country was developing fast, delay in building the capital was not desirable, and contractors were being used because the Public Works Department could not undertake to finish the programme on time. Faced with this unsatisfactory reply, the Committee thought it as well to make its own position perfectly clear, and passed a resolution that 'unless there is full opportunity for natives to be employed on skilled work, it is a waste of public funds and of the Committee's own time to tender advice on their technical training'. Reassurance was received from the Colonial Office representative, but with an important qualification:

It is definitely the policy of His Majesty's Government, as of their predecessors, not to place any legislative obstacle in the way of the advancement of any person in Northern Rhodesia on account of race or colour; and to train and employ natives to the utmost of native capacity in all forms of Government employment. His Majesty's Government are not, however, prepared to limit the freedom of private employers to give preference to any race or colour they may prefer.[2]

The extension of opportunities for Africans in the Government's service was at first almost as difficult as in private industry. When the

---

[1] SEC/NAT/92: Confidential Report by Lord Hailey, undated, probably late 1941 or early 1942.

[2] Edinburgh House Library: Colonial Office, Advisory Committee on Education in the Colonies, Northern Rhodesia and Nyasaland sub-committee, report of meeting on 9 Oct. 1935.

Secretary of State for the Colonies, Sir Philip Cunliffe-Lister, told the House of Commons in 1933 that the retrenchment of administrative staff in Northern Rhodesia could be relieved by the increased training and use of African civil servants,[1] there was an outburst of protest in the territory. The Governor, Sir Ronald Storrs, reassured the Legislative Council:

There is a field for the employment of natives in the Government Service (as in other services) as there has been for many years past; and there is no intention on the part of this Government prematurely or artificially to extend that field. ... There has not been cited one scrap of evidence of a single instance hitherto of any such Africanisation whatever, or of any indication that such a policy is contemplated. And I will take this opportunity of pronouncing a categorical, authoritative, and, I trust, final refutation of statements to the effect that this Government or the Home Government intends to adopt any policy prejudicial to the legitimate interests of the white inhabitants of Northern Rhodesia.[2]

By 1939 the Administration was firmly committed to training Africans as clerks, telegraphists, and post office workers, but the Governor remained conscious of European criticism: 'To charge this Territory with going too fast in this respect is farcical. We are going, of necessity, painfully slowly.'[3]

While the railways, the building trade and even Government service supported restrictive labour practices, the mining industry afforded African workers a chance of progress. Before the depression the standard of locally recruited labour had been very low, and mine managements paid careful attention to improving its quality. Several hundred Africans with experience of underground mine work were acquired from a Southern Rhodesian recruiting agency to act as instructors.[4] Medical care, a supervised diet and the successful campaign against malaria in the mine townships had a noticeable effect on the physical condition of the workers, and in turn on their efficiency. The depression was a turning-point, for where before labour was in short supply and workers were often unreliable, jobs became scarce and desertion decreased.[5] There was also a marked rise in the number of men who brought their families to the Copperbelt and spent a longer period working there. The proportion of married

[1] *Hansard*, 5th series, H. C. Deb., vol. 277, 1933, 850.
[2] *Legislative Council Debates*, 20, 29 May 1933, 88–9.
[3] SEC/NAT/92: John Maybin to Secretary of State, 13 July 1939.
[4] F. Spearpoint, 'The African Native and the Rhodesian Copper Mines', p. 8.
[5] *Annual Report Upon Native Affairs, 1933*, pp. 30, 32.

employees at the mines averaged 40 per cent of the total work force by 1933,[1] and at the Roan Antelope mine where there was a deliberate policy of encouraging longer settlement, by 1935 over 50 per cent of the workers were married, with an average stay of almost two years.[2]

The wholesale dismissals of employees in the depression weakened the position of the European workers who remained at the mines, and enabled a few Africans to make rapid progress. In 1933, for example, 'in a testimonial given to a native of Kasempa District, a European miner praised the man's accuracy in drilling in so many thousandths of an inch and expressed a doubt as to whether five other natives equally skilled could be found in the whole of South Africa.'[3] About this time the Nkana mine prepared Africans for the Government blasting licence examinations with considerable success, 112 gaining certificates in 1934 compared with 274 Europeans,[4] despite the fact that for Africans 'this examination is a harder one than that put to Europeans for obvious reasons'.[5]

Though African skills increased, wages did not follow suit. In 1929 starting pay on the mines had been 12s. 6d. for a thirty-day ticket for surface labour, and 17s. 6d. for underground work. During the construction boom the demand for labour pushed the rates up to 17s. 6d. for surface and 30s. for underground workers, but in 1932 they were reduced to 12s. 6d. and 22s. 6d. respectively. Wage rates were kept low by the plentiful supply of African labour after the depression, and mine managers, aware that wages were already above the average rates in the territory, were not disposed to pay more.

The progress of Africans in mine work attracted unfavourable attention from some of the white miners who came to the Copperbelt when the mining industry re-expanded after the slump. Many of these men were South Africans who were used to the very different labour tradition that had effectively blocked the use of 'cheap labour' on the Rand. The proximity of the Katanga mines to the Copperbelt was a constant reminder that African labour could, if permitted, undertake skilled work for very low wages. Equally important, the widespread

[1] *Annual Report Upon Native Affairs, 1933*, p. 32.

[2] This compared with a total average service of three months at Roan Antelope in 1927, when 20 per cent of the labour force had wives with them. (Spearpoint, p. 53.)

[3] *Annual Report Upon Native Affairs, 1933*, pp. 31–2.

[4] Evidence to the Russell Commission, 1935, vol. ii, p. 840: Sydney Bray, Assistant Inspector of Mines.

[5] Evidence to the Russell Commission, 1935, vol. i, p. 494: George Lange, Nkana Corporation Safety Officer.

expectation of another depression and the memory of the sudden dismissals in 1931 fostered insecurity and suspicion of the managements among European labour, giving rise to an enduring militancy in labour relations.

In 1936 Charles Harris, the General Secretary of the South African Mine Workers' Union, visited the Copperbelt and helped to found a branch of the union there. Shortly afterwards the South African union discovered that its constitution did not provide for branches outside the country, and an independent Northern Rhodesia Mine Workers' Union was founded late in 1936. The mine managements were slow to recognize the new union, and its leaders contacted Clement Attlee in London, threatening a strike if the Colonial Office did not protect their interests.[1] When the Colonial Office heard of this approach it consulted the Ministry of Labour and informed the mine managements that recognition should be granted when the union had a membership of 55 per cent of the eligible workers, rather than 60 per cent as the mines had stipulated.[2] The union was recognized by the mining companies in September 1937. It was still far from securely established, and although it took up the white worker's burden promptly, most of its activity was devoted to strengthening its own organization. Branches were established at Broken Hill, Roan Antelope, Nkana, Mufulira, and Nchanga, but in 1939 the union's membership had dwindled to less than 1,000 out of some 2,500 eligible daily paid Europeans,[3] and a rival organization existed at the Roan Antelope mine.

From the beginning the Mine Workers' Union demanded equal pay for equal work, a favourite device in South Africa for excluding African labour from certain job categories. At this early stage the Northern Rhodesian union was also concerned to keep unqualified white workers out of craftsmen's jobs, and was worried by an influx of aliens and refugees from Europe, 'foreigners' who were 'a serious menace to the British workmen in this territory in the matter of competitive employment'.[4] Another basic demand was for a closed shop, partly to protect the union from disunity within its own ranks and

---

[1] C.O. 795/93/45116: Minute by T. W. Davies, 31 Mar. 1937.

[2] Ibid., Minutes by J. A. Calder, 8 Apr. 1937, 23 Apr. 1937, 28 May 1937.

[3] Evidence to the Bledisloe Commission: Northern Rhodesia Mine Workers' Union, Ndola, 20 July 1938.

[4] Evidence to the Bledisloe Commission: Luanshya Amalgamation Enquiry Committee, Ndola, 18 July 1938, also Nchanga Amalgamation Enquiry Committee, Nkana, 22 July 1938; Gann, *History*, pp. 331–2.

partly for protection against cheap labour.[1] In the recognition agreement of 1937 the union was accepted by the managements as representing European workers only. Since compulsory membership for all daily paid workers, together with the rate for the job, would have amounted to an effective bar against Africans advancing into European job categories, neither the companies nor the Government wanted to see a closed shop established.

Equal pay for equal work was an orthodox trade-union principle designed to stop employers using cheap labour. It assumed a special importance in Northern Rhodesia, where cheap labour was African labour. Africans were customarily employed at rates much lower than those received by Europeans, and no employer would consider hiring them at European rates when there was an ample supply of African labour at the low wage levels offered. The machinery of government and of industry had been established on this basis, and employers were prepared to resist any efforts to alter it. No serious effort was made to relate African wages to European wages in terms of comparative efficiency or job content. Where Africans were capable of doing similar work to Europeans, employers justified wage differentials on the grounds that Africans lacked adaptability or a sense of responsibility, or by reference to a dual economy in which the needs of the African were less than those of the European. At a later date some mine officials might have been prepared to consider 'equal pay for work of equal value', a formula favoured by the International Labour Organization which left room for negotiation, but European mineworkers steadily resisted this flexible definition.

The European workers felt their own position and their children's future as settlers were at stake. The large South African element in the population[2] saw history repeating itself: the employment of semi-skilled African labour at low wages was the issue which had caused the great Rand strike in 1922. Closer to the Copperbelt white workers noted the security of European trade-unionists working for

[1] At this time the generally accepted definition of a closed shop in the United States and Britain was one in which all the employees hired had to be members in good standing of the trade union representing the jobs concerned. A union shop was one in which all persons employed had within a given time to become and remain members in good standing with the union. By these definitions, the European union was fighting for a union shop, although its demands always referred to a 'closed shop'.

[2] In 1931 Northern Rhodesia had 417 people from South Africa in every thousand European inhabitants, compared with 305 from the United Kingdom and Ireland. (Gann, *History*, p. 443.)

Rhodesia Railways Limited, which adhered to Southern Rhodesian employment practices even in the northern territory. Equal pay for equal work was a convenient slogan, for it made no specific mention of colour, and as a fundamental principle of trade-unionism it assured the support of trade-unionists abroad.

The union's desire to protect the white worker's position went further than the field of industrial relations. In evidence to the Bledisloe Commission in 1938 it was complacent about its relations with the mine managements, and pointed to the Government as the real enemy:

Now, we feel that when that day comes, when the interests of the natives and the whites clash, there is nothing to stop the Colonial Secretary and Governor starting large industrial schools for natives, and to turn round to the Mining Companies and say, 'the interests of the whites and the natives are now clashing, you must employ a larger proportion of native artisans year by year,' and gradually put us out of work.[1]

The Government had told the union that it would oppose any attempt to establish a closed shop on the mines,[2] but it was anxious to avoid a clash on the question at a time when the electorate's pressure for amalgamation with Southern Rhodesia was rising. The Senior Provincial Commissioner said to the Bledisloe Commission that 'the Government does not wish to cross swords on such an issue' while a member of the Legislative Council explained that the relations between European trade unions and skilled natives were 'the greatest problem of the whole lot' and doubted 'whether there is any other serious point of difference (with Southern Rhodesia) except that of skilled native labour'.[3] This over-simplified the issues at stake, but a sense of insecurity among white workers about employment policies in the territory was certainly an important force behind the pressure for amalgamation.

The policy aims of training Africans for semi-skilled work were still unsettled at this time and the publication of the *Bledisloe Report* provoked further debate within the Administration. Officials found it difficult to strike a balance between the legitimate needs of developing the Reserves and the need to provide opportunities for advance-

Evidence to the Bledisloe Commission: Northern Rhodesia Mine Workers' Union, Ndola, 20 July 1938.

[2] Evidence, T. F. Sandford, Senior Provincial Commissioner, Lusaka, 12 July 1938.

[3] Evidence, T. F. Sandford, Lusaka, 12 July 1938, and Lt.-Col. A. Stephenson, Ndola, 18 July 1938.

ment in urban areas. The latter policy seemed likely to encourage permanent settlement along the line of rail, and was felt by the European population to threaten its established fields of employment. In 1940 the Governor, Sir John Maybin, reviewed the situation at length in a minute to his Chief Secretary which provides a valuable insight to the Government's attitude:

The European will always require the native labourer, and the reserves must depend for a long time to a considerable extent on the money brought back as earnings in the European area.

I am also convinced that as the native is essential to the white area he cannot for ever be kept from skilled work there, or allowed to use his skill only where he does not compete with the European. Whatever the Government may attempt to do, it seems to me inevitable that artificial bars to the natives' industrial advancement, whether open colour bar or by fixing the wage so high that the employer will not engage him, are bound eventually to fail. The African, in the Gold Coast cocoa hold-up and in the mining strikes in Nigeria has shown his capacity to combine. If he is driven to it, he will combine in Central Africa, there will be serious industrial troubles, and in the end the native will win. It seems to me, therefore, that as a complete and permanent solution the policy of parallel development is bound to fail.

What is the alternative? Are we to adopt outright the policy of the open door, and by a vigorous policy aim at training the native in mass for industrial skilled work? That would meet the claim that there should be complete equality of opportunity. I think that we must examine carefully the results of such a policy for the European and the Native and its effect on their relations with each other. We could in a few years turn out a considerable number of natives with a very reasonable degree of industrial skill. This would ensure them employment on the Mines at rates much higher than any income they can now make in the Reserves. That would accelerate the drift from the native areas to the industrial areas and tend strongly to create a stabilised native industrial population. The men needed for the development of the Reserves both politically and economically would become urbanized and subject to all the fluctuations of industrial employment. We should then have serious social, economic and political problems to face.

The European would suffer from a sudden and intense competition. He would resent that and resist it both by political and economic action. He would feel bitter against the Government. Racial bitterness would spring up and the cooperation of the European in native development would be lost.

It may be said that I have already shown this development to be inevitable. That is true. We must educate and train the native, and however much we might want to keep him, when trained, for work in the native areas, it is inevitable from the start that some will slip off to work in the industrial areas. Eventually there must be competition between the races. I feel, however, that if the process is a gradual one both races can adjust themselves to it without serious friction. If the main drive is for development of the Reserves, an alternative series of careers will be created there, the standard of living will steadily rise as will the culture of the native. The competition for skilled work will not be between a race prepared to accept any wage as an alternative to a life of semi-starvation, and a race with a high cost of living. The standard of African life and wages will rise until the competition is a fair economic one. It will be very many years before the African's output except in certain monotonous jobs approaches that of the European, and the wages of the two will depend on output. If the process is only gradual and carefully directed I see no reason why a reasonable economic partnership should not result.

If the process is gradual we can proceed with our development of the Reserves. I think we all agree on the urgent necessity for this. In the long run the basis of native life must be agricultural and rural. Such a policy will fit into our scheme of political development also.[1]

Maybin appreciated the dangers of competition between Africans and Europeans in the industrial areas, and his solution was delay. It was firmly endorsed by the conservative Secretary for Native Affairs, T. F. Sandford, who found that

In the economic sphere it will be impossible to eliminate for all time competition between the European and the native. It is, however, desirable that this should be reduced to a minimum as long as possible. One can say, without any hostility, that friction betweeen the European and the native is based entirely on the economic factor. While we cannot refuse, nor should we desire to refrain from, education of the native, we can at least refrain from affording him training en masse in those directions which would inevitably increase competition.[2]

A 'holding' policy seemed possible because it was widely believed that European farming and the mining industry had reached their furthest development, and that the climate of the territory was unsuitable for permanent European settlement. Economic development appeared to be arrested at the existing level. Development of the Reserves was a logical way to extend opportunities for Africans in a stagnant economy, at the same time enabling the Administration to evade a thorny political problem. Not surprisingly, in these circumstances the Governor came to the conclusion that 'we can go a long way to meet Southern Rhodesia in the question of native policy'.[3]

[1] SEC/LAB/92: J. A. Maybin to Chief Secretary, 4 Mar. 1940.
[2] SEC/LAB/92: T. F. Sandford to Sir John Maybin, 7 Feb. 1940.
[3] SEC/LAB/92: J. A. Maybin to Chief Secretary, 4 Mar. 1940.

THE COLOUR BAR ON THE COPPERBELT

Sir John Maybin's solution to the colour bar in industry, a gradual integration of employment opportunities on the line of rail while African pressure for advancement was siphoned off by the provision of opportunities in the Reserves, was quickly overtaken by a crisis on the Copperbelt. On 18 March 1940, only two weeks after his minute was penned, a European strike broke out on the mines, followed by an African one, with consequences which were to force the Government to reconsider its concepts of labour policy. The racial situation, in one industry at least, was shown to have passed beyond the possibility of a 'back to the country' solution. The strikes forced the Government to pay much closer attention to the future of the African in industry. Ironically they also led to the establishment of a colour bar on the mines by industrial agreement, with no opposition from the Government or the Colonial Office. The importance of Northern Rhodesia's copper supplies to Britain's war effort outweighed adherence to the wavering principle of equal opportunity.

During the first years of the war more than half of Britain's copper supplies came from North America, but by 1945 Northern Rhodesia was able to provide 67·9 per cent of them.[1] After the Ministry of Supply arranged in 1939 to take up most of the Protectorate's copper output there was strong pressure to increase production, and the industry had difficulty in meeting required targets. To ease the situation the American and British Governments supported the expansion of the Nchanga mine, the Ministry of Supply advancing £750,000 towards the cost while the American Government promised priority for equipment. Only in the second half of 1943 did the Allies feel they had secured copper supplies roughly equal to consumption, and in April 1944 commitments in Northern Rhodesia were reduced.[2] The pressure on production in the war years, when a sense of emergency reached even Central Africa, contributed to a sudden change in the nature of industrial relations on the Copperbelt.

The industrial situation on the mines with regard to job demarca-

---

[1] C.I.S.B.: Evidence to the Guillebaud Arbitration, 1953, from the Chamber of Mines on Northern Rhodesia's production of copper as a proportion of United Kingdom consumption, 1945–51; J. Hurstfield, *History of the Second World War: The Control of Raw Materials* (London, 1953), p. 291.

[2] Gregory, pp. 454–5; L. H. Gann, 'The Northern Rhodesian copper industry and the world of copper, 1923–1952', *The Rhodes–Livingstone Journal*, no. 18 (1955), pp. 8–9.

tion, equal pay, and the 'closed shop' demand was still fluid at the beginning of the war, when the European union raised a claim for a pay increase for lower-paid workers and a cost of living allowance. The recognition agreement with each company required any dispute to be referred to conciliation. Negotiations had hardly begun when this procedure was bypassed by the workers at Mufulira. At a public meeting union officials told them that the management had granted nothing. The workers asked the union representatives to stand down, and then elected some of these union officials and other men as representatives of the 'Mufulira Mine Workers', who did not consider themselves bound by the recognition agreement. On the following day this action committee presented fourteen demands, most of them new, to the management with a request that negotiations start in a day's time. On 17 March 1940, after the company had said it could not negotiate at such short notice, the workers came out on strike. At a meeting at Nkana on 19 March, attended by some of the Mufulira men, a similar course was followed. A 'Nkana Mine Workers' Committee' including officials of the union was elected in place of the union negotiating team; thirteen of the Mufulira demands were submitted to the management, which refused to consider them in the short time allowed; and a strike was declared on 21 March. On the following day the management agreed to conciliation proceedings, provided the Mine Workers' Union represented the workers' committees that had instigated the strikes. The men returned to work on 27 March, after agreement had been reached on many of the points in dispute and the claim for a pay increase had been referred to arbitration.[1]

African workers had been idle during the European dispute, as their work was dependent on white supervision. Before the end of the strike the Acting Labour Commissioner learned at Mufulira that Africans planned to ask for an increase in wages after the European demands had been settled.[2] The Government warned the General Managers at Mufulira and Nkana, and the companies decided to award a cost of living bonus of 2s. 6d. per ticket of thirty working days to all African employees. This had no effect, and on 29 March Africans at both mines came out on strike, demanding increased wages varying between 2s. 6d. and 5s. a day at Nkana to 10s. a day at

---

[1] *Northern Rhodesian Copper Mines Wages Arbitration*, July 1940, pp. 24–5.

[2] SEC/LAB/78, vol. i: Record of discussion with His Excellency the Governor and the Chief Secretary at Kitwe on 26 Mar. 1940.

Mufulira. The Secretary for Native Affairs, Thomas Sandford, and Colonel Stewart Gore-Browne, the Legislative Council Member for Native Interests, hurried to the Copperbelt to reason with the strikers, whose leaders had achieved remarkable control over the crowd. Gore-Browne later wrote that 'it would surprise people who only know the obsequious Government employee or house-boy to see what a tough crowd of Bantu, fired by a long-felt grievance, really can be like'.[1] At Mufulira the strikers rejected the compound elders who normally acted as intermediaries between the workers and management, and appointed a Committee of Seventeen to put forward their claims. Neither management nor Government officials took the demand for such a large pay increase seriously, and there was no real negotiation between the parties. The impasse was broken on 3 April, when a crowd of strikers at N'kana, provoked by the sight of a line of Africans about to draw pay at the compound office, began to stone the building. Troops and police had previously been called in to protect mine installations, and half an hour after the onslaught began they opened fire, killing thirteen men and wounding seventy-one, four of whom died later. The shooting broke the strike, and three days later the Africans began to return to work.[2]

As had happened after the disturbances of 1935, the Government found labour affairs in the Protectorate under sudden scrutiny from home. A Commission headed by Sir John Forster[3] came out from Britain and recommended various improvements in African wage rates at the mines: the surface and underground starting rates of 12s. 6d. and 22s. 6d. respectively for a ticket of thirty days' work were to be increased by 2s. 6d., no deductions from bonuses were to be made for disciplinary purposes, and overtime rates ought to be based on the same percentage of pay as for Europeans.[4] Most important of all, the Commission indicated that an important factor in the unrest had been the bitterness among African mine-workers about their exclusion

[1] Stewart Gore-Browne to Dame Ethel Locke-King, 11 Apr. 1940, cited in Robert L. Rotberg, *The Rise of Nationalism in Central Africa* (Cambridge, 1966), p. 173.

[2] SEC/LAB/104: Report on Native Labour Strike, Apr. 1940, by the Secretary for Native Affairs.

[3] Sir John Forster, Kt. 1939, cr. 1st Baron Forster of Harraby 1959. Chairman of the National Arbitration Tribunal from 1944; Judge, Administrative Tribunal of the International Labour Organisation, 1957–60.

[4] *Report of the Commission appointed to inquire into the disturbances in the Copperbelt, Northern Rhodesia, July 1940* (Lusaka, 1941), p. 51. (The *Forster Commission Report*.)

from certain jobs. The mine managements, Mine Workers' Union, and representatives of Government were advised to meet and consider to what positions, not now open, Africans should be encouraged to advance.[1]

The 1940 strikes were a turning-point in labour affairs from both the African and European viewpoints. The African strike was significant because, unlike the spontaneous protest in 1935 against the Government's tax increase, it was clearly an industrial dispute. It was not, admittedly, an independent dispute, as it was triggered by the European strike immediately preceding it. Yet despite the absence of 'organized labour' in a conventional sense, the strike leaders' firm control of the mass of African workers at Nkana and Mufulira, largely through intimidation, was a formidable weapon, and the brief appearance of Mufulira's 'Committee of Seventeen' showed that there were spokesmen for the workers' side. Most significant of all, the two issues which emerged from the African strike were to be the major elements in the country's turbulent history of industrial relations throughout the remainder of the colonial period, and even after Independence. These issues, the relationship of African wages to those earned by Europeans, and restrictive practices which imposed a colour bar in industry, had been moulded over the previous decade and were now bluntly articulated during the strike. The claim for 10s. a day at Mufulira was not a demand for equal pay (the lowest-paid European workers received £1 for a daily shift at this time) but it was a demand justified in relation to the work of European supervisors. The Committee of Seventeen 'demanded 10s. a day saying that the White men had learned the work from them and did no work. The natives did all the work'.[2] The Governor emphasized this resentment of the front-line European supervisors when he informed the Secretary of State that the demand was a definite racial challenge to the European workers:[3] the issue concerned status and ability, and the Committee of Seventeen had stated 'that they could work as well as the Europeans and they were prepared, if a European Surveyor was provided, to undertake all the work of one shift, and prove they could produce more ore'.[4] This challenge by African workers, however

[1] *Forster Commission Report*, p. 53.

[2] SEC/LAB/78, vol. i: Notes taken by the Governor from Mr. Sandford's statement to the Executive Council, 4 Apr. 1940.

[3] SEC/LAB/78, vol. i: Governor to Secretary of State, 4 Apr. 1940.

[4] SEC/LAB/104: Report on Native Labour Strike, Apr. 1940 by the Secretary for Native Affairs, p. 3.

momentarily organized, anticipated the future course of development and introduced an important new element into Copperbelt labour affairs. At the same time the African protest at the beginning of the Second World War suddenly placed the hitherto insecure white Mine Workers' Union in an almost impregnable position.

NEGOTIATIONS WITH THE MINE WORKERS' UNION

Immediately before the European strike in 1940 the Mine Workers' Union had reached a critical stage in its fortunes. It was some £600 in debt,[1] it had failed to secure amalgamation with the rival Mine Workers' Federation at the Roan Antelope mine, and it seemed to be losing support on the other mines. At Nkana membership was, at most, only 30 per cent of those eligible.[2] No substantial gains had been won from the companies, and although the union's executive blamed the managements for delays in negotiation it was clear that they were not yet in a strong enough position to impose demands. The rebellion in March 1940 in which workers' committees were elected in place of the union's officials before the strike was either a revolt by militants against the union's inability to get results, or a move by union leaders to get results quickly by unconstitutional methods. Some of the union's officials naturally claimed that the former was the case and that they had been unable to control the discontented members. They pointed out that with a closed shop they would have more power to deal with dissent and maintain their own position.[3] But in evidence to the Forster Commission Brian Goodwin, union branch chairman at Nkana, who was also the chairman of the workers' committee, said the strike was not caused by the rising cost of living but by difficulties in securing a revision of the union's recognition agreement from the management.[4]

The strike itself was only partly successful. The union won a cost of living allowance and gained some procedural points, but the management turned down a demand for a closed shop. Later at arbitration the claim for an increase in basic wage rates was rejected. The immediate results were outweighed by the value of the African unrest to the Mine Workers' Union. Both the Government and the companies had to face the embarrassment of a public inquiry for the

[1] Evidence to the Forster Commission, 1940, p. 478: Mine Workers' Union, Nkana branch.
[2] Evidence, p. 476.
[3] Evidence, p. 476.
[4] Evidence, pp. 456–8, 481.

second time within five years, and both were convinced that for a considerable time to come any European strike would inevitably be followed by another African disturbance, possibly at all the mines on the Copperbelt. For this reason alone any European strike was undesirable, but it was doubly so at that time, when vital war supplies of copper would be interrupted. From a state of immediate crisis the strikes of 1940 placed the Mine Workers' Union in a position of strength.

A month after the disturbances the executive of the union again presented a draft of a revised agreement to the companies. The managements were alarmed by a new clause reading 'Non-European labour is to be at all times under direct European supervision other than that of a Shift Boss'.[1] At that time labour on the mines was organized on the basis of European supervisers or 'gangers' in charge of small gangs of unskilled African labour, but already a small number of Africans was supervising gangs or had moved up from the gang system to work demanding some degree of skill. A small number of jobs were handled by Europeans at one mine and by Africans at another.[2] The new clause would have blocked African progress by establishing union members' positions in the mine hierarchy between those of Africans and lower management officials, and it became known in the negotiations as the 'colour-bar' clause.

The local managers turned for guidance to their Managing Directors in London, who were in contact with British Government officials over national copper supplies. The general attitude of the London managements was typified by a message from the Managing Director of Roan Antelope and Mufulira on 18 May 1940: 'We feel strongly that in this time of crisis we should not quibble over words and should try to make an arrangement on the broad principle that if the men are prepared to play the game we are prepared to help in making it possible for them to establish themselves.' Subsequent negotiations in May ended in deadlock, and at the beginning of June the General Manager of Rhokana consulted the Governor, but received little practical help. The Governor was concerned that the uneasy relations between the union and the companies might lead to

[1] C.I.S.B., 100/20/9A, vol. ii: Memorandum, 'Colour Bar' Clause in Agreement between the Companies and the Northern Rhodesia Mine Workers' Union, 4 Jan. 1950.

[2] For a list of such jobs, taken from the *Report of the Commission Appointed to Enquire into the Advancement of Africans in Industry* (Lusaka, 1948), Ch. V, see Appendix A, p. 233.

further disturbances at a time when copper production should be maintained at a high level. When the General Manager pointed out that the main difficulty was the 'colour-bar' clause, the Governor replied 'that he realized the position fully and also the fact that there could be no question of a colour bar in Northern Rhodesia'.[1]

At the end of June a further meeting with the union was attended by senior company officials from London. The 'colour-bar' clause was the main topic of discussion, and the union also raised the question of equal pay, adding that some line must be drawn to protect the white man's livelihood and standard of living. Rhodesia Railways practised discrimination for this purpose, and the union felt that the mines should do so as well. The managements were reluctant to agree, and referred to the shortage of European labour caused by the war, which seemed likely to occasion the use of African labour in further 'white' jobs in the near future. The meeting adjourned after the parties failed to find a common basis for negotiation. Roy Welensky,[2] then an elected member of the Legislative Council and branch chairman of the Railway Workers' Union at Broken Hill, was on the premises where the talks were being held and was invited by the management representatives to consider the position. He was a member of the Government's Man Power Committee appointed in 1940 to deal with the labour shortage, so his interest in the matter was more than that of a committed trade-unionist. Welensky and the representatives of the companies decided that, although there might be a serious problem to face after the war if Africans were used for the dilution of labour, this option should be kept open and a promise made that existing conditions would be restored after the war. The management officials then left while Welensky put the proposition to the union, and when the full meeting was resumed, the 'colour-bar' clause and a restrictive labour clause to limit the amount of work done by Europeans were dropped, and a clause on the dilution of labour was drafted and accepted. As finally incorporated in the agreement signed in July 1940, it read:

Both parties agree that during the War dilution of labour may be necessary, in which case it will be carried out after mutual consultation between the Union and the Company. After the War, working conditions on each

---

[1] Memorandum, 'Colour Bar' Clause, 4 Jan. 1950.
[2] Sir Roy (Roland) Welensky, b. 1907. Member of the Legislative Council of Northern Rhodesia, 1938–53; Minister of Transport, Communications and Posts, Federation of Rhodesia and Nyasaland, 1953–6; Federal Prime Minister, 1956–63.

of the individual mines will revert to the practice at present existing with regard to the number of machines and scrapers worked by employees, number of places supervised by employees, etc.[1]

This clause was the foundation of the wall of protection which the union built up by industrial agreement during and just after the war. The relationship between European and African labour was frozen at its existing level. The management salvaged one concession from the arrangement, in that the wording of the clause referred to 'working conditions on each of the individual mines'. This recognized that Africans had advanced unevenly in some types of semi-skilled work, and protected their position where progress had been made. The union was prevented from imposing throughout the Copperbelt the lowest level of African advancement on individual mines, and years later the anomalies created by the 'ragged edge' jobs were still bitterly attacked by its members. Meanwhile the dilution of labour became an increasingly sensitive matter, and the likelihood of trouble after the war seemed so serious that in the end no move was made to use African workers in additional 'white' jobs. At a meeting of the War Supplies Committee on 7 April 1941 the possibility was discussed, but the Governor 'was afraid that to attempt this might involve labour troubles which he had no desire to contemplate'.[2]

A further indication of the strengthened position of the Mine Workers' Union was the fate of the conference on African advancement which the Forster Commission had recommended should take place between the union, the companies, and the Government. The proposal was at first generally accepted. The Governor minuted in August 1940 that the discussions were necessary, likely to be difficult, and that a fair balance between European and African interests should be sought.[3] The Executive Council gave its approval.[4] The Labour Commissioner felt that the Forster Commission was so much on the minds of the more skilled Africans that the conference must be held.[5] The London Directors of the mining companies informed the Colonial Office that they had no objections.[6] The local managers, however, wrote to the Governor that any direct negotiations with the

[1] Memorandum, 'Colour Bar' Clause, 4 Jan. 1950.
[2] SEC/LAB/191: Minutes of meeting of War Supplies Committee, 7 Apr. 1941.
[3] SEC/LAB/79: Governor's Minute to Chief Secretary, 26 Aug. 1940.
[4] SEC/LAB/79: T. F. Sandford to Chief Secretary, 15 Jan. 1941.
[5] SEC/LAB/79: Minute enclosed by R. S. Hudson, Labour Commissioner, to Chief Secretary, 30 Aug. 1940.
[6] SEC/LAB/79: Secretary of State to Governor, 22 Nov. 1940.

union could only result in the union establishing a colour bar at as low a point as possible in the industrial hierarchy.[1] The negotiations which led to the dilution clause in the agreement of July 1940 had been followed by a new demand in September for a closed shop, and the local managers felt they had reason for caution. The 'ragged edge' jobs performed by Africans were still at stake. The managers declared their willingness to negotiate with the Government alone, but refused to discuss the matter directly with the union.[2]

Shortly after hearing the companies' views, the Governor, Sir John Maybin, wrote to the Secretary of State that at the end of the war the Government and the companies would be under an obligation to reinstate European mine employees who had gone into the army, while Europeans at present performing their jobs also had claims to employment: moreover a slump in the copper industry was generally feared at the end of the war. In these circumstances it would be impossible for Africans to retain jobs they might have taken over from Europeans during the war, and therefore it seemed unwise to press for African advancement at all 'in view of its short duration and consequent dissatisfaction'. Maybin felt that to hold the conference with the union would merely raise bad feelings without producing results, although he concluded enigmatically that it would of course be made clear to the union 'that this Government would not countenance restrictions against Africans'.[3]

The Secretary of State replied within the week that, despite the inevitable difficulties which would arise at the end of the war, the suggestion to defer the conference until then would be too great a disappointment for African opinion. He thought that there would be a definite advantage in initiating discussions with the managements and the union, even if immediate results were not obtained.[4] Maybin did not agree, and at the beginning of February notified the Colonial Office of the pessimistic statement he planned to issue when the Forster Commission's report was published:

The Government hopes in due course to initiate discussions as recommended by the Commission, but it must be realized that the present posi-

[1] SEC/LAB/79: R. M. Peterson, General Manager, Roan Antelope Copper Mintes Ltd. to Chief Secretary, 4 Jan. 1941; A. Royden Harrison, General Manager, Rhokana Corporation to Chief Secretary, 4 Jan. 1941.
[2] SEC/LAB/79: A. Royden Harrison to Chief Secretary, 4 Jan. 1941.
[3] SEC/LAB/79: Governor to Secretary of State, 25 Jan. 1941.
[4] SEC/LAB/79: Secretary of State to Governor, 30 Jan. 1941.

tion is complicated by the fact that many Europeans have gone off from the mines to active service with the forces. The great majority of them were promised by the Companies when they went that they would be reinstated in their employment provided that the scope for mining activities after the war permitted. Numbers of them in the meantime have been replaced by other Europeans and these also will have a claim to continued employment after the war as well as those who have been denied the privilege of active service and have been retained in this war time essential service. A reduction in copper output has also to be contemplated. It is therefore very clear that at the end of the war Government will be hard put to it to secure re-employment or continued employment for all who have such just claims to it. During the war some dilution with African labour has been accepted but it would be impossible to maintain Africans in posts previously occupied by Europeans to the exclusion of previous holders returning from the war.[1]

The Government took six years to initiate the discussions recommended by the Forster Commission.

While the conference was postponed indefinitely, a further barrier to African progress was raised. Only two months after the new agreement with the mining companies was signed in July 1940 the union had renewed its demands for a closed shop.[2] Despite the fact that all the parties concerned were aware that the granting of a closed shop would block African advancement, the Colonial Office instructed the companies that the advancement issue raised by the Forster Commission and the closed shop demand were to be dealt with independently, the former by the Governor and the latter by the companies in their industrial negotiations.[3] In April 1941 Ernest Oppenheimer wrote to his son about the situation:

The union is making a great deal of trouble . . . they propose to take [the 'closed shop'] whether we agree or not and it is for the Government to deal with the men, because the Government objects to a closed shop because it is tantamount to a 'colour bar'. . . . The labour position is developing on the same lines as the position on the Rand during the last war. In the Johannesburg case gold was essential for war purposes, and in Northern Rhodesia copper is essential for war purposes. The men know that we do not want a strike, and would not allow a strike to develop out of patriotic reasons, and they make the most of it.[4]

On 8 May London officials of the two mining groups had an interview

[1] SEC/LAB/79: Governor to Secretary of State, 3 Feb. 1941.
[2] Memorandum, 'Colour Bar' Clause 4, Jan. 1950.
[3] C.I.S.B., 90. 38, vol. i: Notes regarding draft 'closed shop' Agreement.
[4] Gregory, p. 472.

at the Colonial Office with the Parliamentary Under-Secretary of State, George Hall. The British Government did not want to be drawn into the dispute and hoped that in exchange for other concessions the union might postpone the demand for a closed shop. The companies' representatives formed the opinion that if a strike was threatened they would be asked by the Government to give way. Meanwhile they warned the managers in Northern Rhodesia that they could not be party to an interruption of copper production. The local managers, who were strongly opposed to granting a closed shop, replied by cable on 16 May: 'Government should take an active interest in matters and if they do not then Companies should make a definite decision and as a matter of expediency and a further war effort it would seem that the granting of closed shop is necessary however much we dislike doing so.'[1] A week later the London offices replied that after discussing the position with the Colonial Office they were prepared to grant a closed shop in principle provided the union agreed to make no further demands about increases in basic pay for the duration of the war. The union successfully opposed the suggested embargo on pay increases, and the 'closed shop' agreement was made in September 1941.[2] Under the 1941 Emergency Powers Regulations it could not be strictly enforced during the wartime labour shortage, but it was understood that at the end of the war all daily-paid (non-management) European employees who refused to join the union would be dismissed.

The extreme caution with which the Colonial Office, the Northern Rhodesia Government and the mining companies treated the Mine Workers' Union was not the result of the 1940 strikes alone. The union's General Secretary, Frank Maybank, was an outspoken, unpredictable man with strong communist sympathies. After the 'closed shop' victory he continued to agitate for action on a variety of industrial and other issues, making vigorous attacks on the Administration and threatening industrial trouble if his demands were not met.[3] Although Copperbelt support for the war effort was widespread the possibility of further trouble at the mines could not be discounted. The Governor threatened to deport Maybank early in 1942, but it was not until September, after he had tried to involve the European miners and the Railway Workers' Union in an industrial dispute at

---

[1] Memorandum, 'Colour Bar' Clause, 4 Jan. 1950.
[2] Memorandum, 'Colour Bar' Clause, 4 Jan. 1950.
[3] Gann, *History*, pp. 341–2.

the Katanga mines, that he and two supporters were arrested.[1] The Governor acted in close consultation with the British Cabinet over Maybank's deportation, and despite strong protests by the British Trades Union Congress that he had been victimized on account of his trade-union activities, the Colonial Office refused to allow him to return until the end of the war in Europe.[2]

TRADE-UNION LEGISLATION

The threat to the war effort of radical agitation in the Mine Workers' Union coincided with a lesser crisis concerning trade-union affairs. Although it was conducted entirely in a constitutional manner, it was a sharp warning to the Government of the problems raised by the growing political influence of the European trade-union movement. In 1926 Northern Rhodesia had had only five electoral areas which returned one candidate each to the Legislative Council,[3] and the Northern Area covered both Ndola and Broken Hill. By 1941 Ndola, Nkana, Luanshya, and Broken Hill, with their surrounding districts, all had separate representation and the number of electoral districts had risen to eight.[4] The influence this gave to white workers in the urban areas was reflected in the result of the 1941 election, in which five of the eight districts returned members of Roy Welensky's newly formed Labour Party, three of them trade-unionists, to the Legislative Council.[5] As luck would have it, one of the first matters requiring attention by the new Council was a trade-union Bill, and the Administration found itself promoting a highly controversial piece of legislation.

The Trade Unions and Trade Disputes Bill was drawn up in 1938 at the request of a member of the Legislative Council to consolidate the seven British trade-union Acts which had been applied to the Protectorate.[6] The Bill contained some new pro-

[1] Gann, *History*, pp. 342–3; Zambia Expatriate Mineworkers' Association, Mine Workers' Union miscellaneous correspondence, 1940–54; F. Murray, M.W.U. President, to C. R. Attlee, Stafford Cripps, E. Bevin, and others, 18 Aug. 1942.

[2] *Report of Proceedings, Annual Trades Union Congress*, 1944, p. 123, and 1945, p. 145.

[3] Davidson, p. 23.

[4] *Legislative Council Debates*, 79, 21 Oct. 1953, Appendix B, pp. 19, 22.

[5] Davidson, p. 43.

[6] English statute law had been applied to Northern Rhodesia in 1911, and protection for trade unions was therefore provided by the British trade union Acts of 1871, 1876, and 1906. After the European Mine Workers' Union was formed an

visions.[1] In setting out previously unseen and unused British legislation, however, it also included sections based on parts of the Trade Disputes and Trade Unions Act of 1927, passed after the General Strike, which British trade unions bitterly opposed. The clauses to which Northern Rhodesian trade-unionists took particular offence protected people who refused to join illegal strikes or lock-outs; made members of a trade union subscribing to a political fund give their consent in writing; prevented local or other public authorities from requiring that employees should or should not be trade-union members; and made a strike illegal if it had any object apart from furthering a trade dispute within the industry concerned, or was designed to coerce the Government.[2]

The Bill was not introduced in the Legislative Council until after the 1941 election, partly because of long consultations between the Government, representatives of industry, and the unions on its provisions, and partly through delays caused by the need to refer points raised in the discussions back to London for advice, as there was no expert on trade-union law in the Administration. The trade unions' hostility to the Bill, which had been apparent since 1938,[3] increased sharply when they failed to secure a substantial revision of its contents. Maybank took up a threatening attitude towards the Government (from which the Mine Workers' Union later dissociated itself),[4] and in September 1942 Roy Welensky, speaking for the Labour Party, made a fiery attack on the Bill in the Legislative Council.[5] After the debate the Bill was referred to a Select Committee of the Council, which had among its five members Welensky and F. J. Sinclair, both

---

Imperial Acts Extension Ordinance was passed in 1937 to apply the British trade union legislation of 1913, 1917, and 1927, together with the Industrial Courts Act of 1919, to the territory. (B. C. Roberts, *Labour in the Tropical Territories of the Commonwealth* (London, 1964), pp. 260–1.)

[1] The new provisions in the Bill were those for the compulsory registration of trade unions; for arbitration as well as conciliation proceedings in a trade dispute; and for making a strike or a lock-out illegal unless there had been an attempt at conciliation.

[2] SEC/LAB/111: H. W. Wilson, Attorney-General to Chief Secretary, 23 Feb. 1940; same to same, 28 Apr. 1941.

[3] An article in the *Rhodesian Railway Review* in Nov. 1938 attacked the Bill as unwarranted state interference in trade-union affairs, while another article in the *Mine Workers' Union Bulletin* of Feb. 1939 labelled it as class legislation.

[4] SEC/LAB/111: Telegram, D.C., Kitwe to Chief Secretary, 4 Sept. 1942; telegram, D.C., Mufulira to Chief Secretary, 23 Sept. 1942.

[5] *Legislative Council Debates*, 43, 18 Sept. 1942, 210–13.

Railway Union branch chairmen, and Marthinus Visagie, the elected member for Nkana and an official of the Mine Workers' Union.[1]

Before the Committee had a chance to meet, Frank Maybank's detention in October, followed by the threat of a strike on the Copperbelt, created a situation in which the Administration considered it wise to postpone further consideration of the Bill. In March 1943, after Visagie had been elected as the new General Secretary of the Mine Workers' Union and the position on the Copperbelt was quiet, the future of the Bill was re-examined. The Chief Secretary, George Beresford Stooke, felt that as the wartime Emergency Regulations provided for industrial conciliation and arbitration, and as the points with which the trade unions disagreed were contained in the existing law, the draft legislation was scarcely urgent. He also noted that the question of applying the Bill to Africans had not been considered, although Africans were now likely to be involved in three-sided disputes with managements and European workers over advancement.[2] The Attorney-General seized on the point and developed it into a strategy.

I would suggest that the Select Committee should meet. If the opposition should appear to be so great that the passing of the Bill into law was likely to cause any sort of disturbance it should be possible for the Government Members of the Committee to recommend that the Bill should not be proceeded with on the grounds that it was not suitable for native Unions. I assume that the Labour Commissioner could give evidence to justify such a conclusion. So far as the native position is concerned I find it difficult to envisage the possibility that any legislation in this Territory for native Trade Unions will be necessary for a long time and I would not recommend postponement of the Bill on that account except as a subterfuge.[3]

In the end the subterfuge was not produced for the benefit of the Select Committee, but for the Colonial Office. When the Secretary of State inquired about the progress of the legislation, the Governor replied that in view of the opposition of the Labour Party, the danger of unrest in the unions, and the lack of urgency in the matter, the Select Committee would not be convened and the Bill would automatically lapse at the end of the current Council. An African Trade

---

[1] *Legislative Council Debates*, 43, 21 Sept. 1942, pp. 327–8.

[2] SEC/LAB/111: Note on Trade Unions, Conciliation and Trade Disputes Bill by George Beresford Stooke, 6 Apr. 1943.

[3] SEC/LAB/111: H. W. Wilson, Attorney-General to Chief Secretary, 28 Apr. 1943.

Union 'may make its appearance at any time', and he felt that in view of the possibility of three-sided conciliation and arbitration proceedings in the future, further consideration of the legislation and expert advice were desirable.[1] Thus the Bill died, and the Government was rid of a considerable embarrassment.

THE STABILIZATION OF AFRICAN LABOUR

While the Government came under increasing pressure from European workers to protect their interests, the Colonial Office was pressing for a review of the position of African mine labour. After the strikes in 1940 drew attention to the Copperbelt situation, the Secretary of State informed the Governor that the copper industry must be regarded as permanently established, and that the Government's policy towards a settled African industrialized community at the mines should be defined more closely.[2] Sir John Waddington's[3] reply showed that the Administration had not lost its bias against urban settlement: he was not anxious to hasten stabilization 'with the resultant loss to the tribal areas', although he admitted that it was probably inevitable.[4]

The Government recognized that social changes were taking place in the urban areas. Two studies made during the war at Broken Hill and on the Copperbelt showed that a growing number of Africans were adopting the towns as their homes for long periods.[5] Officials feared that any substantial improvement in urban living conditions would not only encourage the permanent settlement of existing residents but would result in an uncontrollable influx of people from the villages, looking for work. Stress was therefore placed on the need to foster stabilization in the rural areas if it was also to be encouraged in the towns, in the hope that agricultural development and better social services in the provinces might reduce the flow of people to the

[1] SEC/LAB/111: E. J. Waddington, Governor to Secretary of State, 30 Aug. 1943.

[2] SEC/LAB/27: Oliver Stanley, Secretary of State to Sir John Waddington, Governor, 28 Apr. 1944.

[3] Sir Eubule John Waddington, 1890–1957. Colonial service, Kenya, 1913–32; Colonial Secretary, Bermuda, 1932–5; British Guiana, 1935–8; Governor, Barbados, 1938–41; Governor, Northern Rhodesia, 1941–7.

[4] SEC/LAB/27: 'Stabilisation of Native Labour', at (23) in file.

[5] G. Wilson, *An Essay on the Economics of Detribalisation* (Livingstone, 1941–2); A. Lynn Saffery, *A report on some aspects of African living conditions on the Copper belt of Northern Rhodesia* (mimeo.) (Lusaka 1943).

Copperbelt.[1] Ideally little permanent settlement should take place in the towns: model villages were again suggested for long-term workers, but the number of inhabitants would be strictly limited, in the few having ownership of their houses, and on retirement they would be encouraged to return to their tribal villages.[2] This policy was accepted by the Colonial Office in 1944,[3] but there was subsequently some disagreement with the Administration over the nature of the balance that was to be sought between rural and urban interests. Leading members of the Administration thought priority should be given to rural progress in development plans,[4] a bias which echoed Sir John Maybin's idea that new opportunities in the rural areas would provide the solution to colour-bar problems in the towns. The Colonial Office was doubtful about whether rural and urban development could ever be precisely balanced, and the Secretary of State felt that progressive development of the countryside could not be expected to keep pace with progress on the Copperbelt, or with the more elaborate services required for both stabilized and temporary workers in the towns.[5] The Government was reluctant to give way to the Colonial Office view. Official policy became 'what is known—and it is admittedly rather a vague phrase—as balanced stabilization'. This was defined by the Secretary for Native Affairs as 'stabilization in the rural areas by such means as we are now adopting by encouraging peasant settlements . . . and in the urban areas to such a degree as the industry warrants'.[6]

The mining companies were as hesitant as the Government about encouraging a stable labour force. Sir Ernest Oppenheimer, the Chairman of the Anglo American Group, was convinced of the need to encourage workers to return home after about eighteen months of

---

[1] *Lynn Saffery*, p. 62; SEC/LAB/27: Report of the Fourth Meeting of the African Labour Advisory Board, 19–20 July 1943, and Note on Stabilization of Native Labour at (23) in file.

[2] SEC/LAB/27: R. S. Hudson, P.C., Western Province to Chief Secretary, 29 June 1944; and Sir John Waddington, Governor to Oliver Stanley, Secretary of State, 2 Jan. 1945.

[3] SEC/LAB/27: Oliver Stanley, Secretary of State to Sir John Waddington, 21 Apr. 1944.

[4] SEC/LAB/27: P.C., Western Province to Chief Secretary, 29 May 1945; also Joint Development Adviser and Commissioner for Native Development to Chief Secretary, 2 July 1945.

[5] SEC/LAB/27: Oliver Stanley, Secretary of State to Sir John Waddington, 29 Mar. 1945.

[6] *Legislative Council Debates*, 61, 17 June 1948, 233.

work.[1] The cost of feeding and housing a worker's wife was calculated at 12s. 8d. a month,[2] almost as much as a labourer's wage, and
although some 40 per cent of the workers had their wives with them
at Nkana Oppenheimer was not keen to have the company incur the
expenses of housing and management involved in a policy of long-
term settlement.[3] Roan Antelope and Mufulira were both anxious to
encourage married labour to stay longer at the mines, but the available accommodation steadily deteriorated because of the wartime
shortage of building materials.[4] None of the mines embarked on a
plan to provide housing suitable for a stable labour force. At least
part of their caution came from their lack of knowledge of the work-
potential of their labour: Oppenheimer thought that African workers
might suffer from progressive exhaustion after eighteen months on the
job, while William Scrivener, the Nkana compound manager, was
uncertain if it was economic to keep them longer than five years.[5]

During the war the companies began to co-ordinate their labour
policies. They agreed that the high turnover of African workers was
uneconomic, but that the permanent settlement of labour at the mines
was unwise. It suited them to acknowledge the prevailing Government view that the labour force's rural connections should be maintained, and that eighteen months to two years was a desirable average
length of service; but they took no active steps to enforce Government
policy, beyond providing travel allowances and unpaid leave to encourage workers to keep up their rural contacts.[6] The companies'
interest in promoting longer periods of work on the Copperbelt was
limited to a number of skilled senior men. At the end of the war 15
per cent of all their African employees left after completing 3 tickets
(90 days' work); 30 per cent of the total had gone by the end of 6
tickets; 55 per cent after 12 tickets; and 75 per cent after 18 tickets.

---

[1] SEC/LAB/49: Labour Commissioner R. S. Hudson's memorandum of
Copperbelt tour 25–30 Aug. 1941, meeting with Sir Ernest Oppenheimer, 26 Aug.
1941.
[2] C.I.S.B., 100.23, vol. i: W. J. Scrivener, Memorandum . . . 26 Mar. 1943.
[3] SEC/LAB/49: Labour Commissioner's memorandum, 26 Aug. 1941.
[4] Lynn Saffery, pp. 50 ff.
[5] SEC/LAB/49: Labour Commissioner's memorandum, 26 Aug. 1941; C.I.S.B.,
100.23, vol. i: W. J. Scrivener, Memorandum on Native Travel Allowance, 18 Nov.
1941.
[6] C.I.S.B., 100.23, vol. i: Memorandum on native labour policy, by Mufulira
Mines African Compound Manager H. H. Field, 1 Sept. 1942; Memorandum on
native labour policy by Roan Antelope Mines African Compound Manager C. G.
Spearpoint, 25 Aug. 1942; Memorandum, undated, on above reports by Rhokana
Corporation Chief Compound Manager W. Scrivener.

Only 10 per cent of the original number stayed on to complete 30 tickets, while 4 per cent reached 42 tickets.[1]

These low figures for length of service at the mines were not incompatible with the growing trend among Africans towards longer residence in the towns. A research worker noted in 1942 that longer residence might be more pronounced outside the company compounds because of the poor mine housing, which was unsuitable for large families.[2] Mine statistics on labour turnover took no account of the total number of engagements a man might work with short or long leaves between them; of the growing number of men who did not return to their villages during leaves, preferring to stay on the Copperbelt; or of workers who moved from one mine to another, or to work outside the mines. After the war the mine managements were still reluctant to recognize the trend. They agreed that longer periods of settlement in their compounds should not be encouraged yet, and that no mine would begin to build additional married accommodation without consulting the others.[3]

The need to maintain industrial peace on the Copperbelt resulted in a policy of *laissez-aller* towards the Mine Workers' Union, and the deportation of Maybank was an emergency measure which pointed up the contrast of the Administration's general policy line. After the 1940 strike, when the union had claimed that it could not control its members, Sir John Maybin was inclined to favour strengthening the union's position to remove some of the discontent among European workers and prevent further unofficial stoppages.[4] The union was quick to exploit this attitude, and the Government was too compromised by the overriding need to maintain copper supplies for the war in Europe to resist. The settlement of the colour-bar issue on the mines by industrial negotiation provided an unfortunate precedent for the future treatment of the problem, while the emergence in the Legislative Council of a bloc of elected members sympathetic to the

[1] C.I.S.B., 100.23, vol. i: P. H. Truscott, Manager of Chamber of Mines to Secretary, Mufulira Copper Mines Ltd., London, 19 Dec. 1946.

[2] Lynn Saffery, p. 4.

[3] C.I.S.B., 100.23, vol. i: P. H. Truscott, Manager of the Chamber of Mines to the Secretary, Mufulira Copper Mines Limited, London, 19 Dec. 1946.

[4] SEC/LAB/111: Sir John Maybin to Chief Secretary, 20 June 1940, and Frank Ayer, General Manager, Roan Antelope Copper Mine Ltd. to Messrs. Ellis & Co., 24 July 1940.

European trade-union movement did not make the outlook for a post-war solution hopeful.

A difficult, potentially dangerous situation had developed at the mines, and the Government was aware that this added a new dimension to the policy of short-term labour migration which it had earlier favoured for cheapness of administration and as a solution to rural economic difficulties. Now that African advancement was blocked, to encourage Africans to remain longer at the mines and acquire industrial skills or increased efficiency might lead to a clash with European workers.[1]

[1] SEC/LAB/27: H. A. Cartmel-Robinson to Governor, 23 Nov. 1944.

CHAPTER V

Labour Supervision and African Trade Unions

THE European Mine Workers' Union made rapid strides in organization and political influence during the Second World War. The representation of African workers was in a much less advanced state. The Colonial Office, under the Labour Government's Secretary of State, Lord Passfield, had stated in 1930 that the introduction of trade-unionism in the Colonies was desirable.[1] The subject was raised again by a Conservative Secretary of State, William Ormsby-Gore, in a circular dispatch sent out in 1937.[2] But despite official approval in London, trade-unionism was not easily accepted in many territories. Its introduction for African workers in Northern Rhodesia illustrates the slow process by which separate strands of local and imperial policy combined, over a considerable period of time, to reach Lord Passfield's objective.

The Northern Rhodesian Government's leisurely approach to the question of African representation in industry reflected both the crippling economic effects of the depression on its policies, and the nature of its relation with the Colonial Office. In the early 1930s Downing Street exercised a minimal influence on matters such as labour policy, and Lord Passfield's interest in labour affairs between 1929 and 1931, when he was Secretary of State, was unusual. At the Colonial Office Conference of Governors and Officials in 1930 his Parliamentary Under-Secretary, Dr. T. Drummond Shiels, put forward forceful views on the revision of labour legislation, the necessity for 'decent' wages, and the progressive development of trade unions.[3] However when Passfield sent out a circular dispatch after the

---

[1] Foreign and Commonwealth Office Library, C.O. 323/1096/70967/3: Circular Despatch from Lord Passfield, Secretary of State for the Colonies, 17 Sept. 1930.

[2] Foreign and Commonwealth Office Library, C.O. 323/1429/1766: Circular Despatch from W. Ormsby-Gore, Secretary of State for the Colonies, 24 Aug 1937.

[3] Colonial Office, *Conference of Colonial Governors and Officials* (Cmd. 3628 of 1930), 10 July 1930.

conference reminding Governors that the highest standards should be maintained in the conditions of employment of native labour, he circumspectly added that His Majesty's Government would 'bear in mind the necessity of not enforcing in British Dependencies conditions of which it is not possible to secure the enforcement in foreign territories which may enter into economic competition with them'.[1]

Little was done in response to the Colonial Office's advice about improving conditions. An effort by Passfield to eliminate penal sanctions for breaches of native labour contracts met with solid opposition from East and Central African Governors, who claimed they were essential to the maintenance of a reliable labour force.[2] Ordinances were passed to fulfil obligations incurred by Britain under International Labour Conventions, but some were not immediately relevant to local conditions, and others, which were, aroused considerable hostility in territorial legislatures. An instance was seen in Northern Rhodesia, where the Minimum Wage Ordinance of 1932 was passed only after the Chief Secretary promised that it was 'not the intention or the policy of the Government to use this empowering Ordinance in the immediate or indeed the near future'.[3] The lack of Colonial Office direction of labour policy reflected the general trend of British Colonial rule at this period. 'Broadly speaking the tendency was to accept the advice of the man on the spot unless there was some positive reason to the contrary. . . . This was not of course the result of inertia or indifference in the Colonial Office; leaving the initiative to the man on the spot was part of the traditional British attitude towards overseas administration.'[4]

Nevertheless the Colonial Office had a strong respect for the development of an institutional framework in dependent territories, and towards the middle of the decade it began to exert increasing pressure for the supervision of conditions of employment through a special government department, the regulation of relations between employers and employees by conciliation machinery, and the recognition of trade unions. The question of the supervision of labour condi-

[1] Foreign and Commonwealth Office Library, C.O. 323/1071/70093: Circular Despatch from Lord Passfield, Secretary of State for the Colonies, 6 Aug. 1930.

[2] Rhodes House Library, 100·441 s $\frac{12}{1930}$ (3)A: C. H. Dobree, Acting Governor of Northern Rhodesia to Secretary of State, 11 Oct. 1930; Governor of Tanganyika Territory to same, 29 Mar. 1931; Governor of Uganda to same, 6 Mar. 1931; Governor of Nyasaland to same, 17 Jan. 1931.

[3] *Legislative Council Debates*, 18, 16 Dec. 1932, 54.

[4] Sir Andrew Cohen, *British Policy in Changing Africa* (London, 1959), p. 82.

tions brought the Northern Rhodesian Administration into conflict with London officials, and on this issue the Colonial Office made its first decisive intervention into labour affairs in the territory.

THE ESTABLISHMENT OF A LABOUR DEPARTMENT

As the web of migrant labour grew increasingly complicated, and a clash of interests developed between European and African labour in the towns, the Government persisted in supervising labour matters through the district administration. The reluctance to set up a new department to deal with labour was, of course, partly concerned with economy; but senior officials were also suspicious of any innovations which might undermine the position of the political officers of the Government. The idea of a special labour department was not easily accepted, despite strong pressure from the Colonial Office, and by the time the department was belatedly established labour relations on the Copperbelt had reached a crisis point.

The direction which control of labour affairs should take had been given a firm prompting shortly after the unrest on the Copperbelt in 1935. The Secretary of State for the Colonies sent out a circular dispatch urging regular inspection of places of employment, and noting that mining developments were particularly in need of attention. He was 'unable to regard as satisfactory a system under which the machinery of government is invoked only to the extent of investigating complaints'.[1]

In Northern Rhodesia the existing provisions for attention to labour affairs by the under-staffed Provincial Administration were far from adequate. On the copper-mines it had the assistance of two Inspectors of Mines and a small number of Medical Officers, but there was 'no co-ordinating direction from anyone whose principal concern it is to deal with labour problems and conditions'.[2] The Native Industrial Labour Advisory Board considered this question in 1935 and recommended against setting up a special Labour Department. Representatives of industry felt that the proposed department would not have sufficient staff to provide much control in the rural areas, and would tend instead to devote attention 'to precisely those areas which were least in need of supervision'.[3] The Board advised

[1] SEC/LAB/35: Circular Despatch from Malcolm MacDonald, Secretary of State for the Colonies, 9 Nov. 1935.
[2] *Chairman's Report of meetings of the Native Industrial Labour Advisory Board held at Ndola on November 7th and 8th and December 16th and 17th, 1935*, p. 8.
[3] Ibid., p. 9.

that the Provincial Administration should be strengthened to enable it to have proper contacts with the African working population, while one officer should be appointed 'to study labour problems not only in the industrial areas but also in the districts from which labour is drawn; to co-operate and keep under constant review the work of departments dealing with labour matters; to keep records and statistics; and to travel freely about the country for the purpose of having first hand knowledge of his work.'[1]

The mine managements' view that a fully-fledged Labour Department might concentrate too heavily on mine labour matters had its counterpart in the Government's suspicion that a specialist department might participate in affairs which were properly the concern of the Provincial Administration. This prospect had caused Sir James Maxwell great anxiety when the establishment of a Labour Department had been considered in 1930, and the Chief Secretary wrote for information to Tanganyika Territory, where a Labour Department had been established since 1925. Maxwell was doubtless reassured to learn that although a Labour Officer, 'being constantly the guest of planters and farmers on their estates, may be inclined to view things from their angle', at least he did not come between the District Administration and the African population: '. . . naturally a Labour Officer who is likely at some future date to be serving again as an Administrative Officer under the local Provincial Commissioner will be careful not to tread on the Provincial Commissioner's corns if he can help it'.[2] Fears of specialist and technical departments persisted among political officers, and the convention to which the Northern Rhodesian Government subscribed, that technical advisers should be responsible to their Provincial Commissioner while under the general supervision of the Head of their Department, was a somewhat unwieldy arrangement.

Shortly after the Native Industrial Labour Advisory Board recommended in 1935 that a labour department was not necessary, the Nyasaland report on migrant labour was published. After considering its account of the damaging results of the migration of workers, the Board changed its mind, and decided that for the effective control of recruiting and migrant labour such a Department was essential; but

[1] *Chairman's Report* . . .1935, p. 9.
[2] SEC/LAB/35: D. J. Jardine, Chief Secretary, Tanganyika Territory to H. C. D. C. MacKenzie-Kennedy, Chief Secretary, Northern Rhodesia, 27 Nov. 1930.

the Department itself should be under suitable control. 'The Board would support the setting up of a Labour Department under a Secretary for Native Affairs, which post should be reconstituted to control Native Affairs generally. The department should act in close co-operation with the Provincial Administration and personnel would operate in any district under the general control of the District Commissioner.'[1]

The Colonial Office held a different opinion of what was expected in labour administration. A dispatch from the Secretary of State, William Ormsby-Gore, dated 24 August 1937 expressed disapproval of efforts to handle these matters through the Secretariat, Native Affairs Department or district administration of a large colony. He instructed that

Colonial Governments should forthwith consider the desirability of setting up a labour organization consisting of officers whose sole duty shall be to inspect and examine labour conditions generally and make suggestions for their improvement, and whose services can be called upon when necessary by the district administrations. I consider that it would generally be advisable that these officers should be under the control of a chief labour inspector who would act as an adviser to Government.[2]

Despite this advice a decision on the form labour administration should take was postponed. The Governor had previously decided that, in view of the questions of policy raised by the Nyasaland report, an expert should be engaged to make a study of Northern Rhodesia's labour situation.[3] Major Granville Orde Browne, who had been head of the Labour Department in Tanganyika from 1925 until 1931, and who was shortly to become Labour Adviser to the Secretary of State for the Colonies, accepted the appointment in the autumn of 1937 and spent six months studying conditions in the territory. He found that the existing system of labour administration 'achieves at best little more than an inspectorate. There is hardly any machinery for securing the constant review and consideration of all sociological problems involved [sic] and the collection of statistics and other materials requisite for their study.'[4] He recommended the appointment of

[1] SEC/LAB/34, vol. ii: Chairman's Report of the Meeting of the Native Industrial Labour Advisory Board held at Ndola on 19 June 1936.

[2] SEC/LAB/35: Circular Despatch from W. Ormsby-Gore, Secretary of State for the Colonies, 24 Aug. 1937.

[3] SEC/LAB/35: Governor to Secretary of State, 1 July 1936.

[4] Orde Browne Report, 1938, p. 80.

a Labour Commissioner, with rank equivalent to a Provincial Commissioner, and the creation of a Department staffed by seven Labour Officers, four stationed on the Copperbelt and one each at Lusaka, Fort Jameson, and Livingstone. A further officer would be posted to represent the interests of migrant labour in Southern Rhodesia.[1]

Orde Browne's recommendations on the posting and status of Labour Officers were submitted to the Native Industrial Labour Advisory Board, which still maintained that on the mines at least, the work should be done by specially seconded District Officers operating under the general control of the District Commissioner.[2] The Board recommended other changes in Orde Browne's proposals, notably a reduction from four to two in the number of officers posted to the Copperbelt. It also felt that an officer at Lusaka was unnecessary, as the needs of the Central Province were less urgent than elsewhere. Finally the position of the Labour Commissioner himself was considered, and the Board 'was of the opinion that friction would be avoided from the outset if this officer was a member of the staff of the Governor's Chief Adviser on Native Affairs'.[3]

Both the new Governor, John Maybin, and the Provincial Commissioner for the area in which the mines lay, H. P. Cartmel-Robinson, expressed doubts about how the new department would be integrated with the existing Copperbelt administration. Cartmel-Robinson felt that Labour Officers might not lighten the work of his District Officers in the Western Province. 'They might in fact increase it if their activities tended to draw attention to any things which were wrong and required administrative action by the District staff to put them right.' He also noted that Major Orde Browne had not included in his list of Labour Officers' duties such items as native registration, settlement of master–servant disputes and claims for compensation for injuries, time-consuming tasks which the district administration would have been happy to relinquish.[4] In contrast, the new Governor held that the duties proposed for Labour Officers were so comprehensive that District Officers would not have enough to do. 'If they are relieved by the appointment of Labour Officers, Asst.

---

[1] *Orde Browne Report*, 1938, p. 86.
[2] SEC/LAB/34, vol. ii: Native Industrial Labour Advisory Board, Minutes of Meeting held at Ndola on 14 Nov. 1938, p. 5.
[3] Ibid., pp. 6–7.
[4] SEC/NAT/16: H. P. Cartmel-Robinson to Chief Secretary, 14 Sept. 1938.

Taxation officers & an extra R.M. [Resident Magistrate] it is inevitable that they will not have a day's work.'[1]

The problems of dividing the work-load of the Copperbelt administration, together with a shortage of Government housing and office accommodation in the area, led to a decision that Copperbelt District Officers should take over the duties that had been proposed for Labour Officers.[2] The economies which might be achieved appealed to the Government, and the establishment of the Department was postponed until 1940, when it was planned that a Labour Commissioner and one Labour Officer, stationed at Livingstone, would be appointed.

Meanwhile the the Chairman's Report of the Native Industrial Labour Advisory Board meeting in November had been submitted to the Secretary of State in January 1939; further progress was delayed until his comments were received on the changes it recommended in the Orde Browne proposals. The reply was late in coming, and was highly critical of the Board, which had been appointed to advise on industrial matters only, for dealing with the general matters of policy covered in Major Orde Browne's report. The alterations were not acceptable:

The Board appears to have regarded the Labour Officers as virtually a part of the District Administration, but, as you will have gathered from my confidential despatch of the 9th June, I consider that the Labour Department should be a distinct organization. This is desirable, amongst other reasons, to prevent a tendency to frequent changes or reallocation of duties to suit the requirements of ordinary District work.[3]

There was a suspicion in the Secretariat that Major Orde Browne, now Labour Adviser to the Secretary of State, had helped to draft the dispatch, unwilling to see his proposals altered by a body he had criticized in his report.[4]

The Secretary of State's reproof was dispatched on 2 August 1939. Within the week the Governor telegraphed the Colonial Office suggesting that the formation of a Labour Department might again be postponed, because of the declaration of war against Germany. He was informed that war conditions made the establishment of a Labour

[1] SEC/NAT/16: Governor's minute to Chief Secretary, 31 Oct. 1938.
[2] SEC/NAT/16: Minute by the Chief Secretary, W. M. Logan, 1 Feb. 1939.
[3] SEC/LAB/34, vol. ii: Malcolm MacDonald, Secretary of State, to Officer Administering the Government of Northern Rhodesia, 2 Aug. 1939.
[4] SEC/LAB/34, vol. ii: J. H. Wallace, Assistant Secretary, to Senior Provincial Commissioner, 11 Sept. 1939.

Department even more desirable than before.[1] Maybin felt that he had come under unreasonable pressure from Downing Street, and particularly resented the August dispatch criticizing the Advisory Board's role in labour affairs. 'This is one of the rare cases in which there is an element of unjustifiable "interference". I see no occasion for the S of S to read me a homily because I consulted NILAB . . .'[2]

The pressure from the Colonial Office could not be resisted indefinitely. Towards the end of 1939 an Acting Labour Commissioner was appointed, and the sum of £6,512 was earmarked for the Department's expenses in 1940, to cover the Commissioner's office in Lusaka, the posting of an officer to Livingstone, the half-time services of a District Officer at Fort Jameson, and the expenses of representation at Salisbury and Johannesburg.[3] The duties of Labour Officers on the Copperbelt were to be carried out by the staff of the Provincial Administration in the meantime. Anticipating criticism of this arrangement, the Governor justified it to the Secretary of State on grounds of economy, the difficulty of getting extra staff in wartime, and the desirability of using the administrative officers' experience of both tribal and industrial conditions.[4] He hoped it would be considered a 'reasonable start',[5] unaware that within four months it was to be tested by European and African strikes on the Copperbelt. At the Colonial Office, where comment had already been passed on the possibility of a confrontation between 'an indifferent type of European immigrant' and 'an undisciplined and floating native labour force', there were doubts about the appropriateness of Maybin's reply. One official minuted that the Governor 'appears to be somewhat piqued at the amount of prodding he has had from this end in the matter of getting ahead with a progressive labour policy. In these circumstances it would, I feel, do more harm than good to criticize his present proposals even though they may not be regarded here as being entirely adequate.' Another noted that the decision to limit the new Department for reasons of economy read very strangely in view of recent improvements in revenue, and a third, anxious to see Maybin

[1] SEC/LAB/34, vol. ii: J. A. Maybin to Malcolm MacDonald, Secretary of State, 20 Dec. 1939.

[2] SEC/LAB/34, vol. ii: Minute by J. A. Maybin, 12 Dec. 1939.

[3] SEC/LAB/36: Sir John Maybin to Malcolm MacDonald, Secretary of State, 14 Dec. 1939; and same to same, 28 Feb. 1940.

[4] SEC/LAB/36: Sir John Maybin to Malcolm MacDonald, 14 Dec. 1939: SEC/LAB/34, vol. ii: same to same, 20 Dec. 1939.

[5] Loc. cit.

pushed harder, argued with considerable foresight that serious labour troubles were likely to arise in wartime.[1]

The Colonial Office's concern for the establishment of the Department was part of a general drive covering many territories. Between 1937 and 1941 the number of dependencies with special labour departments or staff increased from 11 to 33.[2] This development was considered to be the keystone of colonial labour policy, on which all further progress depended, and was held to be of more fundamental importance than the rapid growth of workers' organizations. Trade-unionism in the Colonies was a long-term goal, to be reached without undue haste. The foundations of its natural growth were a conscientious Labour Department, suitable legislation, assistance if necessary by an experienced trade-unionist, and time. Colonial Office officials were hesitant about an artificial stimulus to trade-unionism, but felt that a favourable background would eventually produce healthy and spontaneous labour movements. Northern Rhodesia's slow progress in developing trade unions for Africans was acceptable by these standards, but its reluctance to set up a Labour Department could not be allowed to pass unchallenged.

WARTIME DEVELOPMENTS IN LABOUR POLICY

In 1940 the Northern Rhodesian Government believed that the formation of trade unions for African workers, most of whom were illiterate migrant labourers, would be premature. The Labour Adviser to the Secretary of State, Major Granville Orde Browne, was sympathetic. Three years earlier he had written of labour organization in Africa that normal European methods were unsuitable because the great bulk of labourers were primitive and uneducated men, and would be an easy prey to dishonest schemers.[3] The Russell and Forster Commissions which had investigated the disturbances at the mines in 1935 and 1940 put forward similar views about the situation in Northern Rhodesia.[4] It was too soon to introduce trade-unionism,

---

[1] C.O. 795/110/45233: Minute, G. Seel, 10 Apr. 1939; 795/109/45109: A. R. Thomas to E. Boyd, 18 Jan. 1940, and minutes by E. Boyd, 19 Jan. 1940, and J. G. Hibbert, 3 Jan. 1940.

[2] *Labour Supervision in the Colonial Empire, 1937–1943* (Colonial No. 185 of 1943), p. 4.

[3] Orde Browne Papers.

[4] *Russell Commission Report*, 1935, p. 57; *Forster Commission Report*, 1940, pp. 41–3.

when a reliable labour force did not yet exist. In fact the Employment of Natives Ordinance made it a criminal offence for African workers to leave their job without permission.[1] The Russell Commission glossed over this legal embarrassment at the time of the 1935 disturbance by finding that no Africans had been arrested for striking, and that detentions had been made solely on charges relating to riot and intimidation.[2] The Colonial Office had information to the contrary, but noted that the Commission felt it was right for striking to be an offence in that part of Africa.[3] Major Orde Browne had written in 1933 that respect for an employment contract was a necessary forerunner of industrial organization.[4] Only a few observers believed that Africans in Northern Rhodesia should be introduced to trade-unionism in the near future, among them two missionaries attached to the United Missions in the Copper Belt, who incurred the displeasure of the mining companies for activities 'which do not appear within the scope of missionary activities as normally understood'.[5]

African workers at the mines were not entirely without representation. The compound manager at Roan Antelope, F. Spearpoint, had established a council of tribal elders there in 1931. The system was later adopted in various forms at other compounds on the Copperbelt. The elders acted as assessors in domestic quarrels among their tribesmen, and as a council met from time to time with the compound manager to receive information on behalf of their people or to report grievances.[6] They served a useful function, but their dual role as representatives of workers and management placed them in an invidious position.[7] Many workers came to consider them as the representatives of the management, while the managements were uncertain of their value. H. H. Field, the compound manager at Mufulira, who had more faith in them than the compound manager at Nkana, felt that the elders' role was limited by the ambiguous duties

---

[1] Section 74(2) of the *Employment of Natives Ordinance 1929*, which made absence from work without leave a penal offence for Africans, was dropped in the *Employment of Natives (Amendment) Ordinance 1940* (No. 28 of 1940).

[2] *Russell Commission Report*, 1935, p. 58.

[3] C.O. 795/76/45083, part 2: Minute by A. B. Cohen, 11 Nov. 1935.

[4] Orde Browne, *The African Labourer*, p. 73.

[5] J. V. Taylor and D. Lehmann, *Christians of the Copperbelt* (London, 1961), pp. 43, 161.

[6] F. Spearpoint, 'The African Native and the Rhodesian Copper Mines', pp. 19–20.

[7] A. L. Epstein, *Politics in an Urban African Community* (Manchester, 1958), p. 65.

assigned to them by the mine managements.[1] During the disturbances at Mufulira in 1940 the African workers rejected the elders and chose a 'Committee of Seventeen' instead to put forward their demands. Despite this, and although the elders' industrial role was not well-defined, the Forster Commission suggested that the system should be gradually developed as a preliminary step towards collective bargaining.[2] The Government subsequently encouraged the Nkana and Nchanga mines to adopt the system of elected elders already in use at Roan Antelope and Mufulira, and the term 'elder' was replaced by 'Tribal Representative'.[3]

The disturbances in 1940 forced on the Government a close examination of the problems of industrial representation. Although the 'elder' system was hastily reinforced at all the mines, difficulties raised by the lack of more sophisticated machinery for presenting grievances were brought to light. The strikes at Nkana and Mufulira revealed long-standing complaints over pay and promotion prospects, but workers returned to their jobs only after troops opened fire on the disorderly crowd at Nkana, and little progress in conciliating them had been made. The Government suddenly discovered that it was not easy to act as the protector of African interests in an industrial dispute. Before the shooting at Nkana officials were driven to unusual expedients to try to secure a return to work. Afterwards there was little scope for informal intervention, and the Government found that its efforts to negotiate on behalf of African workers were subject to criticism in London.

When the strike began, the Secretary for Native Affairs had been sent to the Copperbelt to try to find the exact cause of the discontent and to act as an unofficial conciliator. As a helpful insurance Chitimukulu, the Bemba paramount, and other chiefs were asked to send messages advising their tribesmen at the mines not to join in disturbances.[4] Meanwhile in Lusaka the Executive Council considered the possibility of arbitration, but concluded that the African workers would not understand the process and would feel cheated if their wage demand were not met. It decided that an 'arbitral inquiry'

[1] Evidence of H. H. Field to the Forster Commission, 1940, p. 621; and closing speech by the companies' counsel, R. Stratford, pp. 650–3.

[2] *Forster Commission Report*, 1940, pp. 41–3.

[3] SEC/LAB/163: W. M. Logan, Acting Governor to Lord Moyne, Secretary of State, 5 Aug. 1941.

[4] SEC/LAB/78, vol. i: P.C., Kasama to Chief Secretary, 2 Apr. 1940; and Chief Secretary to P.C., Kasama, same date.

should be held instead.[1] The Governor later explained that this misleading term merely implied an effort by the Government to bring the two sides together and suggest a solution.[2] The Secretary of State was informed of the proposal, but in the wake of the shooting at Nkana warned that the arbitral inquiry might be open to charges of collusion between the Government and the companies, while the absence of African nominees to the arbitral committee would almost certainly attract attention in Britain.[3] The Governor in turn warned the Secretary for Native Affairs that his intervention in the dispute must be only that of 'a friendly intermediary', and that the Government's impartiality must be beyond suspicion.[4] He finally decided that the managements must investigate the workers' grievances alone while the Government awaited the report of the official Commission of Inquiry into the shooting.

The Government had resorted to these improvisations because it assumed that the African mine-workers would not understand the principles of industrial conciliation and arbitration, or the conventions of collective bargaining. However, the strikers had at least the rudiments of organization. The real leaders were never identified, and it is not clear whether they were among the Committee of Seventeen who were chosen to present the wage demand at Mufulira.[5] The Kawambwa and Fort Rosebery workers from the north-west of the territory were thought to be the ring-leaders, while many Nyasa, Bemba, and Ngoni workers were lukewarm in their support.[6] Despite this threat of tribal factions the strike was conducted in an orderly manner and affected most of the workers at Mufulira and Nkana. The District Commissioner at Nkana described the situation there as follows:

The mob . . . seemed to be completely hypnotized, and . . . it was in effect in control of the Compound. How this control was exercised we could at

[1] SEC/LAB/78, vol. i: Executive Council Minutes, 4 Apr. 1940.
[2] SEC/LAB/78, vol. i: Governor Sir John Maybin to Lord Lloyd, Secretary of State, 7 Apr. 1940.
[3] SEC/LAB/78, vol. i: Secretary of State to Sir John Maybin, 5 Apr. 1940.
[4] SEC/LAB/78, vol. i: Executive Council Minutes, 9 Apr. 1940; and Chief Secretary to D.C. Nkana, 7 Apr. 1940.
[5] Interview with W. F. Stubbs, former Labour Commissioner in Northern Rhodesia 1944–8, Oxford, 21 Feb. 1969.
[6] SEC/LAB/136, vol. iv: A. T. Williams, D. C. Nkana, Report on the strike of African employees of Rhokana Corporation, 28 Mar.–5 Apr. 1940, p. 18; evidence to the Forster Commission 1940, W. F. Stubbs, D. C. Mufulira, p. 404.

that time only guess but there was obviously some strong sanction behind the orders that were so freely given in our presence. . . . The position seemed to be that the leaders of the strike, with those who willingly followed them, and others who were unable to resist these stronger personalities who had emerged during the five days of the strike, were cut off to all intents and purposes from the ordinary normal life of the Compound.[1]

Whether by hypnotism or by intimidation, the strike leaders wielded impressive power.

The representatives of the strikers at Mufulira, the Committee of Seventeen, were chosen informally at the suggestion of the District Officer, because the workers felt that the tribal elders had become too closely associated with the management. The District Officer felt that they were reluctant to follow his advice at first, 'possibly owing to fear that any such committee might be regarded as ring-leaders'.[2] The committee members were chosen in numbers roughly proportional to the size of the five main language groups at the mines, Bemba, Nyanja, Tonga, Lozi, and Lovale.[3] The Secretary for Native Affairs had offered to meet any spokesmen for the strikers at the Mine Welfare Hall: '. . . representatives started to arrive—others drifted in from time to time saying they also had been sent as representatives. They demanded 10s. a day saying that the White men had learned the work from them and did no work. The natives did all the work. Sandford argued that the Mines could not pay such rates explaining the cost. They refused to listen.'[4] The evidence to the Commission of Inquiry shows that educated, senior workers such as *capitaos* (overseers), hospital orderlies, clerks, and former teachers were prominent among the committee members and among strike leaders at Nkana, and that they were drawn from a variety of tribes.[5] Lawrence Katilungu, later the first president of the African Mineworkers' Union, was said to have been one of the Nkana leaders.[6] Some of these men were not entirely ignorant of the principles of industrial bargaining,

[1] SEC/LAB/136, vol. iv: A. T. Williams, Report on the strike . . . p. 27.
[2] Interview, W. F. Stubbs, Oxford, 21 Feb. 1969.
[3] Interview, W. F. Stubbs.
[4] SEC/LAB/78, vol. i: Notes taken by the Governor from the Secretary for Native Affairs' statement to the Executive Council, 4 Apr. 1940.
[5] SEC/LAB/104: Report on Native Labour Strike Apr. 1940 by the Secretary for Native Affairs, T. F. Sandford (note of interview with strike leaders at Nkana, 16 Apr. 1940, and at Mufulira, 18 Apr. 1940); evidence of Yaphet Gerusi to the Forster Commission 1940, p. 445 and of other members of the Committee of Seventeen, p. 502 ff.
[6] Ronald Segal, *Political Africa* (London, 1961), p. 129.

and pointed out to the Commission that, having made a claim they knew to be too high, they expected the management to put forward a lesser offer.[1] Instead the Secretary for Native Affairs told them their demand was unacceptable, while the mine management did not offer to bargain at all. After its brief moment of prominence the committee disintegrated.

The *Forster Commission Report* recommended in 1941 that the lowest basic wage rates should be raised by 2*s*. 6*d*., and that higher rates should be revised. The Secretary of State for the Colonies decided that the Government of Northern Rhodesia should be responsible for supervising this revision. Northern Rhodesian officials had no experience of such a complicated subject, and hoped that the mines themselves would produce a plan on which they could pass judgement.[2] When the mines were slow to do so, the Governor was pressed by the Secretary of State to undertake the revision, and even to investigate wage rates in other industries.[3] The Governor pointed out that he had no authority to set wage rates other than minimum wages, and that Government could not prepare detailed wage scales for the mines without expert help from the mine managements.[4] The London directors of the companies finally gave the local managers authority to settle the question, and a plan was published giving a new structure for African labour in which workers were divided into four groups—'special', A, B, and C—with pay graded accordingly. The Government was not satisfied with the plan, which provided selective, not general, pay increases, but accepted it in order to be able to publish details of a settlement when the Forster Commission's *Report* was released.[5]

As a result of the strike the Government appointed a single Labour Officer to cover the Copperbelt towns and Broken Hill. A second officer was not appointed until August 1941. These men devoted their time to familiarizing themselves with the working and living conditions of the labour force, and to winning the confidence of the workers and managements. They felt that 'in some cases the first was easier

[1] SEC/LAB/104: Note by T. F. Sandford on interview at Mufulira, 18 Apr. 1940; evidence of Herkos Sikwanda to the Forster Commission, 1940, pp. 503 ff., 517.

[2] SEC/LAB/79, vol. i: Sir John Maybin to Lord Lloyd, Secretary of State, 19 Dec. 1940.

[3] SEC/LAB/79, vol. i: Secretary of State to Sir John Maybin, 23 Dec. 1940.

[4] SEC/LAB/79, vol. i: Sir John Maybin to Secretary of State, 7 Jan. 1941.

[5] SEC/LAB/79, vol. i: Secretary of State to Sir John Maybin, 11 Jan. 1941; Sir John Maybin to Secretary of State, 3 Feb. 1941; and same to same, 4 Feb. 1941.

than the second'.[1] They were particularly concerned with improving housing, rations, and general living conditions; with the establishment of camps and food depots along labour routes; with investigating the causes of desertion; and with conciliation in 'master and servant' disputes which, from the beginning, took up an inordinate amount of time. Although the Department occasionally made representations to employers about wage levels, it believed that the improvement of working conditions should take priority over wage increases in the Copperbelt, since the region had the highest wage rates in the country.[2]

THE BIRTH OF AFRICAN TRADE UNIONS

A Marxist writer has suggested that British authorities were forced to introduce trade-unionism in the Colonies as a response to the rising tide of labour unrest.[3] This theory contradicts the conventional view that the introduction of trade-unionism was a progressive act of colonial policy, introduced from a belief in its desirable social value, as well as from concern about local conditions.[4] The history of trade-unionism in Northern Rhodesia provides some evidence for both sides, but the establishment of African trade unions owed less to black unrest (for which there was great potential) or to theories of social policy than to the ever-present tension between the Government and the white Mine Workers' Union.

The attention attracted by individual outbreaks of trouble in the Colonies tended to be short-lived. The shooting at Nkana in 1940 drew questions in the Commons, the usual crop of letters to *The Times*, and protests from such bodies as the Anti-Slavery Society and the Fabian Colonial Bureau; but pressure was insufficient to force a change of policy.[5] The Colonial Office was naturally concerned, but

[1] Interview, W. F. Stubbs, 21 Feb. 1969.
[2] Interview, W. F. Stubbs.
[3] Jack Woddis, *Africa, The Lion Awakes* (London, 1961), pp. 36–43.
[4] This view is put forward in B. C. Roberts, *Labour in the Tropical Territories of the Commonwealth*, pp. 176–200; Jean Meynaud and Annisse Salah-Bey in *Le Syndicalisme Africain* (Paris, 1963), pp. 33–5, examined Woddis's arguments and concluded that he exaggerated the influence of sporadic local disturbances on the Colonial Office, since there was often no sustained organization behind the unrest.
[5] *Hansard*, 5th series, H.C. Deb., 1940, vol. 364, 191, and 1289–90; 1940, vol. 367, 931–2; 1941, vol. 369, 1259–60; 1941, vol. 370, 1732–61. *The Times*, 11, 13, 18, 24 Mar. 1941 and 3 Apr. 1941. *Memorandum by the Anti-Slavery and Aborigines Protection Society on the Report of the Commission Appointed to Enquire into the 1940 Disturbances in the Copperbelt of Northern Rhodesia, September 1941*. Fabian Colonial Bureau papers.

its wartime interest in labour organization rested on broad considerations of the goals of colonial government and the form social development should take.

During the war working conditions for Africans steadily deteriorated and discontent over wages grew. Starting rates at the mines, which had been cut during the depression, in 1932, to 12s. 6d. and 22s. 6d. for surface and underground workers, remained constant until 1940. In that time there was no official inquiry into the cost of living. Early in the war Rev. R. J. B. Moore investigated the price of basic commodities on the Copperbelt, and came to the conclusion that a simple household budget would require a wage of 25s. a month if employers provided rations for workers' families, and 35s. if they did not. The starting rate of an underground mine-worker was 25s. after the increase in 1940, but the lowest surface wage was 15s. with rations, and wage levels outside the mines were generally lower still.[1] After the *Forster Commission Report* was published the Government, conscious of a steady wartime rise in prices, authorized an official investigation into the cost of living for Africans on the Copperbelt. The preliminary report issued in 1943 noted that there had been selective wage increases at the mines in 1942 and that a 5s. per month cost of living allowance was now given. The average monthly income of a mine-worker's family was estimated at £4. 14s. 7d., of a domestic servant at £3. 12s. 6d., and of a worker in secondary industry at £2. 5s. 10d. The investigator calculated that the minimum income necessary to support a man, woman, and two children on the Copperbelt was £6. 11s. 7d. a month. He felt that the discrepancy between the cost of his budget and real wages gave great cause for alarm, in terms of the potential for unrest and the growing bitterness of the workers.[2] Officials felt that the study involved a subjective judgement on a desirable standard of living which they found unrealistic.[3] The report was not made public.

Outbreaks of African labour trouble underlined the dangers of the

[1] Rev. R. J. B. Moore, 'Native Wages and the Standard of Living in Northern Rhodesia', in *African Studies*, vol. i, no. 2, June 1942, pp. 142–8.

[2] A. Lynn Saffery, *A Report on Some Aspects of African Living Conditions on the Copper Belt of Northern Rhodesia*, pp. 1–20.

[3] In 1947 the Government's estimate of the minimum annual income required in urban areas was £28, or £2. 6s. 8d. a month, substantially less that Saffery's estimate of £6. 11s. 7d., despite price rises in the intervening years. The 1947 estimate was based on the findings of an Advisory Board set up to investigate the wages of contractors' labour on the Copperbelt. (SEC/LAB/190: Sir John Waddington, Governor, to Arthur Creech Jones, Secretary of State, 25 June 1947.)

situation. In 1941 troops opened fire on strikers at Union Minière's Lubumbashi compound who were protesting at the sharp rise in the cost of living. Six Northern Rhodesians were killed and four wounded. The Administration feared that unrest might spread across the Congo border to the Copperbelt.[1] In 1942 a cut in maize rations caused a strike at the Shabani mine in Southern Rhodesia. In 1943 Lozi workers at the Zambezi Saw Mills in Livingstone also struck over rations: as a result the Tribal Representative system was introduced in the compound.[2] In 1945 strikes over wages broke out at the lead and zinc mine in Broken Hill, and among Rhodesia Railway workers in Northern and Southern Rhodesia. At the end of the year the Government was worried in case unrest in the Congo reached the Copperbelt.[3]

Despite this uneasy background the Administration maintained a conservative attitude towards labour representation until after the war. The only major innovation was the setting up of boss boys' committees at the mines for the senior Africans who supervised gangs of labourers. This was done in 1942 at the instigation of the recently formed Labour Department, which had to overcome some hesitancy on the part of both managements and the African workers themselves.[4] Further progress was hampered by the European Mine Workers' Union. In 1943 a rumour spread on the Copperbelt that the Colonial Office intended to send a British trade-unionist to organize African workers. The European union responded by offering to form a branch for Africans. In view of the Government's wartime difficulties with the union, the suggestion was hardly welcome, and the Labour Commissioner announced that it was too early to think of organizing African labour.[5] The attitude of the Provincial Administration was also unhelpful. The Labour Department was more favourably inclined towards African industrial representation than local administrative officers, who were suspicious of the policy.[6] A

[1] SEC/LAB/140: Provincial Commissioner, Western Province to Copperbelt District Commissioners, 10 Dec. 1941.
[2] SEC/LAB/142: Report of strike from Labour Commissioner to Chief Secretary, 18 Feb. 1943.
[3] SEC/LAB/140: Sir John Waddington, Governor, to H.M. Consul-General, Leopoldville, 9 Jan. 1946.
[4] SEC/LAB/62: Report on meetings with Nkana and Mindolo Boss Boys, W. F. Stubbs, Labour Officer, Ndola, 20 Oct. 1942; J. R. Hooker, 'The Role of the Labour Department in the Birth of African Trade Unionism in Northern Rhodesia' in *International Review of Social History*, vol. x, pt. 1, 1965, p. 9.
[5] Hooker, op. cit., p. 10.   [6] Ibid., p. 15.

revealing incident occurred at Kitwe in 1946, when the first Government Social Welfare Officer on the Copperbelt, A. H. Elwell, met a request from the Kitwe African Society to give a talk on forms of social organization, including trade-unionism. The District Commissioner objected to his comments and he was promptly transferred to Livingstone.[1]

In 1946 the Colonial Office sent an official from the Ministry of Labour, M. A. Bevan, to investigate the labour situation on the Copperbelt. He concluded that African workers were still unready for trade-unionism, but suggested that the existing boss boys' committees should be reformed as broader works committees with representatives from all the departments at the mines.[2] The desirability of this transitional stage in trade-union development became questionable after a new intervention from the Mine Workers' Union. Its President, Brian Goodwin, announced in the Legislative Council that African mine-workers were entitled to the assistance of the European union, which would not shirk its responsibilities towards them.[3] As the union wanted to secure a stricter colour bar on the basis of equal pay for equal work, and had had a long and bitter strike over a wage demand in 1946, the Government feared both its motives and the consequences of its suggestion on industrial peace. The need to forestall action by the European union became the incentive to faster progress in leading African workers towards collective bargaining.

Bevan's plan was discussed when the Governor and Northern Rhodesian representatives were in London for a constitutional conference on Northern Rhodesia held at the Colonial Office in June 1946. His transitional scheme was supported by the Colonial Office Labour Adviser, Major Orde Browne, who felt that the development of trade-unionism should not be artificially forced. Roy Welensky, the leader of the unofficial members of the Legislative Council, and Sir Stewart Gore-Browne, a representative of African interests on the Council, both believed that African workers were ready for some form of industrial organization. Gore-Browne favoured the introduction of full trade-unionism as soon as possible, while Welensky had accepted the idea of an interim organization. At a meeting of the Northern Rhodesian officials and Legislative Council representatives

---

[1] R. I. Rotberg, 'Race Relations and Politics in Colonial Zambia: The Elwell Incident', in *Race*, vol. vii, no. 1, July 1965, pp. 17–28.

[2] Hooker, op. cit., pp. 16–17.

[3] *Legislative Council Debates* 54, 6 May 1946, 55.

in London, which Bevan did not attend, it was decided that trade-unionism should be established as quickly as possible, and that a trade-unionist from Britain should be invited to assist the Labour Department.[1] In this case, in contrast to the establishment of the Labour Department, pressure from Northern Rhodesian representatives and officials appears to have overcome doubts at the Colonial Office.

The Colonial Office suggested that the Governor should discuss the decision about trade-unionism with the boards of the mining companies while he was in London.[2] The local managements had earlier been unhelpful towards Labour Department efforts to instruct workers in the principles of industrial representation.[3] After the London consultation, an announcement of the Secretary of State's intention to send a trade-union specialist to Northern Rhodesia was drawn up. It was forwarded to the Chamber of Mines on the Copperbelt, but the Chamber decided to delay expressing an opinion until after a conference of the companies' managing directors in Johannesburg later in the year.[4] The Governor did not wait for the Chamber's reply, and announced in his address at the opening of the Legislative Council session on 30 November 1946 that the Government intended to assist African workers in forming trade unions.[5]

After the major policy decision had been taken, African trade unions were organized with remarkable speed. William Comrie, a member of the Transport and General Workers Union from Greenock, Scotland, was sent out by the Colonial Office in 1947. Later that year he described his work to the Dalgleish Commission as follows: '. . . my job amounts to this—where there is a demand on the part of Africans for some form of organization along trade union lines, I have to guide that demand and to help it and to give all possible assistance to the Africans in building up a proper organisation on proper lines with a reasonable chance of enabling it to succeed'.[6] Comrie found the most promising recruits among Copperbelt shop assistants who had been receiving steady help from the Labour Department since 1942. They formed the first trade union in Northern Rhodesia, the Shop Assistants' Union, in January 1948. At the mines

[1] Creech Jones Papers.   [2] Creech Jones Papers.   [3] Hooker, op. cit., p. 15.
[4] Ibid., p. 17.
[5] *Legislative Council Debates* 56, 30 Nov. 1946, 8.
[6] Evidence to the Commission Appointed to Enquire into the Advancement of Africans in Industry (the Dalgleish Commission), 1947, p. 72: William Comrie, Ndola, 13 Oct. 1947.

Comrie worked with a small group of Africans already prominent as members of boss boys' and clerks' committees and welfare societies. Some familiar names in Zambian history appear among his earliest contacts. Kenneth Kaunda, then an employee in the welfare department at Nchanga, helped to organize one of his first meetings. Matthew Deluxe Nkoloma, later a controversial trade-union leader, was his interpreter.[1] Works committees had been set up at the mines as Bevan recommended, and were encouraged to discuss safety and welfare measures, although they had no negotiating powers.[2] Meanwhile Comrie organized a small team of followers known as the Disciples, 'through whom the gospel of trade-unionism was spread about the Copperbelt'.[3] His activities provoked the European union to try to set up African branches. Brian Goodwin began to hold meetings with African workers, although he did not find his reception favourable.[4] Meanwhile his invective against the Government strengthened official support for Comrie. Pressure was placed on the mine managements to secure their co-operation, and in 1948 the replacement of the works committees by trade unions began.[5]

At the first election at Nkana in February 1948 Lawrence Katilungu was chosen as union president.[6] He had not played an important part in Comrie's campaign, but was influential with Bemba workers as the grandson of a minor chief. He had been a mission teacher, an underground worker at Nkana from 1936, and was currently a recruiting clerk.[7] In March 1949 all of the mine unions amalgamated, and the African Mineworkers' Union (A.M.U.) came into being with Katilungu as its president. Later that year it made its first wage claim, and a recognition agreement was signed with the mining companies. At the end of the year the A.M.U. boasted a membership of 19,000 workers out of an African labour force of 35,000 men. The Shop

[1] Interview with William Comrie, Kitwe, Zambia, 20 July 1967.
[2] Epstein, pp. 89–90.
[3] Ibid., p. 90.
[4] Hooker, op. cit., pp. 20–1.
[5] Loc. cit.
[6] Lawrence Katilungu, 1914–61. Employed as teacher; underground worker at Nkana from 1936–40; paymaster for fish transport firm in the Belgian Congo; re-engaged as clerk, then senior interpreter at Nkana, 1947–9; 1948, chairman, Kitwe branch, National African Congress; 1949–60, president, African Mineworkers' Union; 1950, president, African Trade Union Congress; 1961, Deputy President of the African National Congress. R. Segal, *Political Africa* (London, 1961), pp. 128–30.
[7] Epstein, p. 92.

Assistants' Union had a membership of 1,300 workers, an African Drivers' Trade Union formed in 1948 had a membership of 1,700 men and a General Workers' Trade Union with a membership of about 2,000 had also appeared.[1]

Much of Comrie's remarkable success rested on the earlier work of Labour Officers in guiding boss boys' committees, Tribal Representatives' meetings and works committees towards more efficient and stable organization. Although the Labour Department was an executive rather than a policy-making arm of Government, it appears to have been more progressive than the Secretariat about labour representation. Its officers were not sure that collective bargaining for Africans would necessarily be arranged through trade-unionism, but they did believe that some form of industrial representation was required. They supported this goal despite a lack of co-operation from many employers, and very mixed feelings about it in the Provincial Administration. The labour officers' lack of experience of industry led to charges of reactionary tendencies from progressive critics, but their knowledge of the rural background of migrant labour was a useful supplement to Comrie's industrial approach to labour questions. This was illustrated when the country's first African trade union, the Shop Workers', was established in 1948. It was formed under Comrie's supervision from committees set up six years earlier by the first Labour Officer posted to Mufulira, who happened to be acquainted with tailors' shop assistants there because he had previously served in their home district, Kawambwa.[2]

Despite the speed with which the first trade unions grew, African workers had shown little evidence of a wish to organize themselves independently. Boss boys' and clerks' committees had not shown signs of turning into a mass organization. What had appeared already were élite committees representing senior workers who had a strong sense of self-interest. If any potential for collective bargaining existed spontaneously, it was on the basis of the sectional interests of boss boys and clerks.[3]

Northern Rhodesian workers had shown little interest in the political trade-unionism of the Industrial and Commercial Workers'

---

[1] *Annual Report of the Department of Labour and Mines, 1949,* p. 7.

[2] Interview with William F. Stubbs, Oxford, 21 Feb. 1969.

[3] SEC/LAB/150: Labour Commissioner to Governor, 28 June 1947; J. M. Walker, Labour Officer to Labour Commissioner, 3 July 1947; Labour Commissioner to Chief Secretary, 13 Nov. 1947.

Union in South Africa, or its off-shoot in Southern Rhodesia, which was active from 1928.[1] However, as a result of the southward pull of migrant labour routes, it would have been surprising if some contacts between the northern labour force and more politically active southern workers did not exist. Witnesses gave evidence to the Russell Commission in 1935 about Isaac Ngumbu, who had urged the Bemba not to go to work until they got higher wages. He had boasted that in the past he had 'caused the Shamva Mine [in Southern Rhodesia] to be closed down because of the money and yet he was not killed'.[2] The Governor, Sir Hubert Young, told the Secretary of State that he believed there was planned organization by agitators behind the trouble on the Copperbelt in 1935. 'This is the only possible explanation for the unexpected occurrence.'[3] In a secret dispatch he announced that one of the ringleaders arrested at Luanshya was alleged to be a lieutenant of Clements Kadalie, the leader of the Industrial and Commercial Workers' Union in South Africa. The administration was later alarmed by the appearance of other black trade-union agitators from South Africa in Northern Rhodesia,[4] and a record exists of at least one, John Meshack Chamalula, who attended a trade-union course offered by the Communist Party in Johannesburg.[5] Although such contacts were slight, they were an additional incentive to the Government to foster African trade-unionism under its own control.[6]

A possible reason for the unwillingness of northern Africans to organize, and for their surprising inactivity during a period of static wages and sharply rising prices in the 1940s, is found in the record of the hearings held by the Cost of Living Commission in 1947. An African witness on the Copperbelt pointed out that demands for pay were now associated in the minds of Africans with shooting incidents: 'At our meeting we came to the decision—it was agreed that when Africans make a request for better wages the Government brings guns and shoots the Africans. They do not get anything—they are killed. . . . When we had our meeting it was decided that we must go on strike,

---

[1] J. R. Hooker, 'The African Workers in Southern Rhodesia: Black Aspirations in a White Economy 1927–36', in *Race*, vol. vi, no. 2, Oct. 1964, pp. 142 ff.

[2] Evidence to the Russell Commission, 1935, vol. ii, p. 43, Alimoni Juli.

[3] C.O. 795/76/45083: Sir Hubert Young to Malcolm MacDonald, Secretary of State, 6 July 1935; same to same, 2 June 1935 (secret).

[4] Interview with R. S. Hudson, former Labour Commissioner in Northern Rhodesia 1940–4, London, 18 Feb. 1966.

[5] Hooker, *The Role of the Labour Department* . . ., p. 15, f.n. and p. 19.

[6] Interview with R. S. Hudson, 18 Feb. 1966.

but then we decided to wait because we remembered what happened in the 1935 and 1940 strikes.'[1]

Not only was there insufficient pressure from African workers to force the Government to promote trade-unionism, but the Colonial Office was reluctant to speed up its development. The initiative was the Northern Rhodesia Government's, prompted by its deteriorating relations with the European Mine Workers' Union. Officials felt that it was vital to set up an organization responsive to Colonial Office policies, before the field was taken over by an alien brand of trade-unionism that had developed spontaneously and successfully among European workers in South Africa and Southern Rhodesia, and had aspirations to control the black labour force.

Although the Government's action was determined by political considerations, it also suited other aspects of policy. There had been a muted concern about urban wage levels in the Secretariat since the investigation made in 1943. For some time the Government hesitated to act, reluctant to introduce minimum wages in an area where wages were generally the highest in the country.[2] It was not immediately accepted that workers' needs in urban areas might be unrelated to rural wages and conditions. In 1946 the Government set up an Advisory Board to investigate the wages of Copperbelt contractors' labour, using powers provided in the Minimum Wages Ordinance passed in 1932 to comply with an International Labour Office convention. The move to promote collective bargaining therefore coincided with the Government's first voluntary initiative in regulating urban wage levels.

The decision to organize trade unions on a racial basis was a foregone conclusion. When the M.W.U. was formed in 1937 the mining companies had insisted that its recognition agreement should cover Europeans only. The companies and the Government supported African advancement and opposed equal pay for Africans and Europeans. These aims precluded a united union covering the entire labour force. The decision to divide representation on a racial basis had the support of the Government because it feared that the European union would block African advancement by insisting on equal pay, while gaining control of the African labour movement.[3] The

---

[1] SEC/LAB/150: Evidence of Welford Nurale, undated, to Cost of Living Commission 1947, extract on file; and M. G. Billing, D.C., to Senior Provincial Commissioner, 5 July 1947.

[2] SEC/LAB/98: P. D. Thomas, Assistant Secretary, Memorandum on urban cost of living, 4 Aug. 1945.

[3] R. S. Hudson to the writer, n.d., Feb. 1966.

companies appreciated that it would be preferable to negotiate with a divided, and therefore weaker, labour force. But the decision was also supported by the African workers themselves. Goodwin's efforts to win support among them had little success. African trade-union leaders later claimed that they had not wished to rule out the possibility of a joint union in the future, but wanted to build up their own union first so that it could negotiate from a position of strength with the Europeans.[1] If the European union had succeeded in organizing African branches, it would probably have fought for higher basic pay for Africans. But by also insisting that Africans taking over any part of a European's job should receive the same pay, it would have prevented Africans from advancing into such work. The union would therefore have been divided into two membership groups on different pay scales.

The African Mineworkers' Union grew rapidly, but it had notable weaknesses. Comrie had had to discourage a movement to form a separate African Staff Association by stressing the need for a united front against the employers.[2] The senior workers provided valuable leadership in the early days, but their interests were not identical with those of the union's large following. The organization also faced problems of administration and financial control, and very serious language difficulties. Many African languages were spoken at the mines, and the leaders' command of English was not always fluent. The language barrier bedevilled instruction and negotiation among workers whose acquaintance with the traditions and practices of trade-unionism was of necessity slight. As a result the union was not strong enough in its early years to take up the cause of African advancement, which had been pressed in vain by the Government since the end of the war.

[1] Epstein, p. 91.
[2] Loc. cit.

CHAPTER VI

Failed Negotiations

EARLY in the war the British Government publicly acknowledged the need for African industrial advancement in Northern Rhodesia. The Under-Secretary for the Colonies, George Hall, also admitted the obstacles to such a policy: the slow progress of education for Africans, the Government's obligation to assure employment for European ex-servicemen, and the problem posed by the employment of Africans in 'European' jobs at low rates of pay. 'The very basis of our trade unionism would be blown sky high', Hall told the House of Commons in 1941, 'unless the rights of trade unions, as they are in our own country, are safeguarded when skilled jobs are done by what may be regarded as unskilled persons. For all that, there should be no deterrent to every possible opportunity being given to the African for the purpose of training himself to be fit for jobs when they become available, and I think the difficulties will be overcome.'[1] Despite this assertion of optimism, officials admitted privately that nothing could be done while the wartime demand for copper lasted. 'As long as we must have copper we are in the hands of the Mine Workers' Union', Harold Macmillan, the next Under-Secretary of State at the Colonial Office, told Arthur Creech Jones.[2]

At the end of the war the British Government's commitment to African advancement was no more clearly defined. Many officials in the Protectorate itself recognized a need to provide for African aspirations, but the direction of policy was a matter for debate. The Colonial Office favoured the balanced development of opportunities for Africans in urban and rural areas, but the Provincial Administration retained a strong preference for rural development.[3] European workers found no reason to oppose the rural approach, since development centres such as co-operative settlements 'should be able to absorb all the skilled and semi-skilled artisans from the Urban Areas

[1] *Hansard*, 5th series, H.C. Deb., 1941, vol. 370, 1757.
[2] Creech Jones Papers.
[3] SEC/LAB/27: Oliver Stanley, Secretary of State, to Sir John Waddington, 21 Apr. 1944, and Provincial Commissioner, Western Province to the Chief Secretary, 28 May 1945.

for some considerable time . . . the Social Security of the European Artisans would be correspondingly improved'.[1]

European and African workers participated unequally in the political system and were unequally interested in it. The Government was entrusted with the protection of African rights because the role of Africans in the central political processes was limited. Africans were British-protected persons, not British subjects, and were therefore disqualified from the franchise. Their post-war constitutional progress was marked by the creation of an African Representative Council elected by the various Provincial Councils in 1946,[2] and by the nomination of two of its members to the territorial Legislative Council in 1948.[3] African political awareness was slow to develop, and although the African National Congress was formed in 1948 from an earlier Federation of African Societies, it was not yet influential in shaping African opinion.[4]

In contrast, the European population was vociferous in its demands for a greater share in territorial government. In 1945 a majority of thirteen to nine was granted to the elected and nominated members in the Legislative Council. Discussions on a further constitutional advance began the following year in London, and in 1948 the number of official members of the Legislative Council and the number of elected members were equalized with ten seats each. To these were added four seats for nominated unofficial members representing African interests, of whom two for the first time were Africans.[5] In the Executive Council the unofficial members lacked a majority, but in 1948 a convention was adopted that if the four unofficial members were unanimous in their advice to the Governor, their views would be accepted as the advice of all eleven members.[6] Under this arrangement the Governor's use of his reserve powers in matters affecting African interests could prove embarrassing and might arouse heated political opposition.

As the elected members made progress in the Legislative and Executive Councils the composition of the electorate from which they

---

[1] W. J. Busschau, *Report on the Development of Secondary Industries in Northern Rhodesia* (Lusaka, 1945), Appendix VII, p. 79: Proposals of the British Empire Service League, Luanshya branch.

[2] D. Mulford, *Zambia, the Politics of Independence* (London, 1967), pp. 12–13. The Provincial Councils had been formed in 1943 with a membership drawn from the existing system of Native Authority and Urban Advisory Councils.

[3] Lord Hailey, *An African Survey, Revised 1956* (London, 1957), p. 290.

[4] Mulford, p. 16.   [5] Hailey, p. 290; Mulford, pp. 11–12.

[6] H. V. Wiseman, *The Cabinet in the Commonwealth* (London, 1958), pp. 91–2.

drew their support was changing. During the war the white industrial workers of the Copperbelt and Broken Hill had emerged as an important political force, and under the leadership of the powerful Railway Workers' and Mine Workers' trade unions they were capable of exerting strong pressure on the Government when the interests of white labour were at stake. The Copperbelt had three seats in the Legislative Council in 1948, Nkana, Luanshya and Mufulira-Chingola. These three electoral areas, together with the mining and railway centre of Broken Hill, accounted for some 3,909 registered voters compared with 3,177 in the other six electoral areas.[1] Although the Labour Party had collapsed in 1944, industrial workers were forcefully represented in the Legislative Council by Roy Welensky, chairman of the Broken Hill branch of the Railway Workers' Union since 1933, and by Brian Goodwin, President of the Mine Workers' Union, who had been returned for the Nkana seat.[2]

In its relations with the European political community the Government sometimes appeared as arbiter between European and African interests, and at other times seemed to be acting as a political opposition which represented African interests. In this uneasy dual role officials found their relations with European politicians often strained and distrustful. The surrender of the official majority in the Legislative Council in 1945 and the recognition four years later of the convention equating unanimous unofficial advice in the Executive Council with the unanimous advice of the whole Executive Council, made it constantly necessary for the Government to seek a compromise with the European community in its conduct of business. Although the obligation to protect African interests remained, the Government's ability to do so was substantially undermined by the European population's constitutional advance.

At the end of the war the managements of the four copper-mines found, like the Government, that their freedom of action in matters where European and African interests conflicted had been severely restricted. Since the 'dilution clause' and 'closed shop' agreements had been made in 1940 and 1941, relations with the union had deteriorated further. Claims for wage increases had been resisted during the

[1] Statistics derived from *Legislative Council Debates*, 79, 21 Oct. 1953, 23, Appendix B, Schedule C: Report of the Select Committee on the Delimitation of Electoral Areas.

[2] Welensky and Goodwin were close associates, although in the 1944 election Goodwin won his seat as an Independent Labour member against a candidate put up by Welensky's Labour Party (Gann, *History*, p. 345).

war, the 'closed shop' agreement had not been strictly enforced under the Government's emergency manpower regulations, and the return in 1945 of Frank Maybank, the union leader deported two years earlier for subversive activities, revived militant feelings on the Copperbelt. Fresh demands were raised to protect the position of union members, not only against African workers, but from unskilled or non-union white workers.[1] The union also pressed for direct European supervision of all African employees, for the right to represent Africans, and for European rates of pay for any African employed in job categories in which union members also worked.[2] When conciliation proceedings opened in February 1946 the managements sought, as in the 1940 negotiations, to prevent a union take-over of the 'ragged edge' jobs where work performed by Europeans on some mines was performed by Africans on others.[3] M. A. Bevan, the industrial relations adviser seconded from the British Ministry of Labour to the Northern Rhodesian Government, suggested a compromise formula to replace the dilution clause of 1940:

42. *Dilution of labour.* The Company agrees that work of the class or grade that is being performed or job that is being filled by an employee at the time of the signing of this agreement, shall not be given to persons to whom the terms and conditions of this agreement do not apply.[4]

The new agreement and the rates of pay contained in it applied to European workers only. As it was signed by the union with the management of each mine, Clause 42 preserved the variations in the employment of Africans at individual mines without altering the limitations on further African advancement imposed in the earlier agreement.

Later in the year tension was renewed when the artisans on the mines claimed a wage increase which led to a six-week strike of European workers. The companies and the Government were planning the dispersal of African workers to their homes, in anticipation of a longer stoppage, when agreement to go to arbitration was finally reached.[5] At this time the companies notified the union that they intended to terminate the 'closed shop' arrangement, but after five

---

[1] C.I.S.B., 90.1, vols. ii and iii.
[2] C.I.S.B. 100.20.9A, vol. ii: Memorandum, 'Colour Bar' Clause, 4 Jan. 1950.
[3] Idem.
[4] *Report of the Commission Appointed to Enquire into the Advancement of Africans in Industry* (Lusaka, 1948), p. 28 (The *Dalgleish Report*).
[5] *Legislative Council Debates*, 55, 29 Aug. 1946, 139.

months they reversed the decision, which had seemed likely to lead to another strike.[1]

Before the war the companies encouraged the progress of Africans into the lower European job categories because of the payroll economies which would result. The real cost of European against African labour had risen with the introduction of pension and bonus schemes for Europeans in 1937,[2] and the gradual drop in turnover of African labour, together with an increase in ability, made continued substitution attractive.[3] The dilution clause in the 1940 agreement with the European union blocked this path of advance, but as African wages rose, the incentive to use the African labour force in a more efficient manner also increased. The lowest basic wage, which had been 12s. 6d. for a ticket of thirty shifts before the 1940 strike, had been increased to 30s. by 1948. Investigation revealed a shortage of African workers with a suitable educational or technical background for advanced work.[4] The likeliest fields of progress seemed to lie in the semi-skilled 'ragged-edge' jobs, in an increase in the responsibilities of African boss boys, and in the fragmentation of European jobs for Africans with increased European supervision for a transitional period.[5] The European union was firmly opposed to these alternatives, and the companies felt that if they succeeded in winning some concession from the union it would undoubtedly be a small one, in which any immediate financial advantage in reduced costs might be outweighed by the unrest caused among the European workers. But failure to pursue advancement had also to be balanced against the growing discontent of the African workers who had been denied progress. The manager of the Chamber of Mines informed the mine managers in October 1946 that the records of boss boys' and Tribal Representatives' meetings during the previous eighteen months showed a preoccupation with the question. Boss boys felt they could do the work of the Europeans supervising them, that they were denied prestige for the work they did, and denied jobs of which they

[1] C.I.S.B., 90.1, vol. iv: Record of decisions reached at a meeting of the Executive Committee of the Chamber of Mines, 2 Jan. 1947.

[2] Baldwin, *Economic Development and Export Growth*, p. 89. Baldwin calculates that the ratio of total European to African real earnings rose from 28 to 34 in the years 1937 to 1940, but had dropped back to 28 by 1949 (p. 90).

[3] Ibid., pp. 88–9.

[4] C.I.S.B., 100.15, vol. i: Memorandum on the Dalgleish Commission, P. H. Truscott, Manager of the Chamber of Mines, 17 Sept. 1947.

[5] Loc. cit.; and C.I.S.B., 100.15, vol. i: Dalgleish Commission, outline of evidence to be given on behalf of the Chamber, 1 Oct. 1947.

were capable. He added optimistically that there was reason to think they were more interested in status than money.[1] A conference of Anglo American Group representatives two months later concluded that the concern among some workers about being deliberately held back would almost certainly lead to trouble.[2]

The European union had emerged from the war in such a strong position that the companies felt unable to make any public pronouncements in favour of African advancement, but they also believed that failure to secure even a token measure of progress would increase the likelihood of unrest among African employees. In private they informed the Governor of their dilemma and urged that the Government should take the lead in the matter.[3] In contrast to the pre-war era in which the mines had jealously guarded control of their labour policies, they now looked for Government direction, albeit of a co-operative nature. The Government, however, was as hesitant to cause European political unrest as the mine managements were to incur labour trouble.

THE DALGLEISH REPORT

The position of Africans in industry was among the subjects discussed at the Colonial Office conference on Northern Rhodesia in June 1946 attended by the Governor, Sir John Waddington, together with leading officials, and representatives of the elected members of the Legislative Council. It was decided that the discussions on African advancement suggested by Sir John Forster in his report on the riot of 1940 should now be held, and that independent advisers should be invited to join the Government, the mining companies, and the European union for the talks. The Governor had predicted that a three-party local discussion would break down at once over the union's insistence on equal pay for equal work, to which neither the companies nor the Government could agree. He felt that the participation of independent members to provide an element of conciliation was essential.[4] The union's success in preserving a colour-bar clause

[1] C.I.S.B., 100.23, vol. i: P. H. Truscott to mine managers, 4 Oct. 1946.
[2] C.I.S.B., 100.23, vol. i: Memorandum No. 6 enclosed with P. H. Truscott to Secretary, Mufulira Copper Mines Ltd., 19 Dec. 1946.
[3] C.I.S.B., 100.15, vol. i: R. L. Prain and C. F. S. Taylor, managing directors respectively of the Rhodesian Selection Trust and Anglo American Group copper mines, to Sir John Waddington, 17 Dec. 1946.
[4] Creech Jones Papers.

in the agreement negotiated earlier in the year with the companies did not invite optimism about new developments.

The difficulties of even airing the problem emerged as preliminary arrangements began for the conference recommended by Forster six years before. Senior company officials warned the Governor that if 'the Government does not state publicly that it has accepted the principle of African progression . . . we may find it impossible to appear publicly as being in favour of African progression, for reasons which you will appreciate'.[1] Shortly afterwards the manager of the Mufulira mine pointed out that they did not wish to become involved in another dispute with the union, and needed a clear statement of Government policy as a guide. But the Governor was equally cautious, and the companies described his position as follows:

. . . he could not declare the Government's policy, although it was pretty well known, before the holding of a Conference which was being called specifically to decide upon a policy. Further he wanted to get the parties to attend a conference before making the matter a live issue. To declare a policy might result in all sorts of public commotion and in the refusal of one party or another to attend the Conference. He wanted the Conference to start before any party had publicly committed itself to any definite point of view. He thought that it rested with the Chairman whether or not any good came of the Conference.[2]

The independent chairman chosen to lead the conference was Andrew Dalgleish, a veteran British trade-unionist who had been a member of the Forster Commission in 1940. He was accompanied from Britain by H. O. Smith, a Director of Imperial Chemical Industries, and James Kelly, of the National Union of Mine Workers. The participation of the three independent members in the conference did not have the intended beneficial effect, as they could not agree among themselves on their terms of reference. Kelly applied them to the broad issue of African wage levels, while Dalgleish and Smith limited their concern to African advancement and the appropriate wages for it.[3] They also failed to secure the co-operation of the Mine Workers'

[1] C.I.S.B., 100.15, vol. i: R. L. Prain and C. F. S. Taylor to Sir John Waddington, 17 Dec. 1946.
[2] C.I.S.B. 100.23, vol. i: A. W. Goodbody, Secretary for Roan Antelope Copper Mines Ltd., and Mufulira Copper Mines Ltd., to A. B. Cohen, Colonial Office, 21 May 1947.
[3] Zambia Archives, open file on Industrial Relations Conference, 1947: A. Dalgleish and H. O. Smith to Sir John Waddington, 16 May 1947, and James Kelly to Sir John Waddington, 16 May 1947.

Union and the Chamber of Mines. When the conference opened on 8 May 1947 Frank Maybank read a joint statement on behalf of his union and the Chamber demanding a clear outline of Government policy on African advancement, and the appointment of an official commission of enquiry to investigate the implementation of that policy for the country as a whole rather than for the mining industry alone.[1] Both parties were unwilling to consider the matter at an informal conference.

The breakdown of the talks led to bitter recriminations, with Dalgleish and the Colonial Office placing responsibility on the companies, and the companies blaming the union and the Northern Rhodesian Government.[2] The Colonial Office hinted that the companies did not want a strike while the price of copper was high, and the companies retaliated that 'it is the duty of the Government, who are, as stated in the Forster Report, the guardians of Native welfare, to take the lead in formulating and later implementing a specific policy'. Dalgleish, the companies, and the Government agreed only in the view that serious industrial trouble would result if African aspirations were not met.[3]

After the failure of the conference the Chamber of Mines and the European union continued to press for the appointment of a Commission of Enquiry, with residents of the territory among its members, to examine African advancement on a countrywide basis. The Government was opposed to having residents on a Commission, or allowing it to consider advancement in the territory as a whole, and there was some delay before a compromise was reached.[4] A Commission was finally appointed under the chairmanship of Dalgleish to inquire into the opportunities for advancement and training facilities for Africans in Northern Rhodesian industry. Although residents of the territory were not included, three local assessors were appointed to assist the members. The Government also incorporated into the terms of reference of the Commission the statement of policy desired by the companies and the union. It stated that 'Africans in Northern

[1] Zambia Archives, open file, Memorandum on Industrial Relations Conference, Kitwe, 8 May 1947.

[2] C.I.S.B., 100.15, vol. i: Executive Assistant, Mufulira Copper Mines to Secretary of Chamber, 9 June 1947.

[3] C.I.S.B., 100.15, vol. i: R. L. Prain and S. S. Taylor, respectively managing directors of the Rhodesian Selection Trust and Anglo American Group copper mines, to A. B. Cohen, Colonial Office, 20 May 1947; and Executive Assistant, Mufulira Copper Mines to Secretary of Chamber, 9 June 1947.

[4] Loc. cit.

Rhodesia should be afforded opportunities for employment in more responsible work as and when they are qualified to undertake such work and taking into account the interests of all other persons in employment . . .'[1] The statement was hardly helpful, especially as the Apprenticeship Ordinance excluded Africans from formal training as artisans.

Dalgleish's position had previously been compromised by the absence of a clear lead from the Government, the apparent lack of local support, and the informal status accorded to his mission. Now, accompanied by Henry Main, a former president of the Shipbuilding Employers' Federation, and James Young, General Secretary to the Association of Engineering and Shipbuilding Draughtsmen, he returned to the territory in September 1947. There he found new set-backs. The Mine Workers' Union had decided to boycott the Commission on the grounds that the two trade-union members of the Legislative Council, Roy Welensky and Brian Goodwin, should have been among its members, that its terms of reference should have made specific mention of equal pay for equal work, and that Andrew Dalgleish had in the past shown himself unsympathetic to the interests of European workers.[2] The Government refused to alter the terms of reference or the personnel of the Commission, and the inquiry began without the goodwill of the union, from which co-operation was essential if African advancement was to be implemented peacefully.

Having decided that the lesser industries of the country presented little scope for advancement, the Commission took extensive evidence on the Copperbelt and concentrated its attention on the mines, where it reported that fifty-four categories of work not performed by Africans could be opened to them immediately or after a period of training.[3] Although the number of jobs cited was impressive, the first twenty-seven categories, ranging from carpentry and simple plumbing to the operation of certain winding engines, cranes, and locomotives, corresponded to the controversial 'ragged-edge' jobs and were at this time performed, or had been in the past, by Africans on at least one of the mines.[4] In addition, the report named eleven semi-skilled jobs

---

[1] Government General Notice No. 637 of 1947, in the Government Gazette, vol. 37, no. 37, 29 Aug. 1947.

[2] Legislative Council Debates, 60, 12 Mar. 1948, 87, and Dalgleish Commission Report, p. 4.

[3] Dalgleish Commission Report, pp. 37–41.

[4] Ibid., p. 14.

which Africans with special training could undertake, and a further sixteen jobs which would require advanced instruction.[1] In considering these more advanced jobs the Commission examined the need to provide proper industrial training for them. It recommended that technical education should be extended, stressed the importance of better general education, and suggested that full apprenticeship training should be provided for Africans, under contracts lasting seven years instead of the normal five years.[2]

The mines, wary of the European union's reaction, were pessimistic about the Commission's conclusions and reluctant to press for a wide interpretation of them without the Government's backing. They agreed that certain work was within the capabilities of selected black employees, but claimed that only a small number of jobs would be made available by the Dalgleish formula, and only a few Africans were able to fill them.[3] The management at Nkana thought that if the whole of the Commission's job list was implemented at the mine forty-six Europeans would be replaced by seventy-nine Africans, who would require extra European supervision.[4]

J. D. Rheinnalt Jones, the Anglo American Corporation's Adviser on Native Affairs in South Africa, sent the Copperbelt companies a critical memorandum challenging their assessment. He pointed out that the mines in the Belgian Congo, far from experiencing a shortage of skilled African labour, had engaged illiterate men on work considerably more advanced than that under discussion in Northern Rhodesia. He put forward the view that long trade apprenticeships were obsolescent, and that vocational training for mechanized production methods could be given in a comparatively short time. In the Congo Africans had acquired skills through systematic training programmes, and European workers accepted that it was part of their duties to provide such training. These prospects were so far removed from the situation on the Copperbelt, and touched on so many sensitive issues there, that the Chamber of Mines decided not to give evidence to the Dalgleish Commission on conditions in the Congo

[1] Ibid., pp. 15–17, 24–8, 39–41. The first twenty-seven jobs (discussed earlier at p. 97) are listed as Appendix A at pp. 233–4. The remaining jobs are listed as Appendix B at p. 235.

[2] *Dalgleish Commission Report*, pp. 21–3.

[3] C.I.S.B., 100.15, vol. ii: H. Clark, General Manager, Rhokana Corporation to Secretary of Chamber, 9 Feb. 1949, and C. F. S. Taylor to H. Clark, 7 Apr. 1949.

[4] Evidence to the Dalgleish Commission, p. 379: H. Clark, General Manager, Rhokana Corporation.

unless it was requested.[1] Five years later the number of skilled jobs under consideration in advancement planning was still restricted. The companies told another commission of inquiry that only 331 places could be filled by advancement.[2]

On the crucial question of wages, the Dalgleish Commission sought a compromise between the views of the Government and the mining companies on equal pay, and those of the European union. The report took advantage of the companies' plans to divide operations performed by a European among several African workers to suggest that the European employee's wage (including the cost of his housing) should be divided between the Africans who took over the job, after the cost of any additional supervision was subtracted.[3] The Commission interpreted the Mine Workers' Union's demand for equal pay in the light of 'equal pay for work of equal value', although the union maintained that jobs should not be broken down and that Africans moving into any work previously done by Europeans ought to receive full European pay rates, including equal bonuses, pensions, housing, hospital, and medical services. At the same time the Commission's recommendation removed any financial inducement to the companies to proceed with advancement, and by relating African wage rates, however loosely, to European wages had denied the principle favoured by the companies and endorsed by the Government, that African wages should bear a relation to existing African wage scales and local circumstances. The Civil Service Commission of 1947 had said that while those few Africans who were qualified for posts normally filled by recruitment from Britain should receive about three-fifths of the expatriate civil service rate, in general the application of European rates would restrict the expansion of Government services.[4] Sir Gilbert Rennie, who succeeded Waddington and became Governor in 1948, thought that Africans should be trained for more advanced administrative posts than they then held in Government

---

[1] C.I.S.B., 100.15, vol. i: Notes by the Adviser on Native Affairs on the Memorandum of Evidence of the Executive Committee of the Northern Rhodesia Chamber of Mines, 19 Sept. 1947; also undated notes by R. D. Rheinallt Jones, Adviser on Native Affairs; Record of decisions reached at meeting of the Executive Committee, 11 Sept. 1947.

[2] *Report of the Board of Inquiry Appointed to Inquire into the Advancement of Africans in the Copper Mining Industry in Northern Rhodesia* (Lusaka, 1954), pp. 34–5. (The *Forster Commission Report*.)

[3] *Dalgleish Commission Report*, pp. 35–6.

[4] *Report of the Commission on the Civil Services of Northern Rhodesia and Nyasaland* (Lusaka, 1947), p. 7.

service, with suitable salary increases, but not necessarily involving the principle of equal pay.[1] The companies had planned to double the pay rates of their advanced African employees, by annual increments over five years, to a target of 12s. per shift underground and 11s. per shift for surface work. The rates would be between one fourth and one sixth of those received by Europeans in the same job categories. The companies submitted figures to the Dalgleish Commission showing that the increased supervision required when one European was replaced by several African workers might in some cases result in increased costs for a time, rather than savings. They also pointed out that they could not predict economies in advance of a settlement with the European union.[2]

As well as indicating the jobs which could be opened to Africans, and suitable wage scales for them, Dalgleish suggested that his report should be followed by negotiations between the union, the companies and the Government over the alteration of the agreement between the companies and the union. This repeated Forster's suggestion in 1940 for three-party talks, which had never been implemented. All of the previous negotiations had been between the companies and the union, with the sole exception of the unsuccessful 1947 conference. That four-party meeting had included conciliators, at the suggestion of the Governor and an adviser from the British Ministry of Labour. Dalgleish now ruled out the participation of independent advisers, and suggested that the Northern Rhodesian Government should take a more active role in attempting to reach a settlement.

The Government already found it difficult to take the lead in pressing for African advancement. The constitutional advances of the European population in 1945 and 1948 made a legislative solution unthinkable. The Dalgleish *Report* aroused bitter hostility when it was debated in the Legislative Council. The failure of the Government to get the Mine Workers' Union's support for the Commission before it started its work was a serious liability when it came to implementing its findings. Brian Goodwin told the Legislative Council that the *Report* was 'ridiculous',[3] and Roy Welensky informed members

---

[1] Interview with Sir Gilbert Rennie, London, 8 Dec. 1970. Sir Gilbert Rennie, b. 1895. Financial Secretary, Gold Coast, 1937–9; Chief Secretary, Kenya, 1939–47; Governor, Northern Rhodesia, 1948–54; High Commissioner for the Federation of Rhodesia and Nyasaland in the United Kingdom, 1954–61.

[2] Evidence to the Dalgleish Commission, pp. 596–600: memorandum submitted by the Chamber of Mines on the wage structure for Africans in industry.

[3] *Legislative Council Debates*, 60, 12 Mar. 1948, 86.

that to replace Europeans by Africans would ruin the general economic advance on which African welfare really depended.[1]

THE UNSWORTH CONFERENCE

European mine-workers were concerned not only about the actual jobs mentioned by Dalgleish which Africans might take over at lesser pay, but about the broad principles at stake. They had been assured by the Government that the Africans' progress would not be at the expense of Europeans,[2] by the mine managements that no white worker would be dismissed or placed on a lower pay scale because of advancement,[3] and by Dalgleish that there were wider opportunities in a growing territory.[4] Against these promises they saw realities: the shortage of apprenticeship positions available for white youths at the mines,[5] the reports of poor prospects for secondary industries in Northern Rhodesia,[6] and the threat of widespread African progress in industry—not merely in a few 'ragged edge' jobs—if Africans were given methodical training such as the Congo mines provided.[7] The strong emotions raised by this threat were linked to the settlers' political thrust for responsible government, and they reinforced existing sympathies for Southern Rhodesian policies which protected the rights of the white worker.

The Government's political opponents feared that trusteeship would be used to fend off closer union with Southern Rhodesia, or responsible government for the white community; and the Administration's concern for African progress in industry seemed to underline this possibility.[8] By 1948 Roy Welensky, who had been the leader of the unofficial members of the Legislative Council since 1946, realized that the British Government would never consent to the amalgamation of Northern and Southern Rhodesia. He adopted the idea of a federation as a more promising alternative. The Colonial

[1] *Legislative Council Debates*, 60, 12 Mar. 1948, 77.

[2] Zambia Archives, open file on Industrial Relations Conference, 1947.

[3] C.I.S.B., 100.15, vol. ii: Memorandum on the Dalgleish Commission, P. H. Truscott, Manager of the Chamber of Mines, 30 June 1948.

[4] *Dalgleish Commission Report*, 1948, p. 35.

[5] C.I.S.B., 100.15, vol. i: Memorandum on the Dalgleish Commission, P. H. Truscott, 17 Sept. 1947, p. 4.

[6] W. J. Busschau, *Report on the Development of Secondary Industries in Northern Rhodesia* (Lusaka, 1945); *First, Second and Third Reports of the Advisory Committee on Industrial Development, 1946–48* (Lusaka, 1949).

[7] C.I.S.B., 100.15, vol. i: Dalgleish Commission, notes from J. D. Rheinallt Jones, Anglo American Corporation adviser on native affairs, 19 Sept. 1947.

[8] *Legislative Council Debates*, 61, 24 June 1948, 400–5, 411–12.

Office proved sympathetic, and Godfrey Huggins, who had won a sweeping victory in the 1948 election in Southern Rhodesia, was soon convinced of its advantages over amalgamation.[1] Meanwhile the chances of implementing the *Dalgleish Report* receded as Welensky and Goodwin accused the Government of being firmly anti-settler and of playing off European and African interests to delay further constitutional advance.[2]

Not only were settler interests and the drift of local politics against African advancement, but once again the Mine Workers' Union unexpectedly found its position strengthened by the renewed strategic importance of the copper industry. The British Ministry of Supply had begun to cut back its purchases of Northern Rhodesian copper in 1944, greatly underestimating the post-war demand from home industries. The outlook for the mines seemed bleak, for the cost of deep-level mining was increasing, fuel was scarce, and the necessary machinery and railway stock were in short supply. But the threat of a depression on the Copperbelt, which contributed to the aggressiveness of the Mine Workers' Union immediately after the war, was quickly replaced by an unforeseen rise in demand. The price of copper soared from the controlled wartime level of £62 a ton to £137 a ton by March 1947.[3] In the following year the British Government, faced with a growing financial crisis, became anxious to expand Northern Rhodesian copper production in order to save dollars. In 1950 the Parliamentary Secretary to the Ministry of Supply, which was again taking up most of Northern Rhodesia's copper output, told the House of Commons that the arrangement was saving the United Kingdom the equivalent of some £11 million in dollars annually.[4] Production, which had fallen from a wartime peak of 262,394 long tons in 1940 to 182,289 long tons in 1946, reached 309,141 long tons in 1951,[5] while the sterling price of copper rose by 44 per cent when the pound was devalued in 1949.

The companies later pointed out that from 1947 'copper production was just as important to the United Kingdom Government as it was

[1] Sir Roy Welensky, *Welensky's 4000 Days* (London, 1964), pp. 21–6.
[2] *Legislative Council Debates*, 61, 24 June 1948, 400 ff., speeches by Roy Welensky and Brian Goodwin.
[3] Gann, *History*, p. 361.
[4] *Hansard*, 5th series, H.C. Deb., 1950, vol. 476, 1254–6.
[5] F. L. Coleman, *The Northern Rhodesian Copperbelt 1899–1962. Technological Development up to the end of the Central African Federation* (Manchester, 1971), Table III, p. 145.

during the war', and they did not want to take the responsibility for openly advocating African advancement, which was almost certain to cause a strike by European workers, without Government support.[1] At the same time the danger of unrest among their African employees caused concern. In 1948 the system of employing Africans in three grades and a special group for advanced workers, which had been introduced after the 1940 strike, was widened to an eight-group system with an advanced special group. Wage rates had been substantially increased by the consolidation of a cost-of-living allowance. However the changes provided scope for advancement for the middle grades of workers only, and did not greatly improve the position of the highest and most discontented groups, the clerks and boss boys. The Chamber of Mines felt that as well as taking a lead in negotiation with the European union, the Government should act separately to placate African unrest. African workers had been encouraged to state their aspirations freely before the Dalgleish Commission, and now their claims might ruin negotiations with the European Union, or lead to disturbances at the mines.[2] The manager of the Chamber felt that the Government's vague statement on advancement in the Dalgleish Commission's terms of reference was hardly adequate for the deteriorating situation.[3]

Despite their criticism of the Government, the mines' own course of action was not particularly bold when the three-party conference recommended by Dalgleish met under the chairmanship of the Attorney-General, Edgar Unsworth, on 30 August 1948. In the presence of Brian Goodwin and Frank Maybank, the European union's representatives, the delegates from the Chamber of Mines cautiously stated that they 'did not necessarily accept the principle of advancement' until agreement could be reached with the union, while the chairman interpreted the Chamber's position as 'that certain work could be done by Africans and not that it should be done and that was a very important difference'.[4] Goodwin stated that the union would only agree to advancement with equal pay, after which Frank Maybank cut off further discussion by taking up the case of a management

---

[1] Sir Ronald Prain, *Selected Papers 1953–57* (London, 1958), p. 26.
[2] C.I.S.B., 100.15, vol. ii: Memorandum on the Dalgleish Commission, P. H. Truscott, 30 June 1948.
[3] C.I.S.B., 100.15, vol. ii: Memorandum on the Dalgleish Commission, P. H. Truscott, 12 Aug. 1948.
[4] C.I.S.B., 100.15, vol. ii: Notes on the conference held at Kitwe on Monday, 30 Aug. 1948, by P. H. Truscott, 1 Sept. 1948.

official of the Rhokana Corporation, Rex L'Ange, who had just been elected to the Legislative Council. L'Ange had defeated Goodwin in the contest for the Nkana seat after campaigning as an opponent of African advancement. Maybank claimed that L'Ange's views must represent company policy, and the embarrassed officials of the Chamber of Mines denied it. The conference closed after its members had decided that the Government should negotiate separately with the companies and the union.[1]

Government representatives, again led by Unsworth, met members of the union on 7 January 1949, and representatives of the Chamber on 28 January. For the first time the Government put forward a detailed recommendation, based on the adjustment of clauses 1 and 42 in the union's recognition agreement with the companies. The union had in the past made the removal of clause 42, the dilution clause, conditional on the companies removing the word 'European' from clause 1. The companies had refused because of their fear that the European union would organize African branches. Government officials pointed out that as independent African trade unions had been established at the mines since 1948 this danger was less urgent.[2] If the companies dropped the word 'European', and if clause 42 was deleted, the mines could employ anyone they wished in any job category. The Government hoped that the union would overlook the 'equal pay for equal work' principle if it was made clear that Africans were not doing exactly the same work as Europeans. This could be done more easily if Africans were promoted *en bloc* into a job category and did not take over jobs as individual vacancies occurred.[3]

The Chamber of Mines representatives were pessimistic about the proposals. They pointed out that if clause 42 were to be deleted before the European union had definitely agreed to advancement, the union might well press to take over the African 'ragged edge' jobs instead. The 'equal pay for equal work' principle could not be ignored by the union in the case of the important 'ragged edge' jobs, since it was known that in these jobs Africans were already doing the same work as Europeans. The shortage of capable Africans was such that it was doubtful if entire categories of jobs could be taken over at once. They

[1] C.I.S.B., 100.15, vol. ii: Notes on the conference held at Kitwe, 30 Aug. 1948, by P. H. Truscott, 1 Sept. 1948.
[2] These unions, established at each mine, amalgamated in 1949 to form the African Mineworkers' Union.
[3] C.I.S.B., 100.15, vol. ii: Notes on the conference held at Kitwe on Friday, 28 Jan. 1949, P. H. Truscott; Notes of a meeting held at Kitwe on Friday, 28 Jan. 1949, E. I. G. Unsworth.

added that the union adhered to a very strict interpretation of 'equal pay', and had resisted any suggestion of splitting up or regrading European work to enable Africans to take it over.[1] Nevertheless the managements provided the Government representatives with a list of 'ragged edge' jobs to present to the union in a subsequent, separate meeting,[2] and the Managing Director of the Anglo American Group's copper mines, on a visit from London, privately admitted that the Unsworth Committee had made some 'sensible recommendations' and 'the Governor himself is determined to do all he can to arrive at a peaceful solution'. He advised the local managements that the advancement question 'is so important and the possibilities of action by Maybank so limitless that I think it would be worth considering the Unsworth suggestions in the broadest possible way and not trying to shoot them down by minor criticism.'[3] The London offices of both mining groups informed the Chamber of Mines that if the union demanded the deletion of the word 'European' in clause 1 as the price of the removal of clause 42, they would approve this concession to reach a settlement on the major issue.[4] The local managers reluctantly agreed.[5] By June, however, the Government reported a deadlock in its talks with the European union over the principle of equal pay for equal work, and announced that there was no purpose in continuing negotiations either with the union or with the other interested parties.[6]

When the London offices of the companies were notified by the local managements that the talks had failed, and that the Government's attitude now seemed to be 'to await developments even although it is appreciated that those developments might be violent in character',[7] they contacted the Governor, Sir Gilbert Rennie, who was then in London. On failing to obtain satisfaction, the Managing Directors of the two mining groups sent him a joint statement of their position. After pointing out that Dalgleish had encouraged the African mine-workers to think they would be given opportunities to

[1] Notes, 28 Jan. 1949, Truscott and Unsworth.
[2] Notes, 28 Jan. 1949, Truscott and Unsworth.
[3] C.I.S.B., 100.15, vol. ii: C. F. S. Taylor, Managing Director, Rhokana Corporation and Nchanga Consolidated Copper Mines Ltd., to H. Clark, General Manager, Rhokana Corporation, 7 Apr. 1949.
[4] C.I.S.B., 100.15, vol. ii: Executive Assistant, Mufulira Copper Mines Ltd., to Secretary of Chamber of Mines, 2 May 1949.
[5] C.I.S.B., 100.15, vol. ii: Decision reached by the Executive Committee, Chamber of Mines, 19 May 1949.
[6] C.I.S.B., 100.15, vol. ii: P. H. Truscott to H. Clark, 18 June 1949.
[7] Loc. cit.

advance, and the Government had sponsored an African trade union which could be expected to demand these opportunities as well as increased pay, the London Managing Directors informed Rennie that they did not feel justified in upsetting the whole wage structure of the industry by granting African workers pay increases for their present jobs, nor did they feel this alone would satisfy the discontent:

> The result of the present situation we fear, therefore, may well be a clash between the two races. . . . If it is claimed by Government that this problem is one primarily for the Companies to solve, we must say that we are not, under present conditions, free agents to negotiate new agreements with our European Mine Workers' Union for the elimination of the Colour Bar clause. Normally we could seek to negotiate such an amendment even though, since the attitude of the European Mine Workers' Union appears so uncompromising, the attempt to procure such amendment might be at the risk of a strike. Under to-day's conditions, however, we are under such pressure from the Supply departments in the United Kingdom to produce copper, that we feel we should be charged with irresponsibility in seeking, under these conditions, to revise our Union agreement in the knowledge that such negotiations would probably lead to a stoppage of work.
>
> We also feel that in the last analysis it is not the responsibility of the Companies but of the Government of the Territory to ensure that the terms of employment in a protectorate where no official Colour Bar exists, should be so ordered as to permit of equal opportunity for all according to their capabilities and to the jobs to which they are suited, irrespective of colour.
>
> We would suggest that if the Companies were known to be opposed to progression, and if the Government wished to implement the recommendations of the Dalgleish Commission, Government would have to take positive action to bring about such implementation. We fear that the Companies' actual views, which are known privately by Government, may be influencing the latter to delay action in the expectation that the Companies may be forced by circumstances to make some move.[1]

The companies' attempt to pin responsibility for the situation on the Government met with no success. Soon afterwards the Government found a reason to withdraw completely from direct participation in the advancement negotiations.

THE GOVERNMENT'S WITHDRAWAL

A month after the African Mineworkers' Union was formed, in March 1949, Arthur Creech Jones, the Secretary of State for the Colonies, visited Northern Rhodesia. During the war he had told

[1] C.I.S.B., 100.20.9A, vol. ii: C. F. S. Taylor and R. L. Prain to Sir Gilbert Rennie, 11 Aug. 1949.

George Hall, then Under-Secretary of State, that the Northern Rhodesian Government should restrict the entry of Europeans into the territory, limit European employment, and insist on an increased quota of supervisory jobs for Africans in industry.[1] In office he had to work with less controversial plans, and instead he urged the European and African mine unions to meet and discuss advancement.[2] The meeting had unexpected results, for the African union agreed that no African would take over a European job without European pay, while the European union suggested that in such cases it might represent the African workers involved. Observers were puzzled that the African union had accepted the principle of equal pay, which was recognized as a barrier to advancement.[3] William Comrie, the Government's trade-union officer, who had been present at the meeting, reported that there had been a wider understanding, which also covered the fragmentation of jobs. The European union had apparently agreed that equal pay would not be required when a European job was broken down and performed by more than one African.[4] This second point of agreement, however, was not publicized by either side or included in the published resolutions, and no progress resulted from the joint meeting.

The African union's activities gave the Government an opening for a change of policy which had been tentatively outlined a year before, shortly after the appointment of a new Labour Commissioner, C. E. Cousins, who had a more thorough grounding in orthodox industrial relations principles than his predecessors. He was the first Labour Commissioner appointed from outside the ranks of the Provincial Administration (he was transferred from Palestine in 1948) and the first with any professional knowledge of labour matters in Britain. When the Trade Unions and Trade Disputes bill was under discussion in 1949 the Mine Workers' Union, which was still interested in organizing African workers, and was prevented from doing so by its agreement with the companies, asked the Government to consider inserting a clause in the Bill to make colour-bar arrangements in industrial agreements illegal. The new Commissioner of Labour replied that the Select Committee considering the Bill, which included two trade-unionists, had decided 'that the principle of Government entering in

[1] *Hansard*, 5th series, H.C. Deb., 1941, vol. 370, 1743.
[2] Creech Jones Papers.
[3] Epstein, *Politics*, p. 105.
[4] C.I.S.B., 100.15, vol. ii: P. H. Truscott to Secretary, Mufulira Copper Mines Ltd., London, 14 Oct. 1950.

agreements negotiated freely between employer and employee was
not one that would generally be acceptable to the Trade Union Movement and in these circumstances the Committee was unanimous in
rejecting the suggestion'.[1] Developing this principle during the following year, the Government made it clear that as an African mineworkers' trade union had been launched, the question of African
advancement could be settled inside the industry without Government interference.[2] The Secretary for Native Affairs told the African
Representative Council, in answer to a question on the failure to
implement the *Dalgleish Report*, that as a result of 'this agreement [on
equal pay, in 1950] between the two unions it would appear that the
matter is one for negotiation between all parties in the mining industry and not one to which Government can compel any party to agree'.[3]
Nevertheless the companies remained convinced that the only way to
remove the industrial colour bar was by legislation,[4] while the Labour
Department *Report* for 1951 admitted that

it was not possible to convince the [African] union leaders that this was a
matter for negotiation between their union, that of the European mineworkers and the mining companies concerned. They considered that the
impasse should be removed by some Government action and inevitably the
issues of the 'colour bar', closer association and the definition of partnership became intertangled. The outlook at the end of the year was not
bright . . .[5]

[1] Zambia European Mineworkers' Association, Mufulira Branch Correspondence with Head Office, 1942–59: C. E. Cousins, Commissioner of Labour and
Mines, to F. S. Maybank, 11 Oct. 1949.
[2] *Legislative Council Debates*, 72, 7 Dec. 1951, 498.
[3] *African Representative Council Debates*, 6, 24 July 1951, 61–2.
[4] C.I.S.B., 100.15, vol. ii: S. Taylor to the Chief Secretary, 23 Jan. 1952.
   Report of the Department of Labour 1951, p. 14.

CHAPTER VII

A Plan for African Advancement

THE swift progress of plans to establish a Federation of Northern and Southern Rhodesia and Nyasaland generated a high level of unrest among Africans in the northern territories. African leaders thought that Colonial Office rule and the status of British-protected persons were preferable to closer association with Southern Rhodesia, which they feared might lead to amalgamation and the extension of that country's native policies to the north. They were increasingly critical of their own political status but, to quote one of the two African members of the Northern Rhodesia Legislative Council, they would not agree 'to jump from the frying pan into the burning fire'.[1] According to the Northern Rhodesian Government the new slogan of 'partnership' which would characterize the Federation meant that 'every individual must be free to rise to the level that his ability, energy, qualifications and character permit', but Africans took more heed of Sir Roy Welensky's definition of it as 'a determination to keep a balance between two populations, two peoples in different stages of civilization'.[2]

The mining companies were alarmed by opposition to the establishment of the Federation among African workers and trade-unionists on the Copperbelt. In 1952 the African National Congress set up an anti-Federation Action Council on which trade-union leaders were strongly represented. Shortly afterwards its only European member, Simon Zukas, was deported for advocating a general strike. The Government and the mine managements made plans against a stoppage, and although they over-estimated the cohesion of the Action Council, the background of threatened political disturbances lent urgency to industrial disputes between the companies and the African Mineworkers' Union throughout the year.[3] Leading management officials felt that much of the discontent derived from

[1] *Legislative Council Debates*, 73, 7 July 1952, 237.
[2] *Northern News*, 8 Apr. 1952; *Legislative Council Debates*, 73, 8 July 1952, 310.
[3] C.I.S.B., 100.41, vol. i: Notes of a meeting held at Lusaka on 2 Apr. 1952, by F. B. Canning-Cooke, 7 Apr. 1952.

continued frustration over the advancement question, and that new pressure should be put on the Government to intervene in the matter.[1]

At this point the companies' view of advancement still revolved round theoretical considerations rather than practical ones: they wanted to see the principle of advancement in the industry publicly recognized by both the Government and the Mine Workers' Union before they dealt with actual jobs and wage scales. These priorities were strengthened during the advancement negotiations of 1947–8 and the companies clung to them for several years. The groups felt that advancement was not a suitable subject for bargaining with the European union, because of the danger of strike action and of political repercussions: nevertheless they also felt that until the union conceded the principle of advancement it was useless to make further plans. It was, they believed, the Government's duty to declare a public policy on the matter, and enforce it, since the political implications were as far-reaching as the industrial ones. The expedient the industry later used of creating new African jobs in areas not touched by the European union's agreement was not explored at this stage. Possibly it was felt to be too provocative a move. Discussion was confined to old territory—the take-over of the 'ragged edge' jobs and other low-level European work by Africans; the division of European jobs among a greater number of Africans; on-the-job training for Africans, because formal apprenticeship was a sensitive matter in view of the shortage of places for European youths; and the development of an African wage scale unrelated to existing European wages. The companies were willing to guarantee that no European would forfeit his employment or wages because of advancement, and to proceed with it at a very slow pace to reassure European public opinion, provided the principle was openly admitted.[2]

In the face of the implacable opposition of the Mine Workers' Union both the companies and the Government drifted, with only half-hearted advocacy of the need for African progress. It was not until the African Mineworkers' Union gathered strength and flexed its muscles in a strike in 1952 that some urgency was injected into the situation. Even as late as November 1951 the Chamber of Mines'

[1] C.I.S.B., 100.20.5: Notes of discussions with Messrs. R. L. Prain (RST) and W. Marshall Clark (Rhokana Corporation Ltd.) held at Kitwe, 21 Oct. 1952.

[2] C.I.S.B., 100.15, vol. i: Telegram, Mufulira Copper Mines Ltd., to Chamber of Mines, 26 Feb. 1947; Memorandum, Dalgleish Commission, by P. H. Truscott, 17 Sept. 1947.

Industrial Relations Adviser, F. B. Canning-Cooke, noted critically that the companies had no over-all policy or strategy on African advancement. He warned that the companies might be forced to make endless concessions to the African union as long as the major issue lay unresolved; but he still felt that the Government rather than the companies should make the first move.[1]

Company officials hoped that the loss of revenue to the Northern Rhodesian Government and of copper to the British Government caused by the 1952 African strike might force them to take a renewed interest in the advancement question.[2] The companies were anxious to have the matter raised promptly for political reasons: the rate of South African immigration to the territory, which had consistently outpaced immigration from Britain, had aroused wide comment since 1950, and now led some observers to think that the next terri-torial election in 1953 might produce an Afrikaner majority in the Legislative Council.[3] Sir Ronald Prain of the Rhodesian Selection Trust Group felt that this would end the hopes still entertained by the companies for a legislative solution to the advancement ques-tion.[4] Trade-union affairs provided another reason for action. The Mine Workers' Union was trying to organize European workers employed by mine contractors, and the threat of an extension of the union's influence alarmed the companies.[5] In addition Sir William Lawther, Secretary of the Miners' International Federation (M.I.F.), to which both the European and African mine-workers' unions were affiliated, was expected to visit the territory. It seemed to the com-panies that his visit could only result in an endorsement by inter-national trade-unionism of the 'equal pay for equal work' principle in Northern Rhodesia, which would strengthen the hand of the European union in future negotiations.[6]

The African union's three-week strike late in 1952 concerned a

---

[1] C.I.S.B., 100.15, vol. ii: Memorandum on African labour policy, F. B. Canning-Cooke, 14 Nov. 1951.

[2] Loc. cit.

[3] Creech Jones Papers; *Northern Rhodesia Economic and Statistical Bulletin*, vol. vi, no. 10, Jan. 1954, p. 16, Table 2: Immigrants by Nationality, 1944–53.

[4] C.I.S.B., 100.15, vol. ii: Notes of a discussion with the Secretary of State at the Colonial Office, 20 Nov. 1952.

[5] C.I.S.B., 100.15, vol. ii: Notes of a discussion with representatives of the engineering contractors, 9 Dec. 1952.

[6] C.I.S.B., 100.15, vol. ii: Notes of meeting held at Lusaka on 20 Nov. 1952 . . . (with) R. Welensky and His Excellency the Governor, on the subject of the progression of Africans in industry, by H. A. Watmore, 25 Nov. 1952.

demand for a general pay increase of 2s. 8d. per shift (80s. per ticket of thirty working days). The claim represented a heavy increase on all wage rates, but particularly on the 45s. and 55s. starting rates applicable to the lowest group of unskilled workers, which contained more than half of the mines' African employees. The union eventually agreed to go to arbitration, and with the help of the Miners' International Federation secured the services of Ronald Williams, Labour Member of Parliament and legal adviser to the British National Union of Mineworkers, to represent it at the proceedings. The companies felt certain that Williams would not fail to raise the subject of advancement before the arbitrator. They considered this to be an additional and urgent justification for a new initiative on advancement, as wages were the thorniest part of the problem and they were reluctant to have the matter examined by an 'outsider' in the context of a wage demand.

A meeting attended by the Secretary of State, Oliver Lyttelton, was held at the Colonial Office on 20 November to discuss the Copperbelt situation. The companies' representatives left it thinking that they had won the Secretary of State's support for their view that action should be taken on African advancement in the very near future, and preferably initiated by the Government.[1] On the same day in Lusaka the local mine managers met the Governor, leading officials, and Roy Welensky, leader of the unofficials in the Legislative Council, to discuss the forthcoming arbitration and the problems arising from it. Roy Welensky made the point that any move by the Government or the companies on African advancement would endanger the outcome of the plan for a federation in Central Africa. He also spoke of the danger of opposition from the Railway and Mine Workers' Unions, which might lead to a general strike of European workers. Despite his warnings, the managers of the Nkana and Roan Antelope mines urged the Governor to act before the arbitration proceedings took place, and certainly before the expected delegation from the Miners' International Federation arrived to confer with the two mine unions.[2] They stressed that in new negotiations, by contrast to previous ones, the Government could count on the companies to show publicly that they were in favour of advancement. The Governor, however, did not

[1] C.I.S.B., 100.15, vol. ii: Notes of discussion with Secretary of State at the Colonial Office, 20 Nov. 1952.

[2] As a result of various delays, Sir William Lawther, secretary of the Miners' International Federation, did not visit Northern Rhodesia until Mar. 1954.

commit himself to any action.[1] At a second meeting in Lusaka on 10 December, the mine managers urged the Government to announce the appointment of a commission on African advancement or the calling of a conference on the subject early in the new year, so that the arbitrator on the African wage claim could exclude the subject from evidence presented to him because it was already *sub judice*. Roy Welensky again opposed the companies' suggestions as likely to injure current plans for a federation, and the Government once more refused to give a commitment.[2]

In London the effect of a new initiative over African advancement on the plans for a federation in Central Africa had begun to cause anxiety at the Colonial Office. It was clear that such a move would be unpopular in Southern Rhodesia, perhaps to the extent of affecting the referendum on the federation proposals to be held there early in 1953. In December company officials learned that pressure was being put on the Secretary of State by leading supporters of federation to postpone any action on African advancement in the Copperbelt. At a meeting with Colonial Office representatives on 11 December they tried to counter this threat with the prospect of deliberately allowing the advancement question to be aired in public during the arbitration proceedings. They warned that if the companies decided to follow this course or to give the European union notice terminating the companies' recognition of clause 42 in the agreement, the result might be a lengthy European strike. The Colonial Office representatives seemed unimpressed: they favoured informal lines of action rather than any new public initiative.[3]

Despite the companies' emphasis on the urgent nature of the advancement problem, their willingness to act was largely based on the hope that they could persuade the Colonial Office and the Northern Rhodesian Government to take an initiative which they could follow. Their effort was soon overtaken by political pressure from supporters of federation in Northern and Southern Rhodesia against immediate action on the matter. At the time of the final

[1] C.I.S.B., 100.15, vol. ii: Notes of meetings held at Lusaka on 20 Nov. 1952 . . . (with) R. Welensky and His Excellency the Governor, on the subject of the progression of Africans in industry, by H. A. Watmore, 25 Nov. 1952; and author's interview with Sir Roy Welensky, London, 16 Nov. 1970.

[2] C.I.S.B., 100.15, vol. ii: Notes on discussion with His Excellency the Governor at Lusaka on 10 Dec. 1952, F. B. Canning-Cooke, 17 Dec. 1952; and interview with Sir Roy Welensky, London, 16 Nov. 1970.

[3] C.I.S.B., 100.15, vol. ii: Notes of discussion with Colonial Office representatives on 11 Dec. 1952, dated 12 Dec. 1952.

conference on the federal constitution in January 1953 another meeting
on the Copperbelt situation was held in London at the request of Sir
Ronald Prain, chairman of the RST group. It was attended by the
Secretary of State, the Governor of Northern Rhodesia, Roy
Welensky, and representatives of the mining companies and the
Colonial Office. The company representatives found the Colonial
Secretary much less sympathetic to their case than he had been in
November, and failed to convince him of the need for urgent action.[1]

The company officials left the meeting with the feeling that nothing
could be expected from the Government in the foreseeable future.
They now concentrated their attention on keeping the arbitration
proceedings private, as they feared that a public hearing in which
advancement was discussed might inflame Copperbelt opinion. The
arbitrator, Claud Guillebaud, a Cambridge economist who had
served on wages councils in Britain, was known to favour public
proceedings. The Government, 'in view of African suspicion', refused
to give him firm instructions to the contrary, but the Chief Secretary
reluctantly agreed that if an opportunity arose the Provincial Commissioner at Ndola could point out to him the desirability of private
hearings.[2] In this the companies were at last successful, and their own
case and that of the African union were presented to Guillebaud in
private by Sir Hartley Shawcross and Ronald Williams.

The companies based their case on the social and economic dangers
of increasing African wage levels. High wages would encourage
Africans from the rural areas to settle permanently in the towns. As
the mining industry was based on wasting assets these men's children
might be thrown back on the land and a way of living with which they
had lost all contact.[3] In fact many mine officials at this time believed
in a conflicting theory called the 'backward-bending supply curve' of
native labour: that African workers were accustomed to take work
in order to meet some immediate financial goal, so that if pay was
increased the workers would reach their target sooner and leave
employment, and the supply of labour might even be reduced. Research later showed the response of 'target' workers to low wages
was rational: they had no inducement to remain at work for long

[1] C.I.S.B., 100.20.9A, vol. i: Summary of meeting with the Secretary of State for
the Colonies on 6 Jan. 1953.
[2] C.I.S.B., 100.20.9A, vol. i: Record of decisions . . . of the Executive Committee of the Chamber of Mines, 12 Jan. 1953.
[3] C.I.S.B., 100.20.9A, vol. ii: Address to the Guillebaud Arbitration Tribunal
by Sir Hartley Shawcross.

periods, because it was more profitable for them to divide their labour between work for wages and subsistence agriculture.[1] Ronald Williams mentioned this possibility, then countered the companies' case with impressive evidence of the inadequacy of existing cost of living allowances for African mine-workers, more than half of whom earned little above the sum required to buy minimum necessities listed in a recent report on civil service wages.[2]

Guillebaud awarded substantial pay increases, backdated to 17 November 1952, for all groups of workers, and he was particularly generous to the lowest paid of them. The existing starting rate for Africans on the mines was 45s. per ticket. The companies had offered to raise it to 60s. during negotiations, the union had claimed 125s., and Guillebaud raised it to 80s. At the other end of the scale the starting rate of the special group, the highest paid Africans, was raised from 290s. to 340s.[3] In private Guillebaud stressed to the companies that some measure of advancement, however small, was also necessary to satisfy these workers.[4] The Guillebaud award broke the mining companies' long-held principle that African wages should not be increased without a parallel increase in efficiency, which depended on the implementation of an advancement programme. It also provided temporary relief for the African union's frustration over the issue, although in the eyes of some of its members it seemed to justify a more active use of the strike weapon. The strike that led to the arbitration had been conducted with impressive discipline at all the mines. It marked the entry of a new force on the industrial scene which was intolerant of the leisurely struggle for advancement over the conference table.

ADVANCEMENT ACHIEVED

Unhampered by northern proposals for African advancement, the plan for a Federation won approval from the Southern Rhodesian

[1] This theory has been set out in a West African context by Elliot Berg, 'Recruitment of a Labor Force in Sub-Saharan Africa' (Harvard University Ph.D. thesis 1960). It was applied to the Federation in W. J. Barber, *The Economy of British Central Africa* (Stanford, 1961), pp. 212 ff., and to Northern Rhodesia in Robert E. Baldwin, *Economic Development and Export Growth* (Los Angeles, 1966), Chapter 5. Evidence from Malawi is provided by E. Dean, *The Supply Responses of African Farmers* (Amsterdam, 1966), chapters 2, 4 and 5.

[2] C.I.S.B., 100.20.9A, vol. ii: Address by Ronald Williams.

[3] *Report and Award of the Arbitrator, C. W. Guillebaud, January 1953* (mimeo).

[4] C.I.S.B., 100.20.9A, vol. ii: Notes of a meeting with Mr. C. W. Guillebaud, Ndola, 3 Feb. 1953.

electorate by 25,570 votes to 14,729 in April 1953. Meanwhile the Colonial Office's rejection of the companies' plan for a prompt joint initiative on African advancement at last forced the mining groups to think about independent action. The wage increases given in the Guillebaud arbitration award were so large that a more rational and efficient use of African labour seemed necessary to offset the wage bill. The estimated annual cost of the award was about £873,000,[1] and it followed a sharp rise in the general costs of production.[2] The ending of the British Government's bulk purchases of copper was helpful in timing a move. British control of production from the mines had lasted almost continuously since the beginning of the Second World War, having been prolonged by the post-war domestic shortage of copper, the sterling devaluation crisis, and then by the international shortage of copper caused by the Korean War. On several occasions British pressure to prevent a halt in copper production had undermined the companies' stand in union negotiations. The Rhodesian Selection Trust chairman, Sir Ronald Prain, who felt that the labour situation on the mines was becoming 'untenable in practice and in principle', decided to take advantage of the altered circumstances to press for new talks between the companies and the European union. Copper was released from British Government controls in April 1953 and within ten days the first meeting was held.[3]

At the request of the European union, the African union and the European Mine Officials and Salaried Staff Association (M.O.S.S.A.) were later invited to join the discussions, and the resulting 'four-party talks' began in February 1954. The M.O.S.S.A. representatives confirmed that the Association had no objection to the advancement of Africans into staff categories, even at unequal rates of pay.[4] The European Mine Workers' Union at first seemed willing to discuss the

---

[1] C.I.S.B., 100.20.9A, vol. ii: Notes on the Guillebaud Award.

[2] Between June 1952 and June 1953 these rose by £2·5 million at Roan Antelope, £1·5 million at Mufulira, £0·8 million at Rhokana, and £2·4 million at Nchanga from costs of £7·1 million, £6·6 million, £8·6 million and £5·3 million respectively in 1951–2.

In the same period net profits rose from £2·6 million to £4·7 million at Roan Antelope, £2·6 million to £3·6 million at Mufulira, £7·8 million to £8·3 million at Rhokana and £6·5 million to £8·7 million at Nchanga. (*The Economist*, 5 Dec. 1953, p. 764.)

[3] Sir Ronald Prain, '*Selected Papers 1953–57*' (London, 1958), pp. 29–30; Harold K. Hochschild, 'Labour Relations in Northern Rhodesia', *Annals of the American Academy of Political and Social Science*, ccvi, July 1956, p. 47.

[4] *Forster Commission Report*, 1954, p. 24.

'ragged edge' jobs held by its members, but as a detailed examination of the jobs began the usual obstacles to progress appeared. The companies insisted that with only a few exceptions several Africans would be required to perform the work of one European, and they would be paid at rates appropriate to the existing African wage scale and standard of living. The European union's reaction to this became clear when the job of 'crane chasing' was examined. The job of signalling directions to crane drivers moving heavy loads was done by Africans at one mine, but at the others was performed as part of wider duties by Europeans graded as 'operators'. The union used this case to demonstrate its hostility to the division of work done by individual Europeans, and on 24 July the talks foundered completely on the issues of job division and equal pay.[1] A month later the Government appointed a Board of Inquiry to examine the advancement question once more. Appropriately, the chairman was Sir John Forster, who had led the inquiry into the African strike of 1940 and had first drawn attention to the issue in an official report.

The new inquiry was confined to the copper industry, and Forster had as colleagues on the Board two men of considerable local experience, W. A. Godlonton, a member of the Southern Rhodesia Native Labour Board, and J. H. Gibbons, who had been the first Chief Inspector of Mines in Northern Rhodesia from 1929 to 1938 before transfer to a post in Tanganyika. Forster accepted the conclusions of the Dalgleish Commission about the categories of work Africans were capable of performing, and concentrated his study on the barriers which had prevented them from doing so. The Board's findings, reported in September 1954, endorsed the Government's view that a solution rested 'squarely upon the parties engaged in the industry' rather than upon official intervention.[2] However, the companies' position was upheld in the *Report*'s view that advancement could only be achieved on the basis of a dual wage structure and the 'reasonable fragmentation' of European jobs.[3]

Soon after the Forster Commission urged the industry to try once more to find its own solution to the problem, an important aspect of the Copperbelt situation changed temporarily in the managements' favour. The price of copper soared on the London Metal Exchange and bonus payments to European miners, which were linked to the

[1] *Forster Commission Report*, 1954, p. 11, and Appendices 4 and 5, pp. 46–7.
[2] Ibid., p. 29.
[3] Ibid., pp. 27–8.

Exchange price, rose to 75 per cent of basic wages in 1954–5 and to 103½ per cent in 1955–6.[1] It seemed possible that the prospect of losing wages and bonus payments in these exceptional market conditions might restrain the European workers from strike action, even on a deeply-felt issue.[2]

The Forster *Report* recommended that talks between the companies and the European union should be resumed, but it was soon apparent that the union had not relaxed its position on equal pay or the subdivision of jobs. In November the RST Group took the serious step of issuing to the union the six months' notice required to end its recognition agreement. Although the notice was suspended six weeks later, relations between union leaders and the group's Copperbelt officials remained tense.[3] In January 1955 the European union held a ballot in which 60 per cent of those voting unexpectedly showed themselves in favour of the transfer of low-grade jobs to African workers.[4] Only two branches, at Roan Antelope and Bancroft, voted for the retention of the equal pay principle with no concessions.[5] Despite this mandate the leaders of the union continued to press for safeguards in the transfer arrangements which seemed likely to lead to a new deadlock.

The divided opinions within the union had been inflamed by the RST Group's threat to withdraw the recognition agreement, and also by the effects of a nine-week African strike which began on 3 January 1955. Sir Ronald Prain had commented during the three-week African strike in 1952, which shut down all the mines and put European employees out of work, that the stoppage might bring home to the European workers the dangers of blocking African advancement.[6] The opposite seemed true during the 1955 strike. Although this time European workers were not laid off, considerable resentment built up against the African union's conduct and the companies' supposedly lenient terms for a return to work. The European union's

[1] C.I.S.B.: Companies' statement of case to the arbitration tribunal on the Mines Officials and Salaried Staff Association's wage claim, 1959, p. 2.

[2] Nan S. Waldstein, The Struggle for African Advancement Within the Copper Industry of Northern Rhodesia (mimeo) (M.I.T. Center for International Studies), p. 79.

[3] *Northern News*, 5 Nov. 1954 and 18 Dec. 1954.

[4] C.I.S.B., 100.46, vol. iii: Chamber of Mines to Rhodesian Selection Trust, Lusaka, 4 Feb. 1955.

[5] *Northern News*, 31 Jan. 1955.

[6] C.I.S.B., 100.20.5: Notes of discussions with Messrs. R. L. Prain and W. Marshall Clark held at Kitwe, 21 Oct. 1952.

General Council even decided to hold a second ballot on the transfer of advancement jobs to Africans, in which the previous decision was reaffirmed, but by a smaller majority than before.[1]

The advancement plans of both mining groups hinged on the excision of some twenty-four categories of low-level European jobs from the European union's recognition agreement, including the long-disputed 'ragged edge' jobs identical to work already performed by Africans at some of the mines, and other jobs which required only a small degree of skill. The jobs remaining in the European union's agreement would be listed in 'Schedule A' and those released to Africans in 'Schedule B'. The companies intended to supplement these with the creation of a large number of 'intermediate' jobs more advanced than Africans currently performed but below the level of the lowest European work in the new schedule. There were to be 464 intermediate posts, some created by the division of operations previously performed by Europeans, but many of them entirely new jobs which had never impinged on the European field and which the companies could have introduced at any time without the consent of the European union. The Chamber of Mines gave evidence to the Forster Board of Inquiry that this had not been done in the past because the companies felt it was only a partial solution which would increase the number of aggrieved workers if advancement into the higher jobs in the European field was not also opened.[2]

The advancement plans dealt with the problem of the rate for the job by the simple device of removing low-grade jobs from the European union's agreement, and permitting Africans who might subsequently be promoted to the jobs remaining in that agreement to be represented by the European union and receive equal pay.[3] In addition the RST Group published a proposal by which the gap between the pay of the highest African workers and that of the lowest European operators, from 13s. 6d. to 46s. 6d. per shift, would be bridged by a 'ladder' of intermediate jobs with pay rates ranging from 14s. 3d. to 40s. The rates, to be fixed first in negotiation with the

[1] *Northern News*, 3 Mar. and 7 Apr. 1955.

[2] Evidence of David Symington, Director of the Chamber of Mines, to the Forster Board of Inquiry, 6 Sept. 1954.

[3] *Report of the Commission Appointed to Inquire into the Unrest in the Mining Industry in Northern Rhodesia in recent months* (*The Branigan Report*) (Lusaka, 1956), Appendix 5, pp. 74–9: Agreement between the companies and the Northern Rhodesia Mine Workers' Union, 27 Sept. 1955.

European union and then with the African union, would take into account the principle of 'equal pay for work of equal value' and when, eventually, the efficiency of an African equalled that of European worker he would receive equal pay.[1] These plans repaired the failure of the Unsworth proposals in 1949 to make any reference to 'equal pay' in relation to African wages. The deletion of the word 'European' from the first clause of the Mine Workers' Union's agreement would permit it to represent Africans earning equal pay. It also enabled the negotiators to leave untouched the old provision against dilution, clause 42, as the union 'did not wish to upset its members' by altering it.[2]

As the negotiations progressed, important differences between the Anglo American and the RST Group proposals emerged, caused in part by the Anglo American Group's involvement in the South African mining industry and the Selection Trust's independence of it. The Anglo American Group, sensitive to the pressure of the labour situation on the Rand, had to consider the repercussions of a breach with the Northern Rhodesia Mine Workers' Union on its relations with the powerful Mine Workers' Union of South Africa. The South African Union was active throughout the negotiations in the spring of 1955, after the Northern Rhodesian union had asked it for support and advice on the best way to bring pressure on the Anglo American Group.[3] The two unions' leaders maintained close contacts, their decision to form a permanent liaison committee was well publicized, and in April the South African union voted £5,000 as an initial donation to help their northern brothers in the struggle to maintain European standards.[4] If there had been any doubt about the South African union's interest in the situation on the Copperbelt, its General Secretary, Dan Ellis, removed it during an interview with Harry Oppenheimer, managing director of the Anglo American

[1] *Northern News*, 4 Feb. 1955.

[2] *The Branigan Report*, p. 74: Agreement between the companies and the Northern Rhodesia Mine Workers' Union, 27 Sept. 1955; C.I.S.B., 100.46, vol. iv: Record of Decisions of the Executive Committee of the Chamber of Mines, 11 Oct. 1955.

[3] Zambia Expatriate Mineworkers' Association, Correspondence with the South Africa Mine Workers' Union 1942–58: W. G. Spires, General Secretary, M.W.U., to Dan Ellis, General Secretary, S.A.M.W.U., 17 Nov. 1954; and D. E. Ellis to W. G. Spires, 19 Dec. 1954.

[4] *Northern News*, letter by B. J. Petersen, Acting General Secretary, N.R.M.W.U., 26 Jan. 1955; also *Northern News*, 16, 20, 21, 22 Apr., 2, 7, 30 May; and *Union News*, Special Edition, July 1955.

Group,[1] in July. Ellis claimed he then received an assurance from Oppenheimer that the Group would, if necessary, enter into a separate agreement with the Northern Rhodesian union rather than follow the hard lines adopted by RST's negotiators.[2]

The Anglo American representatives on the Copperbelt had at first suggested that the number of Africans to be advanced in the next five years might be limited to 5 per cent of the number of Europeans at that time on the payroll.[3] This safeguard was replaced by an offer to make each transfer of a European job category to African workers conditional on the European union's approval at the time of transfer.[4] The RST Group would not grant this concession.[5] During July the union's insistence on the veto and the RST Group's refusal to give it seemed likely to lead to a European strike. Union branches voted to raise strike levies, and towards the end of the month negotiations with the Chamber of Mines were shelved so that the union could approach the two mining groups separately.[6] The Anglo American Group's negotiators were now willing to enter into an immediate agreement, to defuse what they believed had become an explosive labour situation which might erupt into violence.[7] On 30 July an agreement was signed by the union and the Anglo American Copperbelt managers involving the transfer of twenty-four categories of European jobs to African workers and incorporating the controversial veto clause.[8] The RST negotiators, who believed that to grant the veto was a substantial surrender of the powers of management, held firm for another six weeks, when the union suddenly gave way and signed an agreement without the clause.[9] On 27 September the two separate union agreements were replaced by

[1] Harry F. Oppenheimer, b. 1908. Son of Sir Ernest Oppenheimer, chairman of the Anglo American Corporation of South Africa. After his father's death in 1958 he became chairman of the Anglo American Corporation, De Beers Consolidated Mines Ltd., and Rhodesian Anglo American Limited, the holding company through which the Nkana and Nchanga mines were developed.

[2] Zambia Expatriate Mineworkers' Association, Correspondence with the South African Mine Workers' Union, 1942–58: D. E. Ellis to B. J. Petersen, 18 July 1955.

[3] *Northern News*, 4 Feb. 1955.

[4] *Northern News*, 8 July 1955.

[5] *Northern News*, 4 Feb. and 8 July 1955.

[6] *Northern News*, 18, 20, 21 July 1955; C.I.S.B., 100.46, vol. iv: Mine Workers Union to Chamber of Mines, 27 July 1955.

[7] Memorandum, D. A. H. Dady, Anglo American Corporation (Central Africa) Limited, 13 June 1969.

[8] *Northern News*, 1 Aug. 1955.

[9] *Northern News*, 12 Sept. 1955.

one common to both the Anglo American and RST mines which omitted the veto provision.

This agreement, achieved after a year of hard and often bitter bargaining, was a symbolic breakthrough, if only a small advance in practical terms. It was widely hailed throughout the Federation as a demonstration of the principle of 'partnership',[1] although of the twenty-four job categories released by the European union, thirteen were of the 'ragged edge' type which had been a source of friction for at least fifteen years, and the others covered work of a low grade. These concessions were not enough to provide a permanent solution, and the agreement provided for the hiring of an independent firm of industrial consultants to undertake a survey of European work as a preliminary to further advancement negotiations at some future date. Meanwhile the European union, which had been deeply divided over the surrender of jobs to Africans, felt that the loyalties of its members would be strained if they were also required to instruct the Africans taking over their work. It announced that its members would not train Africans for the new advancement posts.[2]

After a delay of fifteen years the barriers to African advancement were partially breached. The companies finally challenged the European union and obtained alterations in its recognition agreement. They considered their goals to be in the interests of their African employees, but the African union had not been drawn into the advancement negotiations, except for the brief interlude of the four-party talks. On that occasion it had become clear that the aims of the African union diverged from those of the companies in important respects, and a reconciliation was not in sight. A settlement of the advancement question which would have been welcomed by Africans in the 1940s was less easily accepted in 1955: the companies found that having reached a solution agreeable to the European Mine Workers' Union they faced a new problem in persuading their African workers to endorse it.

[1] E. Clegg, *Race and Politics* (London, 1960), p. 201.
[2] *Northern News*, 17 Nov. 1955.

CHAPTER VIII

The African Reaction

THE companies' advancement plan precipitated a crisis in the affairs of the African Mineworkers' Union. For many years Government and employers had considered advancement on the basis of promotion for senior African workers and the subdivision of European jobs. Now they discovered that the plan did not begin to meet the aspirations of the African labour force. Efforts to implement it caused a wave of African unrest at the mines which led the Government to declare a State of Emergency in the province.[1] The Government had stressed that advancement was an industrial rather than a territorial matter, and that African trade unions were capable of representing African interests in it. It later became clear that this mandate did not include free resort to the strike weapon. A long stoppage could damage national revenues, and, equally important, a strike of over 30,000 African workers concentrated in a handful of company towns on the Copperbelt raised the prospect of disturbances which the police and available military forces might not be able to control. Theoretically African unions were to play a broad role in industrial relations, but in practice the Government became uneasy about possible political influences and what it considered to be irresponsible leadership. In the mining industry the role of the African Mineworkers' Union was limited in another way. Its part in wage negotiations was narrowed by the companies' view that major wage increases should be tied to improved productivity, and were therefore connected with the success of the advancement negotiations. These negotiations in turn depended on a prior agreement with the European union, from which the A.M.U. was excluded.

The Colonial Office had always accepted that trade unions should be subject to some restrictions in the colonies. There had been no suggestion that British trade-unionism, with its tradition of political interests, could be transplanted without modification. In the 1930s the Colonial Office's interest in introducing trade unions had the

---

[1] Appendix C at pp. 236–7 lists, in chronological order, the events in the mining industry which led to the proclamation of a State of Emergency in 1956.

dual purpose of encouraging native employees to participate in bargaining over working conditions, and of preventing the growth of secret political organizations among them.[1] After the war stress was laid on the need for adequate supervision, and in most territories trade unions were required to register with a Government officer, contrary to existing British practice. In 1951 the Colonial Office acknowledged that the post-war effort to establish trade-unionism had met with grave difficulties. Under-staffed Labour Departments had found it difficult to spread trade-union principles among illiterate migrant workers, and the consequences could be seen in the administration of many new unions. The Colonial Office felt that when they were formed too early, organization was weak, financial control deficient, and leadership either lacking or, equally serious, political in its direction.

In Northern Rhodesia the Government was quick to appreciate the danger of political involvement in the African trade-union movement. The Federation proposals had aroused strong African opposition, and out of this the first wave of nationalism was born. A number of African trade-union leaders associated themselves with the African National Congress, and there was a brief threat of a general strike in 1952. In the later disturbances on the Copperbelt in 1956 the suspicion naturally arose that the A.N.C. was involved and had encouraged the African Mineworkers' Union to take strike action. The Government measured the union's political involvement by the yardstick of the narrow role assigned to African trade unions by the Colonial Office, and had little difficulty in concluding that the A.M.U. had exceeded it. Yet positive proof of co-ordination between the union and the Congress, or of demonstrations of solidarity by the union in support of Congress, was lacking.[2] The permissible level of political activity was difficult to define.

DISSENT WITHIN THE AFRICAN MINEWORKERS' UNION

The African Mineworkers' Union had some early successes in wage negotiations. Shortly after it was founded in 1949 it made a substantial wage claim, and eventually won an increase for certain

---

[1] Foreign and Commonwealth Office Library, C.O. 323/1096/70967/3: Circular despatch from Lord Passfield, Secretary of State, 17 Sept. 1930; C.O. 323/1429/1766: Circular Despatch from W. Ormsby-Gore, Secretary of State, 24 Aug. 1937.
[2] E. J. Berg and J. Butler, 'Trade Unions', in *Political and National Integration in Tropical Africa*, ed. J. S. Coleman and C. G. Rosberg, Jr. (Berkeley, 1964), p. 354.

workers and inclusive wages for those in the highest groups, who were given allowances for rations and services previously provided by the companies. After a strike ballot the union secured a profit-sharing scheme for Africans in 1951, and in the same year it succeeded in having the inclusive wage system extended to new groups.[1] In 1952 claims for a general wage increase, first of 1s. 4d. and then of 2s. 8d. per shift, led to the union's first Copperbelt-wide strike and to the Guillebaud arbitration, which awarded large increases to all workers. In this period the union had not participated in advancement nego- tiations, except for its inconclusive meeting with the European union in 1950, when its leaders endorsed the principle of equal pay for equal work. Instead attention had been concentrated on wage and bonus negotiations, and on building up the union's membership and organization. Although the companies would not consider demands for a 'closed shop' similar to that of the European union, they helped the A.M.U. by collecting its 6d. per ticket subscription from wages on a stop-order system. By the end of 1952 these orders covered some 26,000 workers from an African labour force of about 36,000 men.[2]

In the few years in which this substantial record of membership had been built up recognized leaders emerged at the various mines, where large branch committees from the underground, personnel and various surface departments met at regular intervals, and sent repre- sentatives to meetings of the Supreme Council. Among these promi- nent officials were Simon Kaluwa, Robinson Puta, Jameson Chapoloko, and Matthew Mwendapole. The position of Lawrence Katilunga as President was apparently unchallenged at first, but after the Guillebaud award policy disputes and the play of ambitions began to threaten his authority. The wide differences of background and industrial interests among the union's large membership provided fertile ground for discontent.

The union's success in building up its membership, which was in sharp contrast to the weak development of most other African unions in the territory, owed much to the structure of the Copperbelt mining industry. The system of private compounds, with African employees living in company housing close to their work and separated from other local communities, provided unusually favourable circumstances

---

[1] *Annual Reports of the Labour and Mines Department*, 1949, p. 7, and 1951, pp. 8, 13.

[2] C.I.S.B., 100.20.9A, vol. ii: Address by Sir Hartley Shawcross to the Guille- baud Arbitration Tribunal, 23 Jan. 1953, p. 67.

for organization. The enclosed character of mine society out-weighed the effects of the rapid turnover of workers in the lower levels of employment,[1] and sometimes even of tribalism. Tribal authority had begun to weaken early at the mines, and the rapid adjustment of mine employees to their new industrial environment was sharply expressed during the 1940 strike by a gathering of Bemba workers who refused to listen to a message from their paramount chief: 'We do not work for Chief Chitimukulu, we are working for the Bwanas.'[2] In 1953 85 per cent of the labour force voted in favour of the abolition of the main link with their tribal backgrounds, the old system of Tribal Representatives, which trade-union leaders had attacked as a rival centre of authority.[3] Tribal loyalties remained a powerful factor in African social relations on the Copperbelt, but they were often subordinated to the common interests of Africans as mine-workers, or as a community with interests opposed to those of Europeans.[4]

The play of tribal loyalties within the union was affected by the pattern of job distribution at the mines. For a variety of reasons—the theories and preferences held by individual African Personnel Man-agers, the preferences of tribal groups themselves, the background of education in labour supply areas, and local factors affecting the supply of workers from a particular district—certain tribal groups were heavily represented in some types of mine work. There were many men from Nyasaland and from Barotseland, areas where mission schools were well established, among the mine clerks and highest groups of workers. Men from the Lovale area in the west of the country were among the few who would accept sanitation work. The Nyakusa from Tanganyika were thought to be stronger than most workers, and were frequently assigned by Personnel Managers to heavy labouring work underground.[5] The Bemba of the Northern Province, who came from a poor agricultural area and had long-established labour routes to the Copperbelt, were the most numerous

---

[1] The total annual turnover of African labour at the mines was 60 per cent in 1952, but dropped gradually in subsequent years. (See table, p. 208.) The hard core of long-service employees played a prominent part in union affairs. Epstein, *Politics*, pp. 118–19.

[2] Verbatim evidence to the Forster Commission, 1940, of Edward Sampa, Bemba Elder at Nkana.

[3] Epstein, *Politics*, p. 100.

[4] Epstein, *Politics*, Chapter VII, and J. Clyde Mitchell, *The Kalela Dance*, Rhodes–Livingstone Paper No. 27 (1957).

[5] Epstein, *Politics*, pp. 6–9.

tribal group on the mines, followed by the Bisa, who came from the same part of the country. Rivalry between the Bemba-speaking peoples and the Lozi and Nyasa clerks, who enjoyed higher wages and status than most workers, was of long standing, and the consequences spilled over into union affairs. The Bemba predominated in the A.M.U. as they did in the general labour force, and Katilungu, who was distantly related to the Bemba royal family, was labelled by opponents as 'the paramount chief of the Bemba trade union'.[1] The union's General Secretary, Simon Kaluwa, was of Nyasa origin and his dismissal by the Supreme Council in 1952 appears to have been strongly influenced by this fact.[2]

The union faced a difficult problem in imposing unity on a membership of varied tribal origins, but the many different types of job held by members formed an even greater challenge. The union represented all African workers, including about 20,000 men in the lowest of the eight numbered groups, and fewer than 100 skilled employees at the top of the African wage scale in the Special Group. The interests of the different categories differed widely, and this was reflected in the union's indecisive policy about African advancement and 'equal pay for equal work'. To the Africans in the Special and other high groups advancement meant progress into European work with an increase in pay to a level at least approaching European rates, if not equal to them. To the mass of Africans in the lowest grades advancement into semi-skilled European work was of little concern, but the need to raise wage rates for all Africans in recognition of a general advance in both the standard and cost of urban living was an urgent matter. The union's leaders, who maintained international trade-union connections, did not wish to appear to be opposed to the basic trade-union principle of 'equal pay for equal work' and yet had to temper it to local circumstances. Katilungu diplomatically seemed to favour a dual policy of advancement for the small group who aspired to European jobs at equal pay rates, and of advancement for the general mass of workers through a re-evaluation of European and African jobs in which the grading and pay of African jobs would be raised.[3] The strong pressures on either side within the union produced an unsteady line of policy. The stand on equal pay for equal work which the African union had briefly taken in 1950 at a meeting with the European union was renewed in

---

[1] Epstein, *Politics*, p. 92, f.n.
[2] Mitchell, *The Kalela Dance*, p. 34.   [3] Epstein, *Politics*, p. 110.

1954 at the four-party talks, during a discussion of advancement into European jobs. At the same time the African delegation led by Katilungu persistently tried to enlarge the scope of the talks from advancement into European-held work to a review of the low wages and status of the entire African labour force.[1] During the period of these talks a joint meeting was held with the European union on 24 and 25 March under the chairmanship of Sir William Lawther, Secretary-Treasurer of the Miners' International Federation, and the African union again affirmed the principle of equal pay.[2] Then shortly afterwards, when it became clear at the four-party talks that the companies were not prepared to give European wage rates to Africans, the African union leaders agreed to accept the subdivision of European-held jobs at reduced rates of pay.[3] In September union representatives were unable to give unanimous advice on equal pay to the Forster Commission and made a poor impression at the hearing.[4]

By this time the leadership of the union was racked by divisions. Internal rivalries had first become prominent in 1952 when Jameson Chapoloko, the chairman of the Nkana branch, was dismissed from his job at the mine for leading an irregular strike. Simon Kaluwa, who had been Chapoloko's successful rival in the first union elections at Nkana in 1948 and now held the position of Secretary-General, refused to give him a paid union post. Robinson Puta, the union's Vice-President, rallied support for Chapoloko, and Kaluwa was dismissed.[5] By 1954 personal rivalries began to compromise the union's affairs at branch level. In February that year Sylvester Nkhoma, an underground boss boy of mixed Nyasa–Lamba background with twenty-four years of service at the Roan Antelope mine, was elected chairman of its union branch. Nkhoma was noted for his militancy towards Europeans and his readiness for strikes or 'Korea' (war).[6] Chapoloko, now the paid secretary of the branch, held similar views, and the following month they led a strike to try to obtain the dismissal of an unpopular European mine official. The strike was interpreted as a trial of strength with Katilungu and Roan

[1] Harries Jones Papers, Record of the Four-Party Talks.
[2] *Forster Commission Report*, p. 10.
[3] Harries Jones Papers, Record of the Four-Party Talks.
[4] Evidence to the Forster Commission: Robinson Puta, Matthew Mwendapole, Gordon Chindele, 13 Sept. 1954.
[5] *Northern News*, 10 July 1952.
[6] Epstein, *Politics*, pp. 135–41.

became a focus of opposition to his leadership.[1] Later in the year his lack of influence at Nchanga also became apparent. The branch secretary, Matthew Mwendapole, brought the Nchanga workers out on strike in sympathy with a strike of the African General Workers' Union, despite definite instructions against it from Katilungu.[2] In addition to opposition at Roan Antelope and Nchanga Katilungu faced a challenge in the central office. Matthew Deluxe Nkoloma had been associated with the union from its earliest days, when he had worked as the Government Trade Union Officer's interpreter, and although he had never been employed in the mining industry he was elected General Secretary. On his return from a six-month training course at Ruskin College, Oxford, in 1954, he aligned with the more radical elements in the union and acquired considerable influence.[3]

The rivalries in the union developed partly on a personal basis and partly in opposition to the moderate leadership of Lawrence Katilungu. It is unlikely that at this stage support for the African National Congress played an important part in them, although Robinson Puta, the union's Vice-President, was elected Vice-President of the Congress in 1953. Congress was in eclipse for some years after the failure of its anti-Federation campaign, and while individual leaders were prominent on the Copperbelt its organization there was very weak.[4] The controversies within the union were not concerned with territorial politics, but with the degree of militancy to be assumed on industrial questions of advancement, equal pay and opposition to the African Staff Association. The influence of Congress in the union during the first years of Federation appears to have been slight.

THE COPPERBELT STRIKES OF 1955 AND 1956

Before the strikes of 1955 and 1956 the attitude of the Government towards the territory's trade unions had been shaped by the fear that industrial strikes might become a political weapon, and that trade unions were being drawn into association with the African National

[1] *Northern News*, 1 Apr. 1954.
[2] C.I.S.B., 100.20.4B, vol. i: Nchanga Consolidated Copper Mines Ltd., Diary of Events in connection with 'Sympathy Strike' of Africans, 25 Oct.–5 Nov. 1954.
[3] *Northern News*, 9 Nov. 1954; C.I.S.B., 100.20.20, vol. i: undated memorandum, African Union and Congress (1956).
[4] R. I. Rotberg, *The Rise of Nationalism in Central Africa* (Cambridge, 1966), p. 264; Epstein, *Politics*, Ch. 5.

Congress. The Labour Department Report for 1951 noted: 'The picture of industrial relations during 1951 became more and more coloured by political influences as the year advanced. The leaders of the African trade unions were all to a greater or lesser degree concerned with politics and there were periods when political considerations kept union leaders from devoting a sufficient time to normal trade union functions.'[1] In the three succeeding years there were three attempts to hold a general strike, all unsuccessful but each threatening enough at the time to alarm the Government.

The first attempt arose from opposition among Copperbelt Africans to the establishment of the Federation. A young European engineer, Simon Zukas, had become associated with a group of militant members of Congress and was elected to its Supreme Action Council, which had been formed to organize a mass protest against the Federation proposals. In February 1952 Zukas urged his fellow members, who included Katilungu, Puta and Kaluwa, and also Dixon Konkola of the African Railway Workers' Trade Union, to call a general strike.[2] Zukas was arrested and the Government made plans to deal with a long political strike, but the Supreme Action Council proved ineffective.[3] The only outbreak of trouble was at Nkana where Jameson Chapoloko, the A.M.U. branch chairman, was discharged by the mine for leading a short strike in protest at the imprisonment of Zukas.[4]

The following year Harry Nkumbula, the President of the Congress, called for two days of national prayer, which in effect would be a national strike, in opposition to the Federation. Katilungu expressed support for the protest but refused to direct his union to take part, as it was a political matter for individual members to judge.[5] The April stoppage was partially effective in the Lusaka area, but was supported only at the Mufulira mine on the Copperbelt.[6] The Government and the Railways had warned their employees beforehand that they would be disciplined if they went absent from work in support of the two days of prayer. The mines issued no warning because they foresaw unrest if they had to enforce the threat. After

[1] *Annual Report of the Labour Department 1951*, p. 14.
[2] C.I.S.B., 100.41, vol. i: *Freedom Newsletter*, vol. i, no. 3, 4 Mar. 1952.
[3] C.I.S.B., 100.41, vol. i: African labour–political strikes, notes of a meeting held at Lusaka, 2 Apr. 1952.
[4] *Northern News*, 10 July 1952.
[5] C.I.S.B., 100.15, vol. ii: Notes of a meeting, Mufulira, 1 Apr. 1953.
[6] *Northern News*, 2 Apr. 1953.

the protest had taken place, they urged the Government to introduce special measures to deal with future African agitation on the Copperbelt.[1]

In October 1954 yet another general strike was threatened, this time inspired by divisions within the General Workers' Trade Union, and by its lack of success in wage negotiations with the Master Builders' Association. A faction in the union led by Justin Chimba, who had edited a paper called *Freedom Newsletter* with Zukas in 1952, called a strike which coincided with a stoppage by the Government Workers' Trade Union over a wage claim. The African Trades Union Congress endorsed a general strike in support of the two unions, but in the Mineworkers' Union only the Nchanga branch stopped work. The Government issued an ultimatum to its striking workers and those who failed to return by the deadline were discharged, although many were re-engaged as new workers at the bottom of the appropriate pay scales. The Master Builders' Association followed a similar policy.

The persistent threats of widespread labour trouble alarmed the Government, although none of them led to serious unrest. The problem of maintaining order in a large country with limited security forces made many officials take an unsympathetic view of African trade unions, especially when there was any hint of a connection with the A.N.C. Against this unfavourable background of recent industrial trouble, in which the African Mineworkers' Union had never been more than marginally involved, a period of tension at the mines led to the collapse of the industrial relations system there. In January 1955 an eight-week strike began over a demand put forward the previous October by the A.M.U. for a wage increase of 10s. 8d. a shift. This would have increased the pay of the lowest workers, then receiving about £4 for a thirty-day ticket, to the level of £200 per annum income qualification for the franchise. Union leaders denied that this was the reason for the claim: in any case, workers would have had to satisfy the education qualification and to acquire the status of citizens instead of 'protected persons'.[2] The demand was a victory for the faction in the union which interpreted African advancement in terms of a large, general pay increase. This group had been growing since the failure of the four-party talks in July 1954 and

[1] C.I.S.B., 100.15, vol. ii: Notes of a meeting of representatives of the Chamber of Mines with His Excellency the Governor and Government representatives, 4 Apr. 1953.   [2] *Northern News*, 6 Jan. 1955.

gained strength from the union's urgent need for a popular platform to restore a sharp decline in membership.

The loss of support had reached serious proportions during the year. According to union sources, by May 1954 membership was perhaps as low as a third of the labour force.[1] The number of subscriptions in arrears made it difficult to arrive at exact figures. The mining companies' African Personnel Managers thought that only about 26 per cent of their workers still subscribed to the union.[2] A researcher at the Roan Antelope mine also noticed the decline, which he studied during the period of the four-party talks: in a labour force of 10,000 men there, union membership fell from 6,182 to 2,224 (22 per cent of the total) between March and September 1954.[3] There were several reasons for this loss of support. The union had increased its subscription from 6d. per ticket to 2s. 6d. in 1953, and as a result in November the companies ended the check-off system by which they had collected union dues from pay packets. The union had no efficient alternative method of collection, and the increase in the subscription was unpopular. The researcher at Roan Antelope noted as additional reasons for the decline the 'institutional instability' of African urban life; the failure of the advancement talks, with which hopes of a wage increase had been associated; and, paradoxically, a realization of divisions in workers' interests—that advancement might not necessarily bring a general wage increase at all.[4]

The union used the new 10s. 8d. demand to counter its loss of popularity. The wage claim was made on behalf of members only, and this was used as a lever for a membership drive before the strike ballot was held at the end of November. The union claimed 25,000 members out of a total African labour force of about 37,000 men, but only 18,475 workers voted in the ballot, all but 365 in favour of the strike.[5] The leaders of 7,000 Nyakusa workers threatened not to support it, and ministers of the Jehovah Witnesses, who had several thousand followers at the mines, urged them not to join the stoppage.[6] However the union did not implement the decision to strike until 3 January, giving members time to collect their Christmas bonuses and take advantage of the ripening of local crops. When it was

---

[1] *Northern News*, 7 May 1954, quoting figures from the A.M.U. publication, *The African Miner*.

[2] C.I.S.B., 40.4, vol. i: Minutes of meeting of African Personnel Managers' Committee, 22 Apr. 1954.

[3] Epstein, *Politics*, p. 112.   [4] Ibid., pp. 129–30.

[5] *Northern News*, 9 Dec. 1954.   [6] *Northern News*, 21 and 29 Dec. 1954.

enforced all but 4,115 of the 34,000 African employees at the four big mines stopped work.[1] Differences among the leaders seemed to have been temporarily healed and Katilungu was as much in favour of a long strike as Nkoloma or Nkhoma.[2]

The mining companies felt that the Guillebaud award in 1953, which was substantially less than the union's claim for an increase of 2s. 8d. per shift, had unbalanced their wage structure, and they did not look kindly on a new demand four times greater than had been claimed on that occasion. When conciliation proceedings broke down they offered to go to arbitration on the wage claim, but the union refused unless demands for weekly instead of ticket pay, and for the application of the claim to union members only, were also considered. It seemed to the managements that the union had decided to repeat the tactics of 1952 when a strike had preceded the favourable arbitration award: 'It was clear that the Africans regarded a strike as an essential prelude to an increase in wages or a successful arbitration and the Companies could not allow that idea to continue, otherwise there would be a strike every time there was a demand for increased wages.'[3] The extravagance of the wage claim and the refusal to go to arbitration made the local managements determined to put up a stiff resistance. They decided to try to maintain production by keeping their European employees at work and by taking on new African labour.[4] They also issued an ultimatum that employees who had not reported for work by 29 January would be discharged.

As the deadline approached the Government became increasingly concerned about the dispute. On 29 January the Chief Secretary offered the Government's services to try to bring about a return to work, if the companies would provide some concession for the union. The managers were reluctant to bargain with the strikers, for their aim was not only to restore full production but 'to bring home to the Africans that they have been misled by their leaders'.[5] They believed

---

[1] About 2,600 of those at work were employed on essential services. (C.I.S.B., 100.20.5, vol. i: Record of telephone conversation between F. B. Canning-Cooke and C. E. Cousins, Labour Commissioner, 4 Jan. 1955.)

[2] C.I.S.B., 100.20.5, vol. i: Record of a meeting held by the Roan Branch of the African Mineworkers' Union, 30 Dec. 1954.

[3] C.I.S.B., 100.20.5, vol. i: Record of decisions of the Executive Committee of the Chamber of Mines, 26 Jan. 1955.

[4] C.I.S.B., 100.20.5, vol. i: Record of decisions of the Executive Committee . . . 11 Jan. 1955.

[5] C.I.S.B., 100.20.5, vol. i: Record of decisions of the Executive Committee . . . 31 Jan. 1955.

that if the leadership was not thoroughly discredited a similar situation would recur within a few months of the end of the strike. When the deadline passed the mine managers decided that the strikers had in effect discharged themselves. Although the Labour Department accepted this view the Secretariat thought that the men could not be considered as discharged until the companies had issued a general notice on their position. The companies planned to send each man notice of his discharge in writing when arrangements were made for evictions from mine housing, but they did not intend to begin the evictions for a month, when they would enforce them through the courts if necessary.[1] Although there was therefore some doubt about whether the men could be considered to be discharged already, their position was quickly prejudiced by the recruitment of new workers from the pool of unemployed men in the mining districts. By the middle of February 2,000 had been taken on.[2] The companies had no intention of replacing the entire labour force in this way, as they were counting on the eventual return of most of the strikers, but they used the strategy to impress their firmness on the workers and the Government.

The Government was seriously concerned about the possible consequences of discharging a large number of workers on the Copperbelt. Evictions from mine housing would probably cause disorders, and even if the discharges were peacefully accomplished there would be problems of food distribution, unemployment, and repatriation. With the limited transport available the District Commissioner at Kitwe calculated that it would take between seventeen and twenty-six weeks to return one-third of the mine families to their distant home districts.[3] Despite the possible repercussions of the strike the companies were not anxious to have the Government intervene, and the Government was in the difficult position of having no grounds for entering into the normal conduct of the dispute. Both the companies and the African union had acted within the letter of the law and within the terms of their own agreement. Government-assisted conciliation proceedings had failed and arbitration had been refused. The Administration now faced the choice of offering informal advice

---

[1] C.I.S.B., 10.27, vol x: Record of decisions of the Executive Committee . . . 10 Feb. 1955.

[2] C.I.S.B., 100.20.5, vol. i: Chamber of Mines to Anglo American Corporation, Johannesburg, 14 Feb. 1955.

[3] C.I.S.B., 100.20.5, vol. i: Paper prepared by Kitwe District Commissioner's Office, 'Transport of African Mineworkers Discharged', 27 Jan. 1955.

or taking the serious step of appointing a Board or Commission of Inquiry, and the Chief Secretary had indicated earlier that it was desirable to avoid official intervention in industrial disputes: 'The administration is there to maintain law and order, to do all that it can, all in its power by way of its good offices to bring people together, but that is where it must stop.'[1]

The Government urged the General Managers to take back some, if not all, of the discharged workers at the same wage rate as they had earned before the strike: if the companies insisted on re-engaging the strikers at the lowest wage levels in their grades, their old salaries could be restored after a short period of satisfactory service.[2] The General Managers privately admitted that some such concession might eventually be necessary, but they felt it was too early to make an offer in case the union interpreted the move as a sign of weakness.[3] The Deputy Labour Commissioner, Roy Philpott, had approached the A.M.U.'s Supreme Council and found that it too was not ready to compromise.[4]

On 9 February representatives of the Chamber of Mines met the Governor, Sir Arthur Benson,[5] the Chief Secretary, and other officials to discuss the situation. The lack of confidence between the companies and the Government was apparent, although the Government officials stressed that because of shortage of staff, which had resulted in poor contacts with African mine-workers, they relied on the companies' assistance to maintain peace on the Copperbelt. It was clear that the A.M.U. was thoroughly discredited in the Government's eyes because of its refusal to negotiate on the wage demand, and its subsequent insistence on a long strike. Senior Government officers felt that the union deserved to suffer a severe defeat, and one even suggested that the companies should withdraw their recognition of it, since the Government felt that it no longer represented the general mass of Africans working at the mines. This was further than the companies were prepared to go. Their industrial relations adviser pointed out that the union had committed no breach of the agree-

---

[1] *Legislative Council Debates*, 83, 11 Nov. 1954, 65.

[2] C.I.S.B., 100.20.5, vol. i: Record of decisions of the Executive Committee of the Chamber of Mines, 7 Feb. 1955.

[3] C.I.S.B., 100.20.5, vol. i: Record of decisions . . . 31 Jan. 1955.

[4] C.I.S.B., 100.20.5, vol. i: Record of decisions . . . 7 Feb. 1955.

[5] Sir Arthur Benson, b. 1907. Cadet, Northern Rhodesia, 1932; seconded to Colonial Office, 1939; Administrative Secretary, Uganda, 1946–9; Chief Secretary, Central African Council, 1949–51; Chief Secretary to Government of Nigeria, 1951–4; Governor of Northern Rhodesia, 1954–9.

ment with the companies which could justify a withdrawal of recognition.[1]

A week after the meeting with the Governor the companies had engaged enough new recruits and returning strikers to restore production to about 58 per cent of the normal level at the four big mines.[2] Despite pleas from the Governor to slow down the enlistment of new workers, by 18 February the companies had taken on more labourers and raised production to two-thirds of normal output, at which level they were no longer losing money.[3] Meanwhile the Provincial Administration had drafted District Officers and messengers to the mine compounds to open sub-bomas on premises lent by the companies, 'each . . . provided with a flagstaff', where they urged Africans to return to work or leave for their home districts.[4]

It seemed that the companies were about to inflict a crushing defeat on the union when the situation was dramatically altered by an intervention from abroad. Ronald Williams, who had presented the African case to the Guillebaud Tribunal, was again sent to the Copperbelt by the headquarters of the Miners' International Federation in London. Williams had no official status in Northern Rhodesia as a negotiator, but as a representative of international trade-union opinion he was able to exert powerful pressure on the companies and the Government. He made it clear that he would report to the M.I.F. that the companies were using 'scab' labour, and raised the possibility of British trade-unionists refusing to handle Northern Rhodesia's copper, of international trade-union bodies providing extensive financial support for the strikers, and of opportunities arising for intervention by the Communist-controlled World Federation of Trade Unions.[5] He also persuaded the African union to drop its wage claim provided the strikers were taken back in their former jobs.[6]

The local mine managements were still convinced that if the union's current leaders remained in power trouble would soon break out again, but they were willing to re-engage strikers on a basis of

[1] C.I.S.B., 10.27, vol. x: Record of decisions . . . 10 Feb. 1955.
[2] C.I.S.B., 100.20.5, vol. i: telegram to Rhodesian Selection Trust, Lusaka from Chamber of Mines, 10 Feb. 1955.
[3] C.I.S.B., 100.20.5, vol i: same to same, 14 Feb. 1955; Rhoanglo press release for 18 Feb. 1955.
[4] C.I.S.B., 100.20.5, vol. i: telegram to Rhodesian Selection Trust, Lusaka from Chamber of Mines, 15 Feb. 1955.
[5] C.I.S.B., 10.27, vol. x: Record of decisions of the Executive Committee of the Chamber of Mines, 22 Feb. 1955.
[6] C.I.S.B., 10.27, vol. x: Record of decisions . . . 25 Feb. 1955.

demotion with loss of pay.[1] The head office of the RST Group in Lusaka warned its senior Copperbelt manager of the dangers of adverse publicity abroad and urged him to meet the union's approach either by re-engaging the strikers at the bottom of their previous work group or, if Williams would not accept this, at their old rates of pay.[2] Meanwhile R. L. Prain, the Chairman of the Group, arrived in Lusaka from London and W. Marshall Clark, the manager of Anglo American's Rhodesian interests, flew up from Johannesburg. The local managers were instructed to re-engage the strikers at their previous rates of pay and to ignore the strike discharges as far as pensions and leave rights dependent on uninterrupted service were concerned. The large number of new recruits had precedence over the strikers, but those for whom jobs were not immediately available were to be placed in a reserve labour pool at their old pay rates and required to do any work given to them.[3] The African union accepted these terms on 2 March and its members returned to work two days later.

The end of the strike had been brought about without any settlement of the issues at stake. Under the threat of international trade-union action and of embarrassing criticism abroad the leading officials of the mining groups had dictated the terms of agreement to the local mine managers, while a prestigious trade-union representative from Britain had exerted pressure on the African leaders to return to work. The local managers, as well as some high Government officers, still felt that the union leaders had acted in an irresponsible fashion throughout the dispute, while the union leaders had been forced to drop their pay claim in ignominious circumstances. The breakdown of communications between the union and the companies was not likely to be repaired by the conditions under which the stoppage ended. The local managements re-engaged workers on the basis of a labour rationalization scheme that had been under consideration for some time, with the result that the total labour force was reduced in size.[4] The absorption of the 8,000 Africans who had been placed

[1] C.I.S.B., 10.27, vol. x: Record of decisions . . . 25 Feb. 1955.

[2] C.I.S.B., 10.27, vol. x: J. H. Lascelles, Director, Roan Antelope Mines Ltd., Lusaka to J. Thomson, Manager, Roan Antelope Mines Ltd., Luanshya, 27 Feb. 1955.

[3] C.I.S.B., 100.27, vol. x: telegram, Rhodesian Selection Trust, Lusaka to Chamber of Mines, Kitwe, 28 Feb. 1955; and S. Taylor, Secretary of Chamber to R. Philpott, Deputy Labour Commissioner, 1 Mar. 1955.

[4] C.I.S.B., 10.27, vol. x: Minutes of meeting of the African Personnel Managers and Mine Secretaries, 2 Mar. 1955.

in the paid labour pools after the strike was therefore slow, and became a new source of difficulties between the companies and the
union.[1] The wage demand for an increase of 10s. 8d. per day which
had caused the strike was not forgotten. Six weeks after the return to
work the companies received notice of a new claim from the union
consisting of a wage demand of 6s. 8d. per day, together with a
demand for an increase of 1s. 6d. per day in the cost of living allowance and of 2s. 6d. a day in the copper bonus.[2] This thinly disguised
revival of the 10s. 8d. demand confirmed that the companies' view
of advancement as a limited progression of skilled Africans into
European jobs bore little relation to the concept of advancement
through general wage increases which had gained acceptance in
the union.

One of the most important results of the 1955 strike was the
managements' decision to recognize the Mines African Staff Association (M.A.S.A.) as an official negotiating body, to provide an
alternative to the union leadership.[3] The Association had been set up
by senior African workers in 1953. They had considered forming
a similar body in 1948, when the first branch of the union was
formed, but abandoned the idea after the Government trade-union
officer stressed the importance of a unified labour front in early
negotiations with management. The new Association reflected rivalries between prominent Africans as well as differences in workers'
interests: Simon Kaluwa, one of the organizers, had been dismissed
as General Secretary of the Mineworkers' Union in 1952, while
another, Godwin Lewanika, had been defeated by Katilungu for the
chairmanship of the newly-formed trade union at Nkana in 1948.[4]

The African Mineworkers' Union bitterly opposed the Association,
and only two months after Lewanika had formed the first branch at
Nkana in May 1953 Katilungu began to campaign for its abolition.[5]
A.M.U. leaders alleged then and later that the Association was a
'company union' formed with the mines' assistance to undercut their
position. It certainly received strong support from the companies in

[1] *Branigan Report*, p. 16.
[2] C.I.S.B., 100.20.11, vol. i: Record of decisions of meeting of Executive Committee of the Chamber of Mines, 20 Apr. 1955.
[3] C.I.S.B., 10.27, vol. x: Record of decisions of the Executive Committee of the
Chamber of Mines, 10 Feb. 1955.
[4] C.I.S.B., Evidence submitted to the Branigan Commission: Statement of Case
submitted by the Mines African Staff Association, Sept. 1956.
[5] C.I.S.B., 100.47, vol. i: O. B. Bennett, General Manager, Rhokana to Secretary
of Chamber of Mines, 24 July 1953.

1955–6, when relations with the A.M.U. were at their lowest ebb; and the companies realized from the first the advantages which the Association's existence would present in advancement negotiations, since wages for advancement jobs could be separated from general wage demands. However the records of the Chamber of Mines show that the Association was formed spontaneously by senior workers, who had long been aware that their interests did not correspond to those of most of the union's members.[1] The mining companies approved of the development as a logical and necessary step in industrial organization. Years before, at the time of the establishment of the European union, the managements had insisted that supervisors and 'white-collar' workers should be separately represented, and had recognized the Mine Officials and Salaried Staff Association (M.O.S.S.A.) in 1943 despite strong opposition from the union. Now M.O.S.S.A., the European staff organization, supported the companies' belief that dual representation was suitable for African workers:

It may sound like a contradiction in terms to suggest that membership in the African Union constitutes the greatest barrier to African advancement which exists today. . . . It is observed on all sides that the advent of the African Union had a disastrous effect on the efficiency and economic worth of the supervisory African. . . . African supervisors can be, and are, influenced not to exert that authority and responsibility for which they are paid as supervisors or staff employees.

It is our firm conviction that until the African follows the accepted principle of division by category and not by colour, he will get nowhere.[2]

The companies thought that African staff categories should include senior personnel in clerical, health, welfare, and training departments, men trusted with the handling of money or confidential information, and those whose work was equivalent to that done by European staff, as well as supervisors.[3] Despite their interest in the Association, however, the mines at first refused to recognize it because of its small membership. It grew steadily, and by the end of 1954 claimed 493 members at five branches, including the new Bancroft mine.

The African staff organization had legitimate industrial functions

---

[1] C.I.S.B., 100.47, vol. i: Record of decisions of the Executive Committee of the Chamber of Mines, 30 Dec. 1952.

[2] C.I.S.B., Evidence submitted to the Forster Commission, 1954: Memorandum by the Mine Officials' and Salaried Staff Association.

[3] *Branigan Report*, pp. 16–17.

but, unfortunately for its members, it also acquired overtones of Federal political propaganda. The Federal Government, according to the Prime Minister, wanted to create an African middle class:

so that we may get responsible members of this House from African people who have a stake in the country quite apart from a communal one . . . a middle-class to really direct the mob below them, and therefore this recognition of the African Mine Officials and Salaried Staff Association is an essential feature to my mind, in the policy of the Federal Government . . .[1]

The political significance of the split in the trade union movement at the mines was not lost on African workers, and members of the Association were soon known as 'makopo'—stinking fish—throughout the mine townships. African politicians claimed that the Association was on the side of the Europeans, while the organization's moderate leadership and failure to include a strike clause in its recognition agreement were anathema to militant trade-unionists, who objected to any threat to the A.M.U.'s dominant position among African workers.

The bad feeling generated by the African union's strike in 1955 gave the companies a powerful incentive to grant the Association official recognition. Their new determination to press the European union for an agreement on African advancement provided another reason, as they wanted to be able to divide advancement jobs between the African union and the Association in the settlement. The companies could not recognize the Association as a negotiating body before the A.M.U. agreed to give up its right to represent staff categories, which it had held up till then as the sole trade union for African mine-workers. Discussions with the A.M.U. about altering its sphere of representation opened three weeks after the strike ended, but when the companies failed to secure co-operation they issued six months' notice on 12 May 1955 for the termination of the union's recognition agreement. A month before the deadline, on 11 October, the union's representatives signed a new agreement conceding supervisory and staff posts to the African Staff Association, and the companies made it clear that M.A.S.A. would also represent most of the proposed advancement jobs. Shortly before, on 27 September, the long-awaited agreement between the companies and the European union releasing twenty-four job categories to African workers had been signed. When these posts and newly-created 'intermediate' jobs

[1] *Debates of Federal Assembly*, 6, 30 July 1956, 712.

were distributed sixty-two job categories were given to M.A.S.A., two to the Mines' African Police Association, and only eleven to the African Mineworkers' Union. The union made no protest to the companies at the time.[1]

For the five months in which the African union was under notice of the termination of its recognition agreement, the companies were in the awkward position of having decided to recognize M.A.S.A. without being able to conclude formal agreements with it. To strengthen the Association, however, they agreed to accept its concept of staff status, which included the introduction of monthly pay instead of 'ticket' pay for Africans in supervisory work, on the lines of the division between monthly paid staff and daily paid union members among European workers. The companies could not impose this change as long as the A.M.U. continued to represent all African workers. They therefore introduced it in June 1955 as an optional choice, permitting workers eligible for staff status to transfer their 'ticket' pay rate to a monthly payment.[2] As a 'ticket' covered thirty working days while the monthly pay period included days off work, the terms of the offer were really a substantial inducement to change to monthly pay, amounting to an increase of 14 per cent in annual wages.[3] The financial advantage was explained by personnel officers to every worker eligible for the option,[4] but the African union strongly opposed the scheme 'in certain cases by misrepresentation, and in certain cases by threats and intimidation' because monthly pay carried with it the right to join the Staff Association.[5]

In the period between the end of the eight-week strike in March 1955 and the Copperbelt strike of 22 June 1956, which opened a new wave of unrest at the mines, the position of the labour-pool gangs, the new monthly pay plan for senior Africans, and the long-standing wage claim strained the relations between the managements and the union. The 10s. 8d. claim had been outstanding in one form or another since September 1954, and in view of a rise in the cost of living the companies agreed that some adjustment was necessary. On 5 July 1955 the African union accepted a consolidation of the existing cost-of-living allowance into wage rates, with a new cost-of-living

---

[1] *Branigan Report*, p. 19.
[2] C.I.S.B., 100.47, vol. i: Record of decisions . . . 20 Apr. 1955.
[3] *Branigan Report*, p. 22.
[4] C.I.S.B., 100.47, vol. ii: Enclosure with letter from S. Taylor, Secretary of Chamber of Mines to the General Managers, 7 Apr. 1956.
[5] *Branigan Report*, p. 23.

allowance of 14s. per ticket. In addition the cash bonus rates, which ranged from 11s. 6d. to 43s. 6d. per ticket, were doubled. The settlement was the biggest increase made since the Guillebaud award in 1953, although it fell far short of the union's demand. Meanwhile the claim for a wage increase of 6s. 8d. a day had been submitted to unsuccessful conciliation proceedings, and on 9 May 1956 the union agreed to take it to arbitration.[1]

The wages issue which had caused so much trouble in 1954 and 1955 seemed temporarily under control, but the discontent of union leaders had now focused instead on the monthly pay options and the companies' recognition of the Staff Association. African politicians saw the Association as a middle-class organization which might counter the growth of African nationalism. The grievances of the union leaders were more specific. They felt that their senior members were being enticed away by the pay option and by the fact that the new organization would be the main beneficiary of the long-awaited advancement scheme. By July 1956 all but 700 of the 2,740 eligible workers had accepted monthly pay.[2] Those who accepted the option were not compelled to join M.A.S.A., but many union leaders made no distinction between eligibility to join the Association and actually becoming a member, and the union made no use of a strategy suggestion by the Labour Department of persuading workers to accept monthly pay while retaining membership in the union.[3]

Trouble erupted suddenly on 18 June 1956, when the Nkana branch of the union called a strike 'on the grounds that the present attitude of the mine management of the Rhokana Corporation Ltd. is extremely deplorable'.[4] The Assistant Labour Commissioner tried to find out what the union considered 'deplorable', and was told by its officials that they had called the strike because they felt boss boys were being forced to accept the monthly pay option, and because the management refused to discuss the matter with them. On 22 June the union's Supreme Council brought out some 25,000 Copperbelt workers on a three-day strike in sympathy with the Nkana branch. At the end of it the Nchanga branch staged a further two-day stoppage to protest against the compulsory use of protective leg-guards

[1] C.I.S.B.: Companies' statement of case to Arbitration Tribunal on African Wages, Dec. 1956.
[2] *Branigan Report*, p. 23.
[3] Evidence of the Acting Labour Commissioner, R. Philpott, to the Branigan Commission, 24 Oct. 1956.
[4] *Branigan Report*, p. 21.

by Africans working underground. Leg-guards were disliked because they caused wear on clothing and because Europeans did not have to wear them. Their introduction in the 1940s had reduced accidents, but the union now claimed that they contributed to mishaps by restricting circulation and causing fatigue. During this disturbed period the companies announced, on 21 June, that the option which permitted staff and supervisory workers to receive monthly or ticket pay would be withdrawn, and the employees would be obliged to accept monthly pay.[1]

In retrospect the announcement may have seemed poorly timed, but the companies had been considering a withdrawal of the option for some months under pressure from M.A.S.A., and because they felt that the arrangement was reducing the number of candidates available for advanced training.[2] They interpreted the Nkana strike as evidence of the damaging effects of the option, which underlined the need to end it as soon as possible.[3] Instead their action led to further unrest. On 2 July the underground boss boys at Nkana struck for six days in support of some of their number who refused to accept monthly pay, and another strike involving a much larger number of workers lasted for three days at Mufulira.

A series of meetings was held in July between union and management officials to examine the union's grievances, and it emerged from these talks that the union wanted to reverse the agreement of 11 October 1955 which had released the representation of senior workers to the Staff Association. The union revived a suggestion it had made before that agreement, that job demarcation should be abolished and workers given a free choice between representation by the union or by M.A.S.A., regardless of whether they were paid by the ticket or by the month.[4] The union claimed that the companies were trying to destroy it by fostering the growth of M.A.S.A., while the companies pointed out that M.A.S.A. had been founded independently by senior workers and that the union still represented more than 90 per cent of their African employees. No compromise was reached, and five days after the talks ended the 'rolling strikes' began.

Under the direction of the union's Supreme Council the strikes

[1] *Branigan Report*, pp. 20–2.
[2] C.I.S.B., 100.47, vol. ii: telegrams from Chamber of Mines to Anglo American Corporation, Salisbury, on 5 Mar. 1956, 11 May 1956, and 7 June 1956.
[3] C.I.S.B., 100.47, vol. ii: Record of decision of the Executive Committee of the Chamber of Mines, 19 June 1956.
[4] *Branigan Report*, pp. 17, 25.

'rolled' through seven branches in turn, in a protest lasting twenty-five days.[1] When the strikes ended the union introduced a ban on overtime to continue the protest against monthly pay, and on 3 September the companies were informed that Saturday work would also be banned and that Africans would neither wear leg-guards nor present identification discs when going underground. When Africans refused to take these safety precautions at work on the following day, the mines prevented them from going underground, and at some places surface employees stopped work in sympathy with the underground workers. The stoppages continued until 11 September when the Acting Governor, A. T. Williams, proclaimed a State of Emergency in the Western Province, including the Copperbelt, on the grounds that law and order were endangered and the situation at the mines had gone beyond an industrial dispute. Thirty-two Africans were immediately seized under the provisions of the Emergency Regulations, including Matthew Deluxe Nkoloma, the union's General Secretary, and twenty-five members of the Supreme Council.[2] Subsequently thirty-one further arrests were made, including Africans prominent in the Western Province organization of the African National Congress.[3] Lawrence Katilungu was out of the country and escaped detention.

The declaration of a State of Emergency on the Copperbelt raised important questions about the nature of the African Mineworkers' Union's activities. The union had disrupted the normal running of the copper-mines for more than two months, had called fifteen strikes without using the agreed industrial negotiating machinery, and on the few occasions when discussions were held had focused its complaints on rights of representation which it had signed away in the agreement of 11 October 1955. These activities were damaging to the copper industry, which estimated its losses at 12,000 long tons worth over

---

[1] *Branigan Report*, pp. 25–6. The order of the seven 'rolling strikes' was as follows:

Bancroft Mine	30 July – 1 Aug.
Roan Antelope Mine	2 Aug.– 5 Aug.
Rhokana Mine	9 Aug.–12 Aug.
Broken Hill Mine	9 Aug.–12 Aug.
Mufulira Mine	13 Aug.–16 Aug.
Chibuluma Mine	16 Aug.–21 Aug.
Nchanga Mine	20 Aug.–23 Aug.

[2] Ibid., p. 27.

[3] C.I.S.B., 100.20.20, vol. ii: Note on T. MacDonnel Stewart *v.* the Chief Secretary of Northern Rhodesia, 1956; *Legislative Council Debates*, 90, 30 Nov. 1956, 177.

£3,000,000,[1] and to the economy and revenues of Northern Rhodesia and the Federation; but they were not illegal. The territory's industrial legislation was based on principles of voluntary agreement between employers and employees, and contained no coercive clauses to force the parties to follow a given negotiating procedure or submit to Government direction. As in Britain, strikes were permissible even if the normal negotiating machinery had not been used.

The Government maintained, however, that the unrest on the Copperbelt since June amounted to more than an ordinary industrial dispute. It justified the declaration of a State of Emergency by the need to preserve law and order: the actions of the African leaders had been designed to inflame public opinion and had already led to breaches of the peace.[2] At the time the Government acted pressure had been exerted by sections of the European population, by members of the Legislative Council, and by Federal politicians for some drastic measure.[3] Tension was high on the Copperbelt, the situation was expected to worsen, and rumours of an African general strike were current in the week before the Emergency was declared.[4] The Government found it difficult to give precise reasons for the declaration, which was essentially a preventive measure, but the detention of leading members of the African National Congress organization in the Western Province at the same time as the arrest of union officials indicated that the Government did not think the strikes had been entirely industrial in their origin.

The terms of reference of the Commission of Inquiry appointed by the Government to investigate the unrest included not only an examination of any matters likely to cause discontent within the industry, and a review of the adequacy of existing industrial legislation and negotiating machinery, but also a direction to consider 'whether the activities of any person or organizations outside the mining industry have had or may have the effect of producing unrest within the mining industry'.[5] The reference to an organization outside the mining industry was clearly directed at the African National Congress. The Commission, headed by Sir Patrick Branigan, Q.C., formerly Solicitor-General of Northern Rhodesia from 1938 to

---

[1] *Branigan Report*, p. 28.
[2] C.I.S.B.: Companies' Statement of Case to the Branigan Commission, p. 217.
[3] *Northern News*, 8 Sept. 1956.
[4] *Northern News*, 10 Sept. 1956.
[5] *Branigan Report*, pp. ii–iii.

1946,[1] heard extensive evidence on this point but was unable to reach any definite conclusion.[2] It reported:

While we are not satisfied from the evidence adduced before us that the activities of any persons or organizations outside the mining industry have had the effect of producing unrest within the mining industry we must record that evidence was produced which showed that certain leaders of the African National Congress had, in public utterances, expressed strong antipathy to a recognized organization of African mine employees, namely, the Mines' African Staff Association, at a time when delicate negotiations were taking place between the Companies and their African employees regarding their representation by that Association. ... Such interference in the relationship between the Mining Companies and their employees . . . may, in given circumstances, have the effect of producing unrest in the industry and we hold this view because the evidence placed before us showed that a significant number of office holders in the African Mineworkers' Union also held prominent positions in the councils of the African National Congress.[3]

The Government had linked the unrest at the mines to A.N.C. influence because of a revival of Congress activities in 1956, after several years of decline. A vigorous series of boycotts had been conducted in April, May and June in both line-of-rail towns and remote rural centres against stores which practised racial discrimination towards African customers.[4] The European community demanded that the Government take steps to control the boycotts, and a Crown prosecution alleging conspiracy to injure trade was brought against four A.N.C. officials in Mufulira. Unexpectedly, the officials were acquitted by the magistrate, who found that their conduct was justified, and the case was hailed as a notable victory by the Congress.

[1] The other members of the Commission were Judge Heiman Joseph Hoffman, a judge of Southern Rhodesia's Water Court, president of its Town Planning Court and chairman of its Natural Resources Court, and William J. Donnelly, C.B.E., chairman of the Northern Rhodesia Silicosis Compensation Board at Kitwe and a resident of the territory since 1924.

[2] The Branigan Commission heard evidence for five weeks (24 Sept. to 2 Nov. 1956) and signed its report on 12 Nov.

[3] *Branigan Report*, pp. 51–2. In an interview at Bristol on 6 Mar. 1969 Sir Patrick Branigan said that the European public firmly believed that the Congress was involved in the strikes. His own inclination had been to omit any reference to the political connections between the union and the African National Congress in the *Report*, as he felt the companies had failed to prove their case that such a connection existed. Judge Hoffman disagreed and thought that a reference to it should be inserted. Their conclusion quoted above, a compromise between their views, was widely criticized in Northern Rhodesia because it did not find that the Congress had played an important part in the trouble.

[4] Rotberg, *The Rise of Nationalism*, pp. 277–9; Mulford, *Zambia*, pp. 44–6.

The African union's strike action at the mines came immediately after the boycott campaign, and was at once connected with it by the European public.[1]

Whether there was really such a link became a major issue in the evidence presented to the Branigan Commission. Both the Government and company officials were genuinely alarmed by the impressive display of Congress organization, and felt that the outbreak of strikes on the Copperbelt had followed the boycotts too closely to be a coincidence. However, both had additional reasons for presenting evidence to that effect. By proving that the unrest on the mines was politically inspired, the companies could lessen criticism of their forcefulness in pushing through radical changes in their system of worker representation. The Government also had a vested interest in showing that the Copperbelt troubles were political rather than industrial in origin, since it did not want to leave itself open to charges of persecuting a trade union in the course of an industrial dispute. The companies pointed out to the Commission that many union leaders were members of Congress,[2] and presented reports of various meetings where union and Congress officials had expressed support for each others' aims,[3] but they could provide no proof that the union had come under direct Congress control, although the Assistant Commissioner of Police gave evidence *in camera* on the last day of the hearings, supporting the companies' assertion of a link between the two organizations.[4]

The charge of collusion was denied by Lawrence Katilungu, who presented the African Mineworkers' Union's case to the Commission and tried to justify its past conduct, while protecting both his past and present role in union affairs. He stressed that he had been absent from the Copperbelt from 8 June to 24 June, 28 June to 9 August, and 31 August to 14 September in Lusaka, England, and Bulawayo respectively, and that during the summer the union had been under the leadership of Sylvester Nkhoma, the Acting General President, and Matthew Nkoloma, the General Secretary. He was evasive about the union's conduct over the monthly pay options and its opposition to M.A.S.A., and sought to show that much of the discontent at the

[1] Mulford, pp. 45–6.

[2] C.I.S.B., Evidence to the Branigan Commission: Companies' Statement of Case, Appendix 29, pp. 220–3.

[3] Ibid., pp. 224–7: Appendix 30.

[4] C.I.S.B., 100.20.20, vol. ii: F. Canning-Cooke to Chamber of Mines, 24 Oct. 1956.

mines had arisen from the treatment of the pool gangs, in which some 500 men still remained just before the outbreak of the strikes.[1] Katilungu denied that Congress had had any influence over the union's affairs,[2] and while cross-questioning the manager of the Roan Antelope mine made a telling point about the right of British workers to participate in politics without prejudice to their trade-union activities.[3]

Despite the efforts of the companies and the Government to show the Congress's influence in the unrest at the mines, the Branigan Commission concluded bluntly that the cause of the trouble had been: 'the irresponsible opposition of the Northern Rhodesia African Mineworkers' Trade Union to the Mining Companies' recognition of the Mines' African Staff Association as an organisation representing certain categories of the Companies' African employees'.[4] The Branigan Report found that the trouble was mainly industrial in origin and was caused by a dispute over representation by two employee organizations. Such disputes had been a source of bitter discontent in more sophisticated and longer-established unions than the A.M.U., and Branigan felt it was a sufficient explanation for the unrest in 1956. The conduct of union leaders during the strike in 1955 had already prejudiced Government and company officials against them and caused them to be branded as 'irresponsible', but efforts to show that they were also engaged in political agitation did not stand scrutiny. Both the Government and the companies had access to extensive information on African political activities, but they could not show that the Congress had had any direct control, or even substantial indirect influence, over union affairs. There was a certain degree of overlapping leadership between the two organizations, a characteristic of many African associations in the country, but no evidence of a co-ordinated common programme.

Branigan's conclusion that the unrest was primarily within the mining industry itself is supported by the fact that the local managers of the copper mines had realized early in June that to withdraw the monthly pay option for union members might well cause a strike. At that time, well before the first stoppage, the managers knew they were taking a calculated risk. They felt it was difficult to assess the

[1] Evidence of Lawrence Katilungu to the Branigan Commission, 26 Oct. 1956.
[2] Ibid., 27 Oct. 1956.
[3] Evidence of Jack Thomson, General Manager of Roan Antelope Copper Mines Ltd., to the Branigan Commission, 10 Oct. 1956.
[4] *Branigan Report*, p. 49.

union's mood accurately, and they admitted that there was a distinct possibility of strikes if the option for workers to take ticket or monthly pay was withdrawn. They even noted with dismay that Lawrence Katilungu, who was considered to have a restraining influence on his colleagues, would be in England in July.[1] Nevertheless the system of having two forms of payment for the same work, a clumsy device introduced eleven months earlier to boost M.A.S.A. before it had official recognition as a negotiating body, was no longer necessary and had become an embarrassment to both M.A.S.A. and the companies. The managers thought, wrongly as it turned out, that the union would find it difficult to justify a strike over job categories it had ceased to represent the previous October. They also hoped that union leaders would not wish to appear to be opposing advancement and higher wages, and would avoid any action liable to prejudice the wage claim for an increase of 6s. 8d. a day which was still awaiting arbitration.[2] But the African union had concluded the agreement of 11 October 1955 under heavy pressure from the companies' threat to end recognition of it as a negotiating body the following month, and had subsequently regretted the decision. The division of representation with M.A.S.A. was brought home by the fact that the jobs of 66 of the union's 138 officials fell within M.A.S.A.'s sphere of representation under the new monthly pay arrangements, and the men concerned had to be moved to alternative ticket-paid work.[3] The transfer of the bulk of the advancement jobs to the Staff Association was a further grievance, and the members of the Branigan Commission told the company managers privately that unless more opportunities for advancement were provided for ticket-paid employees, this would always be a potential source of trouble.[4]

The African union had acted irresponsibly during the summer of 1956 as the Branigan Commission charged, but it might have claimed in self-defence that the mine managements had exerted undue pressure on it to secure a share of African representation for M.A.S.A. (albeit a small share), and that the companies had acted provocatively

---

[1] C.I.S.B., 100.47, vol. ii: Record of decisions of the Executive Committee of the Chamber of Mines, 7 June 1956.

[2] Loc. cit.   [3] *Branigan Report*, p. 18.

[4] Until the day before it was signed the report of the Branigan Commission contained this recommendation, but it was removed at the last minute in case the African union should misuse it at a later date. Instead it was communicated privately to the mine managers by the Commission's secretary. (C.I.S.B., 100.20.20, vol. ii: J. Thomson, General Manager of Roan Antelope Copper Mines Ltd. to Secretary of the Chamber of Mines, 22 Nov. 1956.)

in giving the majority of the advancement jobs to the Staff Association. In the companies' defence it could be said that their negotiators were themselves under extreme pressure in 1955 and 1956, as they tried to secure the consent of their European and African employee organizations to the advancement plan. In addition, both sides carried over some of the mutual hostility generated during the strike of 1955 into the events of the following year. Even if political factors were excluded, there were enough tensions within the copper industry to account for the unrest at the mines in 1956.

THE REBUILDING OF THE AFRICAN MINEWORKERS' UNION

After the detention of the leaders of the African Mineworkers' Union the Government hurriedly set about its reconstruction. The strong connections of the union with trade-union institutions abroad, including the British Trades Union Congress and the Miners' International Federation, made it necessary to preserve the shell of the A.M.U. and restore its functions under suitable control.[1] Roy Philpott, the Acting Labour Commissioner, stated shortly after the detentions that the Government's policy was to secure the return to work of those Africans who were still on strike, restore law and order, and re-establish good industrial relations.[2] Although the Government considered that the irregular strikes of the past summer amounted to more than an ordinary industrial dispute, and planned to hold the detainees for a lengthy period,[3] it was aware that it had left itself open to charges of crushing a recognized trade union in questionable circumstances and was anxious to restore the semblance of normal industrial relations on the Copperbelt.[4]

An uncertain factor in the situation was the position of Lawrence Katilungu, the union's president, who had been attending a meeting of the Railway Arbitration Board in Bulawayo when the other union leaders were detained. His past role in relation to the union's political connections and to the conduct of the strikes was at best equivocal. He felt that although the union itself should not support the African National Congress individual members and officers could do so; and

[1] C.I.S.B., 100.20.20, vol. i: Chamber of Mines to Rhodesian Selection Trust and Anglo American Corporation, Salisbury, 20 Sept. 1956.

[2] C.I.S.B., 100.20.20, vol. i: same to same, 14 Sept. 1956.

[3] C.I.S.B., 100.20.20, vol. i: same to same, 20 Sept. 1956.

[4] *Northern News*, 17 Sept. 1956; *Hansard*, 5th series, H.C. Deb., vol. 558, 1956, 1428–9.

while he had been frequently absent from the Copperbelt during the summer and had not been as closely associated with the conduct of the strikes as other union leaders, he nevertheless appeared to have acquiesced to them. However he was thought by the Government and by the mine managements to be more moderate and responsible than other leaders, and the managements, on learning after the detentions that Katilungu was returning from Southern Rhodesia and 'was not on the list *yet*', informed Philpott that he was probably the only African capable of persuading the strikers to return to work.[1] Katilungu arrived back in Northern Rhodesia on 14 September, three days after the State of Emergency was declared, and on the following day he issued an appeal approved by the Acting Labour Commissioner urging union members to go back to work.[2] He quickly assumed an important role in the effort to restore order on the Copperbelt, and whereas Philpott had spoken at the time of the detentions of setting up alternative negotiating machinery, within a week the Chief Secretary to the Government was urging the reconvening of the remnants of the union's Supreme Council under Katilungu's leadership so that it could open negotiations with the managements.[3] Meanwhile Katilungu had announced that under the present circumstances the union must press its grievances through negotiation and arbitration rather than by strikes.[4] The Government was determined to keep control of the situation, but Katilungu's co-operation became essential to its plans: in turn Katilungu's personal position within the union was strengthened by the Government's support and by the removal of the turbulent opposition, but the union itself was now a much less powerful body.

The decision to detain the union leaders had been taken by the political officers of the Government,[5] but the task of rebuilding the organization was given to the Labour Department, which favoured voluntary reform rather than control by legislation. The mining companies wanted the Legislative Council to introduce penalties for

[1] C.I.S.B., 100.20.20, vol. i: Chamber of Mines to Rhodesian Selection Trust and Anglo American Corporation, Salisbury, 14 Sept. 1956.

[2] *Branigan Report*, Appendix 8, pp. 89–90.

[3] C.I.S.B., 100.20.20, vol. i: Chamber of Mines to Rhodesian Selection Trust and Anglo American Corporation, Salisbury, 14 Sept. 1956, and same to same, 20 Sept. 1956.

[4] *Northern News*, 20 Sept. 1956.

[5] Evidence to the Branigan Commission by R. Philpott, Acting Labour Commissioner, 24 Nov. 1956, implied that the Labour Department was not consulted before the detention of the trade-union leaders.

breaches of the industry's negotiating procedure, which the union had persistently flouted during the summer.[1] The Acting Labour Commissioner felt that this would not stop irregular strikes and would certainly be difficult to enforce against a large number of strikers.[2] Instead, the Labour Department wanted administrative reforms within the union, a revision of the industry's negotiating procedure, and improved communications with African workers by both Government officials and company personnel officers. The Registrar of Trade Unions was to make frequent inspections of the union's accounts and provide advice on the management of its finances, which were in a poor position.[3] The number of full-time paid union officials, who had come to dominate the organization, was to be cut back. Ten paid officials were now in detention, including militant leaders such as Nkoloma, Chapoloko, Puta, and Mwendapole. Some had been given paid union posts after dismissal by the companies for various misdemeanours, while Matthew Mwendapole and Matthew Nkoloma, the General Secretary of the union, had never been employed in the industry at all. The union's subscription income had dropped from £16,620 to £9,054 between 1954 and 1956, but the cost of officials' salaries had risen from £1,110 in 1952 to £4,360 in 1954 and to about £6,000 for the twelve months ending in August 1956.[4] After the detentions Katilungu combined the paid positions of President and General Secretary, and agreed not to engage any other paid officials or staff other than branch clerks in the immediate future. The Supreme Council was to be reduced in size, and union business undertaken on a voluntary basis by ordinary members of the various branches in their spare time.[5]

Previously disputes had moved quickly into the hands of the paid officials. To counter this trend the Acting Labour Commissioner suggested the introduction of African shop stewards and a revision of the negotiating procedure to encourage the settlement of grievances on the shop floor and at local level.[6] The Branigan Commission en-

[1] *Branigan Report*, p. 36.   [2] *Branigan Report*, p. 48.

[3] Evidence to the Branigan Commission by R. Philpott, Acting Labour Commissioner, 24 Nov. 1956.

[4] Evidence by R. Philpott, 24 Nov. 1956; *Branigan Report*, pp. 45, 48. Figures for the union's subscription income provided by the Office of the Registrar of Trade Unions in Zambia are used here. The final amount for 1956 indicates a bigger drop in income than the estimate of £10,431 which appears at p. 47 of the *Branigan Report*.

[5] Evidence by R. Philpott, 24 Nov. 1956.

[6] Evidence by R. Philpott, 24 Nov. 1956.

dorsed this recommendation, but in practice it proved difficult to implement.[1] The companies wanted only one shop steward in each department, while Katilungu demanded departmental committees of shop stewards, claiming that African workers preferred to settle problems in a group and were suspicious of individuals acting independently. The companies held that the shop stewards should have some knowledge of English, of the union's recognition agreement, and of the work of their own departments. They admitted, however, that since M.A.S.A. had taken over the representation of the higher groups of employees the union might have difficulty in finding even one man in each department with these qualifications.[2] The plan foundered as the damage done to union leadership at all levels by the detentions and the recognition of M.A.S.A. became apparent.

The difficulties caused by the union's weakened leadership were reinforced by its members' disappointment in the result of arbitration proceedings in December 1956. The union's demand for a wage increase of 6s. 8d. per ticket, which had first been put forward in April 1955 after the unsuccessful strike over a demand for 10s. 8d., had dragged through tedious negotiations and was finally rejected by the arbitrator, Sir Walter Harragin. Harragin's finding was contrary to the advice of his assessors, O. B. Bennett, the manager of the Rhokana mine, and William Comrie, the former Government trade-union officer, who had suggested that a small award would help to bolster Katilungu's position.[3] During the following year membership of the union fell to about 6,560 and its subscription income dropped to £6,521.[4] Katilungu was the subject of persistent attacks by the African National Congress,[5] which now seemed to be particularly active at the Roan Antelope mine,[6] and Government officials felt that his influence was waning.

In September 1957 the Senior Provincial Commissioner asked the companies for help in strengthening Katilungu's position, and the Labour Department urged him to hold public meetings at all branches

[1] *Branigan Report*, pp. 53–4.

[2] C.I.S.B., 100.20.20, vol. ii: Record of discussion with the Commissioner for Labour and the Deputy Commissioner for Labour, 12 Feb. 1957.

[3] Interview with William Comrie, Kitwe, 20 July 1967.

[4] Information from Office of Registrar of Trade Unions, Lusaka, 2 Oct. 1967.

[5] Mulford, *Zambia*, p. 64.

[6] C.I.S.B., 100.41, vol. i: Notes of a meeting between the Senior Provincial Commissioner, Western Province, and representatives of the mining companies on 4 Sept. 1957.

to reassert his authority.[1] The Department even opposed an invitation to Katilungu to visit the United States, as they considered he was irreplaceable in organizing the union and that his presence prevented attempts by the African National Congress, which was growing in influence, to penetrate it. In an effort to stabilize his position the Government put pressure on the Chamber of Mines to restore the check-off arrangement by which the companies had deducted union subscriptions from workers' pay until 1953. The Chamber was reluctant, fearing that an increase in the union's funds would result in more paid officials or in new efforts at penetration by the A.N.C., but at a meeting in December 1957 a senior Government official successfully presented the union's case.[2] The companies signed an agreement with the A.M.U. in March 1958 in which they agreed to collect subscriptions not exceeding one shilling per ticket for the union—but stringent safeguards for the use of funds were included: the companies were entitled to end the arrangement on fourteen days' notice if the amount of the subscription was altered without their consent, if satisfactory accounts were not kept, or if the funds or the organization of the union were used for any political purpose.[3]

Fears that the union would engage in nationalist politics were unjustified. In addition to the stringent controls in the check-off agreement, the union was steered on to a conservative path by the detention, in some cases for over three years, of the leaders of the rolling strikes, and by the restrictions placed on their right of entry into mine property after their release. With the approval of the Provincial Commissioner the mining companies decided not to re-employ any of the detainees when they were released, and to exclude them if possible from the private mine townships.[4] In November 1957 the Assistant Labour Commissioner inquired on Katilungu's behalf if the mining companies would employ eight men recently released from detention, with the explanation that: 'Katilungu states that he

[1] C.I.S.B., 100.41, vol. i: A. C. Annfield, Secretary of Chamber of Mines to J. P. Murray, Senior Provincial Commissioner, 6 Sept. 1957.

[2] C.I.S.B., unnumbered file, Proposed Review of Recognition Agreement, record of meeting between representatives of Government and the Chamber, 18 Dec. 1957.

[3] C.I.S.B., Evidence to the Morison Commission, 1962, Companies' Statement of Case, Appendix 1: Agreement of the Companies and the African Mineworkers' Union, 12 Mar. 1958.

[4] C.I.S.B., 100.20.25: Record of decisions of Executive Committee of the Chamber of Mines, 27 June 1957; and note for members of the Executive Committee, by David Symington, 28 June 1957.

has found it impossible to run his Union efficiently due to the lack of experienced trade unionists at his disposal. It would appear that the only Africans capable of assisting him are either members of M.A.S.A. or restricted persons.'[1] The companies remained adamant, and although Katilungu employed two former detainees, Gordon Chindele and Harry Chiyungi, as Assistant General Secretary in turn at the union's headquarters, and later another, Matthew Mwendapole, as a head office clerk, men who had been detained during the 1956 State of Emergency were forbidden to enter the township areas.[2] The ban was not lifted until 1960 when, after Government officials had stressed the shortage of competent union officers to run affairs during Katilungu's absence, the companies agreed to allow Chiyungi and James Namitengo, a senior union member who had also been detained, to enter the mine townships.[3]

In 1959 relations between Katilungu and the African National Congress changed, and he began to take a part in its affairs, even advocating the transfer of A.N.C. headquarters to the Copperbelt and the need for strike action to break up the Federation.[4] His political activities did not seriously damage his relations with Government officials, since the Labour Department had now taken the line that a trade-unionist could participate in politics if he tried to keep his political interests and his trade-union interests in separate compartments. More important, the rapid evolution of African nationalist politics had placed Katilungu and Harry Nkumbula, the President of A.N.C., on the right wing of African opinion. The foundation of a more extreme rival organization, the Zambia African National Congress, by Kenneth Kaunda late in 1958 alarmed the Government. At a time when Northern Rhodesia was embarking on its first elections under a new constitution which gave Africans the right to vote and African politicians a place in the electoral system, Nkumbula acquired a measure of respectability in the eyes of the Government.[5] This derived largely from comparison with the leaders of Z.A.N.C., which was banned shortly before the election in March 1959. Katilungu

[1] C.I.S.B., 100.20.25: Assistant Labour Commissioner to Secretary of Chamber, 18 Nov. 1957.
[2] C.I.S.B., 100.20.25: Record of decisions of the Executive Committee of the Chamber of Mines, 25 Nov. 1957; Secretary of Chamber to General Managers, 26 Dec. 1958; and Chamber to Rhodesian Selection Trust, Salisbury, 7 Sept. 1959.
[3] C.I.S.B., 100.20.25: Record of decisions of Executive Committee of the Chamber of Mines, 11 Apr. 1960.
[4] Mulford, Zambia, pp. 110–11.
[5] Ibid., pp. 86–90.

stood as an independent candidate for a Copperbelt seat. Although he received the largest number of African votes, he was defeated under the complicated new constitutional formula by another candidate who had heavy support from white voters. He then began to take an active part in A.N.C. affairs, but this did not cost him his good standing with the Government. It benevolently sponsored his appointment to the Monckton Commission reviewing the Federal constitution in order to reduce his activities in local politics.[1]

There was no immediate indication that Katilungu planned to involve the African Mineworkers' Union in his own wider ambitions. The check-off agreement between the union and the companies was revised in September 1959 with even stricter safeguards than before against union participation in politics, including definitions of the type of activity which would be contrary to the agreement and, pointedly, a prohibition against union officials advocating strikes in support of any political organization.[2] The union's membership had revived during 1958 to nearly 15,000 workers,[3] and although subscription income remained low because the companies refused to collect more than would cover the union's administrative expenses, a recovery seemed under way which would be jeopardized by the withdrawal of the check-off facilities. The Mineworkers' Union remained insulated from the increasing militancy of African nationalism, and one of the most distinctive aspects of its history during the 1950s is the effectiveness with which it was prevented from participating in politics after its early potential in that direction became apparent.

[1] Mulford, *Zambia*, p. 116.
[2] C.I.S.B., Evidence to the Morison Commission, 1962, Companies' Statement of Case, Appendix 1: Agreement of the companies and the African Mineworkers' Union, 29 Sept. 1959.
[3] Information from the Office of the Registrar of Trade Unions, Lusaka 2 Oct. 1967.

CHAPTER IX

Industrial Relations, Politics, and the Law

'THE main objectives of labour policy in Northern Rhodesia include the establishment of fair working conditions for those in employment, the maintenance of good relations between employers and employees and the peaceful and expeditious settlement of industrial disputes.'[1] The seizure of the African trade-union leaders in 1956 raised important questions about the circumstances that had allowed such a situation to develop. Was the legislation applied to industrial relations in Northern Rhodesia suitable for the Copperbelt? Should the Government continue to allow disputes to be resolved within industry when this policy raised the possibility of disturbances and violence, and the loss of valuable revenues to the country? The rolling strikes intensified public debate on the legislation covering trade disputes and trade unions in the territory.

The number of strikes in Northern Rhodesia had risen since 1950 and, more important, the number of 'man-days' lost had increased substantially (see Table 4). Most strikes concerned African workers, both because they had more reason to be discontented with their working conditions than Europeans, and simply because there were many more of them.[2] The range of African grievances was wide, for employers normally had to make arrangements for their workers' housing and rations, which gave additional scope for disputes. Wages, conditions of work, housing and rations, cases of assault, and the language difficulties between Africans and Europeans were frequent sources of trouble. Disputes over such matters involving a small group of workers for a few days were not of national importance, and in several major sources of employment, such as agriculture and domestic service, it was unlikely that major stoppages could ever take

[1] Philpott papers: Memorandum on industrial relations prepared by the Labour Commissioner, 10 Sept. 1953.

[2] In 1956, about 24,840 Europeans and 265,930 Africans were estimated to be in employment. The total African population was between 2·5 and 3 million at this time. (*Annual Report of the Department of Labour 1956*, Table 1(b), p. 33; *Preliminary Report of the May/June 1963 Census of Africans in Northern Rhodesia* (Lusaka, 1964), p. 1.)

TABLE 4

Disputes Involving Stoppages, All Industries

Year	Stoppages All Industries	Stoppages Mines African	Stoppages Mines European	Workers Involved All Industries African	Workers Involved All Industries European	Workers Involved Mines African	Workers Involved Mines European	Man-days lost All Industries	Man-days lost Mines
1950	74	4	3[a]	4,777	1,732	222	1,732	8,646	2,743
1951	91	3	0	10,896	0	5,582	0	76,606	65,996
1952	114	14	0	45,282	0	35,017	0	669,557	640,065
1953	94	4	2	5,651	770	273	770	24,230	13,812
1954	143	1	5[a]	44,197	334	5,831	135	589,209	35,101
1955	49	2	2	39,811	152	37,987	141	1,548,420	1,546,542
1956	110	26	5	118,065	1,596	107,505	1,500	469,682	460,368
1957	76	8	11[a]	30,376	4,903	26,936[b]	4,903[b]	210,070	205,785
1958	40	1	1[a]	24,303	2,924	260	2,924	1,159,218	1,156,920
1959	23	0	2	2,085	99	0	99	2,185	121
1960	61	8[c]		6,134	107	3,368	20	7,507	3,912
1961	65	13		12,037	25	7,879	25	19,640	16,416
1962	94	23		50,834	499	45,033	499	561,534	552,053
1963	194	57		40,109	1,577	26,222	1,577	409,559	361,096

[a] European disputes put 17,746 Africans out of work in 1950, 101 Africans in 1954, and 21,623 Africans in 1958. In 1957, 165,914 man-days were lost by African workers as a result of the European rockbreakers' dispute in July.

[b] A correction in the 1958 Labour Department *Report*, p. 55, gives these figures in place of the numbers published in the 1957 *Report* (2,881 Europeans and 9,914 Africans).

[c] Labour Department *Reports* do not give racial division of stoppages after 1959.

Source: Table Eleven (a) in *Annual Reports of the Department of Labour*, Northern Rhodesia, 1950–63.

place.[1] The building industry, the railways, and Government service offered more potential for organization, but again African employees were dispersed at scattered places of work and a sense of common interest was lacking among them. The mines, with 36,000 Africans and over 6,000 European employees concentrated on the Copperbelt, were uniquely situated for labour organization and strike action, and were the natural focus for criticisms of industrial relations.[2]

The losses to national revenues from strikes at the mines intensified Government interest in the industry during the successive African and European stoppages between 1956 and 1958, which coincided with a decline in the value of copper on world markets. Its price dropped from a peak of over £400 per ton in 1956 to £158 per ton in 1958, and the contribution of taxes on the copper industry to combined Federal and Northern Rhodesian revenues raised in the territory fell from 66·2 per cent in 1956–7 to 40·2 per cent in 1958–9.[3] The prolonged African strike in 1955 cost Northern Rhodesia just under £2½ million in lost taxes, and the Federal Government lost more than £3¼ million.[4] Subsequent stoppages cost less, but the Government was sensitive to the loss because of its generally declining revenues from the copper industry. The Financial Secretary pointed out in 1957 that with a copper price of £240 a ton, a Copperbelt-wide strike

Major Fields of Employment, 1956

	European workers	African workers
Mining	7,740	45,990
Government Service	4,550	39,110*
Domestic Service	5	34,455
Agriculture	1,360	31,615
Building	1,620	26,610
Railways	2,225	6,415
Native Authorities, etc.	—	21,000

* Includes Federal Government staff in Northern Rhodesia.
Source: *Annual Report of the Department of Labour 1956*, Table 1(b), p. 33.

[2] A study of countries with a more diversified economy than Zambia indicated that the mining industry generally has a high strike rate compared with other sectors of the economy. The authors attributed this to the isolated site of many mining enterprises, which insulates mine-workers from the general community and aids the cohesion of the group. (Clark Kerr and Abraham Seigal, 'The Interindustry Propensity to Strike—An International Comparison', in *Industrial Conflict*, ed. A. Kornhauser, R. Dubin, and A. M. Ross (New York, 1954), pp. 189 ff.).

[3] Hall, *Zambia*, p. 280; Baldwin, *Economic Development and Export Growth*, p. 190.

[4] *Legislative Council Debates*, 92, 2 July 1957, 463.

would cost the Government £660,000 a month in lost mineral royalties, income tax and surcharge. The Federal Government would lose over £$\frac{3}{4}$ million a month.[1] Because the financial well-being of the Government was interlocked with that of the companies, its efforts to improve industrial relations and reduce the number of strikes in the territory were concentrated on the mining industry.

Northern Rhodesia's industrial legislation permitted employers to make their own arrangements for the recognition of trade unions and for negotiating with them. The law merely set minimum standards for the organization of unions, which by convention and Government policy, but not by law, were established on a racial basis.[2] In the event of the notification of a dispute to the Government, the legislative framework provided for conciliation proceedings to bring the parties together and try to aid them to find a solution to the problem themselves. If this failed the matter could go to arbitration, in which an independent authority would make a recommendation after considering the case on its merits.[3] The use of conciliation and arbitration machinery was voluntary, and if the parties did not ask for its application the steps open to the Government consisted of informal approaches to the people concerned, the appointment of a Board or Commission of Inquiry into the dispute, or, as in the 1956 rolling strikes, the assumption of extraordinary powers through the declaration of a State of Emergency.

Northern Rhodesia's legislation was based on British precedents, although it was not an exact reproduction of English law. It was an imported product which had been evolved in circumstances very different from those in Central Africa, and had been applied with small variations to numerous colonial territories.[4] The essential characteristics of the British system, where the law was simply 'a gloss or footnote to collective bargaining',[5] found no parallels in

[1] *Legislative Council Debates*, 92, 2 July 1957, 463. A Government submission to the Honeyman Commission estimated the loss of revenues to Northern Rhodesia from the twenty-six day African strike at Roan Antelope in 1956 at £165,000 and the loss from the European rock-breakers' stoppage in 1957 at about £112,000.

[2] *The Trade Unions and Trade Disputes Ordinance*, No. 23 of 1949.

[3] *The Industrial Conciliation Ordinance*, No. 24 of 1949.

[4] Northern Rhodesia's Trade Unions and Trade Disputes Ordinance was for a time the only colonial legislation which still followed the British practice of not requiring the registration of trade unions. It also contained a very unusual provision that trade unions should follow a stated conciliation procedure to acquire the protection automatically given in Britain for acts done in support of a trade dispute.

[5] O. Kahn-Freund, 'Legal Framework', in *The System of Industrial Relations in Great Britain*, ed. A. Flanders and R. A. Clegg (Oxford, 1954), p. 66.

neighbouring African territories to which labour legislation had been more closely tailored in existing economic and political conditions. In South Africa and Southern Rhodesia the state had intervened to support the industrial colour bar, while in the Belgian Congo the right of Africans to organize in trade unions had been severely restricted.

In South Africa African trade unions had not been recognized under the Industrial Conciliation Act of 1926, and by an amendment to it in 1937 agreements made by white and coloured workers with their employers could be extended to all workers, including Africans, in that trade or industry. The Native Labour (Settlement of Disputes) Act of 1953 provided a new substitute for collective bargaining by Africans. An elaborate system was prescribed in which Europeans appointed by the Minister of Labour would negotiate on behalf of African workers with employers, and the Minister would publish a settlement legally binding on employers and employees. African unions had no role in the statutory bargaining procedure, and strikes were punishable by a heavy fine and three years' imprisonment. The racial divisions in industry were strengthened by the Industrial Conciliation Act of 1956, which compelled existing mixed unions to segregate their membership and permitted the Minister of Labour to reserve work on a racial basis.[1]

The South African system was designed to promote and protect the position of the white industrial worker. In contrast, the mining industry in the Belgian Congo had taken the lead in Southern Africa in training and advancing black workers, but wages had not increased with opportunity, and trade-unionism had been firmly discouraged. European unions were given official recognition in 1921, but Africans were not allowed to organize until 1946. Even then the unions were confined to a local or craft level, membership was limited to those with at least three years of employment in the trade concerned, and the local administration had wide powers over the union's affairs. Collective bargaining was restricted, and by 1954 only 7,500 Africans out of a total labour force of 1,146,000 men were union members.[2]

Southern Rhodesia's Industrial Conciliation Act of 1945 followed

[1] A. Hepple, *South Africa* (London, 1966), pp. 192–3, 241–3; Lord Hailey, *An African Survey* (London, 1956), pp. 1440–3.
[2] Ioan Davies, *African Trade Unions* (London, 1966), pp. 48–9; E. Bustin, 'The Congo', in *Five African States*, ed. G. Carter (Ithaca, 1963), p. 47.

South African precedents by excluding Africans from the definition of employees in connection with registered trade unions and industrial councils. Industrial councils formed by employers and white workers could have their agreements made binding on all workers in the industry. A heavy reliance was placed on state regulation of industrial negotiations, and the law required that full use be made of existing machinery for the settlement of disputes. If the parties would not agree to go to arbitration voluntarily, compulsory arbitration proceedings were enforced and workers could not declare a strike until after the award, when both sides had twenty-eight days in which to reject the findings of the arbitrators.[1] The Industrial Conciliation Act was not amended to permit Africans to join in collective bargaining until 1959, when integrated trade unions were recognized. This change was presented as implementing the policy of partnership, but the Government also felt that integrated unions were less of a threat to European labour than independent African ones.[2] Later a few independent unions were recognized when their interests clearly differed from those of Europeans.[3]

The Northern Rhodesian Government faithfully followed Colonial Office directions against discriminatory legislation for African trade unions. Before the relevant ordinances were passed and even before the first African trade union had appeared, the Government's trade-union adviser, William Comrie, announced that 'it would be wrong to "water down" correct principles for application to Africans and that Africans should be required to conform with the accepted principles from the very start. He [Comrie] would not agree that there should be any "halfway house" in the application of trade union legislation to Africans.'[4] At this early stage, in 1948, the local managers of the mining companies feared that the newly formed African unions would be unable to comply voluntarily with the provisions for trade-union organization set out in the Trade Unions and Trade Disputes bill, and should be subject to some form of compulsory supervision. They also felt that the Industrial Conciliation bill should be fortified by a mandatory conciliation procedure to counter

[1] Philpott Papers: 'Industrial Relations in the Federation', R. Philpott, Dec. 1961.

[2] J. Barber, *Rhodesia: The Road to Rebellion* (London, 1967), p. 44; C. Leys, *European Politics in Southern Rhodesia* (Oxford, 1959), pp. 116–19.

[3] *Rhodesian Perspective*, ed. Theodore Bull (London, 1967), p. 111.

[4] C.I.S.B., 70.7, vol. i: Industrial legislation, notes on an informal discussion which took place on Thursday, 24 Feb. 1949.

irresponsible leadership in the African and European unions.[1] The Government rejected both proposals and the two bills became law in 1949. Most of the provisions in the new ordinances were already in force in Northern Rhodesia through the application of British statutes to the territory,[2] but although the changes in the law were few, the significance of the step was appreciated by the Chamber of Mines' legal adviser: ' . . . the active passing of the legislation means that we must settle principles of the nature of African Trade Unionism on the model of European Trade Unionism—it is an irrecoverable step and if no legislation was introduced now the way would be open for other and more suitable legislation'.[3]

In a more literal sense than the legal adviser had intended, the European Mine Workers' Union served as an influential model for the leaders of African employees on the mines. Formal instruction in trade-union principles was limited. The Labour Department had a general responsibility for the education of African trade-unionists, but a special trade-union officer had been employed for only five years. The formal contacts between the African and European unions were few, but the conduct of the Mine Workers' Union was probably at least as important as other forms of instruction in providing a model for the African union.

Although African trade unions were established by a major act of policy on a 'separate but equal' basis in relation to the existing European unions, and the Government opposed discriminatory legislation, it was impossible to prevent discrepancies arising in private industrial agreements. In the mining industry the most significant difference between the treatment of the two unions by the companies lay in the 'closed shop' agreement with the European union. The managements had granted it reluctantly and refused to make a similar concession to the African leaders. Another difference reflected the traditional organization of the mines: the European union negotiated with the Heads of Departments, but African union leaders met members of the African Personnel Department as well. The

[1] C.I.S.B., 70.7, vol. i: Memorandum by the Chamber of Mines on the Trade Unions and Trade Disputes Ordinance and the Industrial Conciliation Ordinance, 25 May 1948.

[2] The British trade union Acts in force were those of 1871, 1876, 1906, 1913, 1917 and 1927, together with the Industrial Courts Act of 1919. See this volume, pp. 65–68.

[3] C.I.S.B., 70.7, vol. i: H. M. Williams to the Secretary of the Chamber of Mines, 13 May 1948.

managements felt that the participation of African Personnel Officers at various stages in negotiations was important because of language and other difficulties in communicating with union leaders.[1] The European union limited to five men the number of members presenting a complaint to management. The African union preferred to have a much broader representation and was entitled to have fourteen members present in the early stages of local negotiations, rising to twenty-three men at Copperbelt-wide talks. Demands and grievances seemed to move upwards from the members of the European union to the union's executive with remarkable speed.[2] In the African union the process was apparently reversed. Demands often filtered downwards from the Supreme Council leaders, who had little difficulty in raising mass support for them at branch meetings.[3] When strike action was contemplated, the African union's 1949 Recognition Agreement obliged it to obtain the consent of half of the total membership by secret ballot. The European union did not accept a similar strike ballot obligation until legislation was passed enforcing it in 1958.

The African and European unions' recognition agreements provided for local discussion of grievances, but the strong centralization of the managements' side of industrial relations encouraged a similar centralization on the part of the unions. From 1941 the mines coordinated their labour policies through the Chamber of Mines in Kitwe, which was under the direction of an Executive Committee of the general managers of the biggest mines. The headquarters of both unions were also in Kitwe. Wage demands and the question of African advancement were customarily dealt with through the central machinery of the union head offices and the Chamber, although resulting agreements with the unions were signed separately by each mine management, not by the Chamber of Mines. Individual

---

[1] Evidence to the Commission appointed to inquire into the Mining Industry in Northern Rhodesia, 1962 (the Morison Commission), vol. i, pp. 65–90: R. G. Gabbitas, African Personnel Manager, Nchanga, 17 May 1962.

[2] *Report of the Commission appointed to inquire into the Stoppage in the Mining Industry in Northern Rhodesia in July, 1957, and to make Recommendations for the Avoidance and Quick Settlement of Disputes in the Industry* (Lusaka, 1957), pp. 33–4. (The *Honeyman Report*.)

[3] Evidence to the Branigan Commission, 1956, by R. Philpott, Acting Labour Commissioner, 24 Oct. 1956. Philpott's comment refers to the heyday of the Supreme Council's activities. Research eleven years later showed that the process had been reversed, and demands now generally move upwards from branches and union members to the Supreme Council. R. H. Bates, *Unions, Parties and Political Development, A Study of Mineworkers in Zambia* (New Haven, 1971), pp. 103–6.

grievances could be settled at the mine concerned, but the union head offices were often involved as well. The Branigan Commission in 1956, the Honeyman Commission in 1957 and the Leggett conference in 1959 all pointed to the need to restore the settlement of grievances to the lowest possible level through the introduction of effective work-place machinery. The same recommendation was made by the Morison Commission in 1962 when a new wave of unrest over African wages and union representation hit the industry.

African and European union leaders' distrust of the companies was reciprocated and communications within the industry were poor. A mutual lack of confidence had been evident in 1955, during the African wage strike and the difficult discussions with the European union over African advancement, but negotiations had been con-ducted according to the agreed procedures. In the following years these rules were often ignored. The companies could skilfully manipu-late the fine points of a procedural agreement to their advantage, but they were powerless in face of the philosophy expressed by the President of the European union, that 'a Union should strike quickly and embarrass the Companies financially in every way it can.'[1] In the summer of 1956 fifteen African strikes took place without any resort to the procedure for the notification of disputes laid out in the recognition agreement, and between January 1956 and July 1957 there were fourteen irregular stoppages by European workers. It was soon apparent that problems of leadership and organization were not confined to African trade unions. The M.W.U.'s financial posi-tion was much more stable than that of A.M.U., but there had been frequent changes in the top leadership. Some observers felt that the 'closed shop' agreement gave a few leaders too much power, and others thought that the members were not amenable to being led.[2] A British trade-unionist commented that 'we are not dealing with British workers, but they are somewhat similar to Australians, all the forcefulness, brashness of a new country and all the "Jack's as good as his master", "Everyone's a leader" attitudes. It means a loyalty to the union but they are difficult to discipline.'[3]

The partial breakdown of industrial relations on the mines led critics to question the adequacy of the internal organization of the

[1] *Honeyman Report*, p. 24.

[2] *Legislative Council Debates*, 94, 14 May 1958, 838; *Honeyman Report*, p. 32.

[3] Zambia Expatriate Mineworkers' Association, file of M.W.U. Head Office correspondence with overseas unions 1955–8: Walter Hood to Sir Vincent Tewson, General Secretary of the T.U.C., 8 Sept. 1958.

unions, of the recognition agreements within the industry, and of the relevant legislation for the territory as a whole. At the same time the Government was forced to consider taking a more active role in labour disputes.

PRESSURES FOR CHANGE

The Government of Northern Rhodesia endorsed the voluntary settlement of industrial disputes for several reasons. As orthodox British policy it was agreeable to the Colonial Office, and moreover it rationalized the shortage of staff and lack of experience in such matters which would have made state intervention difficult in any case. The principle also permitted the Government to stand aloof from the politically embarrassing problem of African advancement on the Copperbelt. The establishment of an African trade union for the mining industry released it from the duty of representing African interests. As the number of irregular strikes mounted, however, it was no longer possible to maintain a detached attitude.

The Government ventured into the field of industrial relations with caution, for it knew from experience that it could expect resistance from the Mine Workers' Union to any restrictive changes in the law. The European union was well aware that the Colonial Office would not countenance discriminatory legislation, and it therefore felt obliged to oppose amendments aimed at weaknesses in African trade unions as well as those aimed at itself, since the changes would apply to all unions in the country. It did not hesitate to lobby the elected members of the Legislative Council, although they were now much less sympathetic than they had been a decade earlier. With the African Mineworkers' Union, in a rare display of co-operation, it organized support in Britain through the Trades Union Congress, the Miners' International Federation, and the British National Union of Mineworkers: Will Lawther was a leader in all three bodies and a keen observer of developments on the Copperbelt.[1]

While trade-unionists were united against restrictive measures, the supporters of restrictions were not. The mining companies, potential allies of the Government, were firmly opposed to compulsory arbitration, which might have forced them to submit to the recommendations of an 'outsider'. They felt that arbitration was suitable

---

[1] Sir William Lawther, Secretary of the Miners' International Federation, had also been President of the National Union of Mineworkers and of the Trades Union Congress.

for wage disputes, but not for matters which raised other issues of policy. The elected members of the Legislative Council were torn between allegiance to the European mine-workers among their constituents, and consideration of the drain of successive strikes on territorial revenues. The situation had seriously deteriorated before some of them felt able to support reforms. The Federal Government also had a strong interest in loss of revenues, but industrial relations were a territorial responsibility under the Federal Constitution. Southern and Northern Rhodesia had different industrial legislation, and this was left untouched by the Federal arrangements. The Federal Government had to rely on persuasion, diplomatic pressure and indirect intervention when it felt its interests were endangered by events on the Copperbelt.

The Government of Northern Rhodesia was wary of trade-union opposition to change, but prolonged strikes on the Copperbelt brought demands from the companies, the elected members of the Legislative Council and from members of the Federal Government for intervention. The Government's response developed in two stages. During the African mine-workers' strikes in 1955 and 1956 the maintenance of law and order on the Copperbelt seemed to be the vital issue. By the following year the emphasis of arguments for intervention had changed to a need to avoid loss of revenues and to protect the national interest. At first the justification for Government action was simply that African trade unions had proved unable to accept the responsibilities of their role in a permissive industrial relations system. This view was overtaken by the opinion expressed by Government officials, the mining companies and many politicians that the importance of the copper-mines to territorial revenues was so great that special steps should be taken to deal with disputes in the industry.[1] They argued that the same principles of labour relations should not be used for a developed, diverse economy and for an economy dependent on one industry. Proposals for legislative action followed this shift in emphasis. They were concerned at first with setting minimum standards for the conduct of trade-union affairs, but were soon supplemented by demands for some official regulation of negotiating procedures between employers and workers.

After the African General Workers' and Government Workers'

---

[1] *Legislative Council Debates*, 94, 14 May 1958, 804–5; C.I.S.B., Statement of case by the Mining Companies to the Honeyman Commission, 1957; *Legislative Council Debates*, 94, 14 May 1958, 819, 831, 839, 840, 843.

strikes in October 1954 the Associated Chambers of Commerce and Industry took the lead in pressing for alterations in the law concerning trade unions.[1] The Chamber of Mines did not participate, still believing that the troubles in its own industry could be cured by a change of leadership in the African Mineworkers' Union, but it was far from displeased with the Bill to amend the Trade Unions and Trade Disputes Ordinance which the Government published in 1955.[2] The Bill tried to foster stricter accounting in trade-union affairs by setting out the purposes for which trade-union funds could legitimately be used, and by giving the Registrar of Trade Unions the power to inspect the books and accounts of registered unions 'at all reasonable times'. In addition, anyone who had been convicted of fraud within the previous ten years, or who had not worked for at least eighteen months in the industry concerned, was ineligible for office in a trade union. The most important object of the Bill was to make the registration of trade unions compulsory, giving the Government the same powers of supervision that had already been established in all other British colonies.[3]

Both the African Mineworkers' Union and the European Mine Workers' Union objected strongly to the measures.[4] The influential European union exerted pressure on elected members of the Legislative Council, while representations were made to the Colonial Office through trade-union organizations in Britain.[5] The draft legislation was delayed for over a year, but in June 1956 a new Bill was published containing almost all of the previous proposals. The European union renewed its pressure on the elected members and the British Trades Union Congress, and adopted the role of protector of the weaker African unions against Government repression.[6] By this time, how-

[1] C.I.S.B., 70.7, vol. iv: Memorandum from the Associated Chambers of Commerce and Industry to Government and all Elected Members of Legislative Council, 28 Oct. 1954.
[2] C.I.S.B., 10.27, vol. x: Record of decisions of the Executive Committee of the Chamber of Mines, 10 Feb. 1955; C.I.S.B., 70.7, vol. iv: S. Taylor to General Managers, 12 May 1955.
[3] *The Trade Unions and Trade Disputes (Amendment) Bill, 1955.*
[4] *Northern News,* 11, 28 May 1955.
[5] C.I.S.B., 70.7, vol. iv: Federation of Employers of Northern Rhodesia, memorandum on the draft amendments to the industrial legislation, 28 Dec. 1955.
[6] Zambia Expatriate Mineworkers' Association, M.W.U. file, Trade Union Legislation 1949–58: Record of meeting with the elected members of Legislative Council, 11 July 1956; M.W.U. file, Head Office correspondence with overseas unions: J. F. Purvis, Acting General Secretary to the General Secretary, T.U.C., 13 Aug. 1956 and to Walter Hood, T.U.C., 13 Aug. 1956.

ever, unrest had already begun on the Copperbelt which was to lead to the African rolling strikes, and the Government had little difficulty in securing acceptance for the Bill in the Legislative Council.

The strikes on the Copperbelt convinced the local mine managers of a need for stronger measures. In May 1956 they had rejected a Labour Department proposal for local standing conciliation boards as the 'thin end of the wedge' leading to compulsory arbitration,[1] but two months later they asked the Government to consider bringing in legislation similar to that in Southern Rhodesia which made it an offence to strike during negotiations on disputes.[2] The Southern Rhodesian law included compulsory arbitration, a feature specifically recommended to the Government by members of the Legislative Council, and in a public speech made on the Copperbelt by Sir Roy Welensky, then the Acting Federal Prime Minister.[3] However when the Branigan Commission sat in September to hear evidence on the cause of the disturbances the companies said they were still opposed to compulsory arbitration. They wanted legislation to introduce compulsory use of agreement procedures and conciliation machinery, to be followed by voluntary arbitration if necessary.[4] The Labour Department strongly opposed these suggestions, and gave evidence to the Commission against them: 'To introduce legislation creating new criminal offences, the enforcement of which would be extremely difficult, would tend to bring the legislation itself into disrepute. Where many thousands of people were on strike, as happened on the Copperbelt recently, and if that strike were illegal in the terms of the proposed legislation, it would be impossible to invoke the law.'[5] The Commission accepted the Labour Department's view that penal legislation would not prevent irregular strikes, and did not endorse the companies' proposals.[6]

The Government was not in favour of new legislative measures after the African strikes of 1956 because the breakdown in industrial relations seemed to be a local matter reflecting the political effects of African nationalism and the relative inexperience of African trade-

[1] C.I.S.B., 70.7, vol. iv: Record of decisions of Executive Committe of the Chamber of Mines, 21 May 1956.

[2] C.I.S.B., 70.7, vol. iv: S. Taylor, Secretary of the Chamber of Mines, to Chief Secretary to the Government, 20 July 1956.

[3] *Southern Rhodesia Industrial Conciliation Act, 1945*; *Legislative Council Debates*, 88, 5 July 1956, 177–8, and 6 July 1956, 250–1, *Northern News*, 4 July, 1956.

[4] *Branigan Report*, 1956, p. 36.

[5] Ibid., p. 48.   [6] Ibid., pp. 52–3.

union leaders. When these leaders were placed in detention it was expected that better influences would prevail.[1] Events in 1957 forced officials to take a broader view of the situation. The European Mine Workers' Union showed that it was capable of irregular conduct as forceful in its impact as the African strikes of the previous year. For the third year in succession revenues were affected by strikes in the mining industry, and what had seemed to be temporary difficulties in labour relations now appeared to be developing into a general weakness. Between January 1956 and July 1957 the European union had ignored the agreed procedure for the discussion of disputes with the mine managements in fourteen incidents leading to strikes, and on all of these occasions the companies had tacitly condoned the breaches of agreement in order to secure a speedy return to work.[2] These precedents reinforced the confidence of the union's Executive Council when it supported some of the mines' 270 rock-breakers in an attempt to impose shorter Saturday working hours on the companies. The union was shocked when the companies resisted and shut down the mines.[3] All of the mine operations depended on the rock-breakers' work of blasting at the ore walls, and when these key employees refused to work their normal shifts the managers felt they had little choice, under the existing strict safety procedures, but to bar the men from the mines and gradually shut off production. Within ten days a large number of European workers and some 26,000 Africans had been laid off.[4]

When a Commission led by George Honeyman,[5] a member of the British Industrial Disputes Tribunal, was appointed to inquire into the dispute, many irregularities in the union's conduct at branch level and in the Executive Council came to light. As a result, the companies were able to make a strong case for legislative action against unofficial strikes. They repeated their 1956 demand that strikes should

[1] The Government placed great faith in the efficacy of this tactic. On 12 Mar. 1959, the leaders of a new nationalist political party, the Zambia African National Congress, were swept into detention. On the previous day the Governor, Sir Arthur Benson, informed the Colonial Office that 'our plans have been based on the belief that if we declare Zambia to be an illegal society and put out of harm's way the fifty main leaders, the vast bulk of our Africans will be pleased and the few thousand on the fringe will at worst sit tight and gradually come over to our side'. (Mulford, *Zambia*, p. 104.)

[2] *Honeyman Report*, 1957, pp. 12–16, 24.

[3] Ibid., p. 20.   [4] Ibid., pp. 20, 24.

[5] Sir George Honeyman, b. 1898. Kt. 1961. Member, National Arbitration Tribunal, 1949–51; Industrial Disputes Tribunal, 1951–9; Master of the Bench, Inner Temple, 1961.

be made illegal where agreed negotiating procedures had not been followed or where there was no trade dispute. They also asked for compulsory strike ballots, and for legislation to abolish the closed shop because it gave union leaders excessive power.[1] The Honeyman Commission was sympathetic to these proposals but felt that the abolition of the European union's closed shop would cause further unrest at the mines. The Commission recommended that it should be illegal for the members of a trade union with a closed shop agreement to strike before the agreement's negotiating procedure had been exhausted. Such unions would also be required to hold a ballot approving the closed shop clause, and to hold secret ballots before a strike.[2] In addition, the Commission suggested that the companies and the European union be given six months to insert a clause in the recognition agreement giving voluntary consent to go to arbitration if conciliation failed. If they did not comply the Government could consider introducing a system of statutory compulsory arbitration similar to that in force in Southern Rhodesia.[3]

This recommendation was a sharp break from general British colonial practice.[4] Compulsory arbitration had been used to strengthen the colour bar in Southern Rhodesia, but when its introduction in Northern Rhodesia was discussed during the Second World War it was rejected for this reason by the Governor, with the full support of the Secretary of State.[5] As a colour bar was still upheld by industrial agreement on the Copperbelt, and Honeyman felt it was unwise to abolish the European union's closed shop, it was conceivable that under a compulsory arbitration system the Government would have to give official sanction to colour-bar arrangements in the mining industry. The Administration had tried to avoid this

---

[1] *Honeyman Report*, pp. 29–30.   [2] Ibid., pp. 32–3.

[3] Ibid., p. 35. The Southern Rhodesian Industrial Conciliation Act provided that if the parties to a dispute went voluntarily to arbitration the award was binding, but if they were forced by law to accept compulsory arbitration they had the right to reject the award within twenty-eight days. The Northern Rhodesian debate over compulsory arbitration was vague about the desirability of this right.

[4] Lord Hailey, *An African Survey* (London, 1956), pp. 1440–5. The Colonial Office did sanction the introduction of compulsory arbitration in Aden in 1960, but this was a 'measure of desperation' after a wave of political strikes brought normal collective bargaining to a halt. (B. C. Roberts, *Labour in the Tropical Territories*, pp. 331–4.) Provision was made for employers and workers with satisfactory bargaining arrangements to opt out of the new system. (Aden, Industrial Relations (Conciliation and Arbitration) Ordinance, No. 6 of 1960.)

[5] SEC/LAB/124: Governor Sir John Waddington to Secretary of State, Oliver Stanley, 23 Feb. 1943; Secretary of State to Sir John Waddington, 28 Apr. 1943.

embarrassing prospect in the past, but now gave serious consideration to the Commission's views because of the deteriorating situation on the Copperbelt.

The Government had expected trade-union opposition to the proposals, but it also found that the mining companies were less than enthusiastic about some of them, especially compulsory arbitration, which they still feared might undermine the rights of management.[1] At the other extreme, the support of the elected members of the Legislative Council for most of the proposals was so vigorous that it was also likely to cause difficulties. Many members were willing to go further than Honeyman by advocating the complete abolition of closed shop arrangements, even although the Commission's report had pointed out that this would almost certainly cause industrial trouble.[2] The Chief Secretary feared that they might force the Government to act in favour of abolition, a step that had the companies' support.[3]

The Mine Workers' Union was energetic in rallying opposition to the Honeyman proposals, despite its loss of the elected members' sympathy. Its main ally was the African Mineworkers' Union, which had long coveted a closed shop. Together the two unions solicited the British Trades Union Congress, the National Union of Mineworkers and the Miners' International Federation to intervene at the Colonial Office on their behalf. Shortly afterwards the Bill published in February 1958 to amend the Trade Unions and Trade Disputes Ordinance was withdrawn.[4]

After the withdrawal of the Bill the Government was obliged to make an embarrassing disclosure. Officials had publicly stated that the Government would not deviate lightly from the Honeyman recommendations,[5] but now they confessed that there was confusion about the exact meaning of some of them. Certain proposals were 'not absolutely clear'[6] and advice was being sought from George Honeyman himself before a revised Bill was published.[7] Elected

---

[1] C.I.S.B. 70.29: Report on meeting with Government representatives, 3–4 Dec. 1957.

[2] *Legislative Council Debates*, 93, 27 Nov. 1957, 844–58.

[3] C.I.S.B., 70.29: Telegram from Chamber of Mines to Anglo American Corporation, Salisbury, 19 Dec. 1957.

[4] Trades Union Congress: *Trade Union News for Overseas*, 20 Aug. 1958.

[5] *Legislative Council Debates*, 93, 27 Nov. 1957, 858–9 and 94, 14 May 1958, 806.

[6] *Legislative Council Debates*, 94, 25 Mar. 1958, 207.

[7] *Legislative Council Debates*, 94, 14 May 1958, 807–8.

members of the Legislative Council suspected that the Colonial Office, under trade-union pressure, had asked for the revision of the Bill, although the Government denied the allegation.[1] The elected members resented Colonial Office supervision as much as ever, and the United Federal Party, to which a majority of them belonged, was campaigning to secure control of the legislature under new constitutional arrangements to be introduced at the 1959 election.[2] The form of the constitution was still under discussion, and therefore the question of Colonial Office intervention in territorial affairs was a particularly sensitive one. By making representations to the Colonial Office through the British Trades Union Congress the Mine Workers' Union alienated the elected members and turned consideration of the Trade Unions and Trade Disputes amendment Bill into a major issue.

Jack Purvis, the General Secretary of the Mine Workers' Union, and Lawrence Katilungu, President of the African Mineworkers' Union, flew to London on 22 March to further their joint cause, and their progress was followed with rising temper by elected members of the Legislative Council.[3] Shortly before their return on 21 April a revised Bill was published in Northern Rhodesia. The Director of the Chamber of Mines felt that the changes were small,[4] but the British Trades Union Congress thought they were a considerable improvement on the previous Bill.[5] The new proposals simplified the procedure for notifying the Government of a trade dispute, a subject of much controversy in the discussions between the Trades Union Congress and the Colonial Office,[6] and removed penal sanctions for unions which called a strike in defiance of secret ballot requirements, except for unions with a closed shop agreement. The votes needed to approve a closed shop agreement were reduced from two-thirds to half of a union's total membership, but measures to restrain the activities of such unions were retained. Where a closed shop union existed, it would become a criminal offence for members to strike before conciliation proceedings were completed; and members of

[1] *Legislative Council Debates*, 94, 25 Mar. 1958, 207; 14 May 1958, 816–17, 872–3.

[2] Hall, *Zambia*, pp. 167–8.

[3] *Legislative Council Debates*, 94, 14 May 1958, 816.

[4] C.I.S.B., 70.7, vol. v: D. Symington to S. H. Brooke-Norris, 24 Apr. 1958.

[5] Trades Union Congress, Colonial Advisory Committee: *Situation in Northern Rhodesia*, 7/2, 4 June 1958.

[6] Loc. cit.

such a union would have the right to appeal to an independent arbiter if they were suspended or expelled by union leaders.[1]

The two mine-workers' unions felt that the changed proposals were still oppressive, and asked the Government, the Chamber of Mines and the elected members of the Legislative Council for a delay in implementing the Bill, so that voluntary changes in the mining industry's negotiating procedure could be made instead.[2] As an insurance they also contacted the British Trades Union Congress and the Miners' International Federation again, urging them to make a joint representation to the Colonial Office for a delay in the Legislative Council debate on the Bill which was to take place on 14 May.[3] The two unions had not explained what voluntary changes in negotiating procedure they wanted, and a joint statement in support of the concession of a closed shop to the African union was hardly calculated to win the confidence of the unions' opponents.[4] Katilungu and Purvis found the Government and the companies 'extremely hostile' to their proposals for a delay: according to Jack Purvis, 'nothing that they could say or do would convince anyone that the Unions were sincerely seeking to establish a new era in industrial relations.'[5] On 12 May the two unions issued another plea for a chance to establish voluntary machinery in place of the Honeyman proposals 'which strike at the root of the trade-union movement in Northern Rhodesia'.[6] On the same day representatives of the Trades Union Congress, the National Union of Mineworkers and the Miners' International Federation saw the Secretary of State's Labour Adviser in London to ask for more time to allow the unions to negotiate with their employers. They were told that

everything possible had been done at this end . . . the whole situation rested on the meeting of the two unions [that day] with the Unofficial Members. It was the opinion of the Labour Adviser that it would have created a constitutional crisis in Northern Rhodesia if the Secretary of State for the

[1] *Legislative Council Debates*, 94, 14 May 1958, 808–13.
[2] T.U.C., *Situation in Northern Rhodesia*, 4 June 1958.
[3] Loc. cit.
[4] C.I.S.B., 70.7, vol. v: Notes of a special meeting of the Chamber of Mines with M.W.U. and A.M.U. representatives, 8 May 1958; Joint statement of Representatives of N.R. Mine Workers' Union and N.R. African Mineworkers' Trade Union, 28 Apr. 1958.
[5] T.U.C., *Situation in Northern Rhodesia*, 4 June 1958.
[6] C.I.S.B., 70.7, vol. v: The Proposal of the Northern Rhodesia Mine Workers' Union and the African Mineworkers' Union for the Establishment of Voluntary Negotiating Machinery, 12 May 1958.

Colonies now forced a waiting period. The Bill had to come forward on May 14th and much was being said in Northern Rhodesia about the influence of Whitehall.[1]

The representatives of the two unions failed to persuade the unofficial members of the Legislative Council of their good intentions. The Bill was debated as scheduled on 14 May, and in due course it passed into law.

During the controversy over the amendment Bill the introduction of compulsory arbitration had temporarily fallen from view. The *Honeyman Report* had advised the companies and the Mine Workers' Union to accept a clause providing for arbitration in their recognition agreement, and suggested that if they failed to do so within six months the Government should introduce it by law. The Government went even further: on giving the companies and the union the required six months' notice in December 1957 the Chief Secretary, Evelyn Hone, informed them that regardless of their compliance the Government would consider introducing compulsory arbitration on a territorial basis.[2] The Chamber did not send a formal reply until the six months' notice had expired, when it expressed its opposition on the grounds that arbitration would not have prevented the African strikes of 1952 and 1955 when the proper procedures had been followed, and that until 1956 the record of conciliation in European disputes was very satisfactory.[3]

Before any action had been taken, yet another European strike erupted. Labour relations in the industry had been deteriorating under pressure from the effects of the drop in world copper prices. The managements were conscious of the need to hold down costs, and European workers of their declining bonus rates, which were linked to the current price of copper and had dropped from a peak of 103½ per cent of union wage rates in 1955–6 to 55 per cent in 1956–7, and to 17 per cent in the period from March to June 1958.[4]

---

[1] T.U.C., *Situation in Northern Rhodesia*, 4 June 1958.

[2] C.I.S.B., 70.29: Evelyn Hone, Chief Secretary to the Government, to Secretary of the Chamber of Mines, 11 Dec. 1957.

[3] C.I.S.B., 70.29: A. C. Annfield, Secretary of the Chamber of Mines, to Chief Secretary to the Government, 9 June 1958. The Chamber hoped that the Government would not recollect that the Chambers' Executive Committee had favoured compulsory arbitration during the African strike in 1955 (Telegram, Chamber to RST, Salisbury, 10 Dec. 1957).

[4] C.I.S.B., Statement of case by the mining companies to the Hoffman Arbitration Tribunal, 1959, on a wage claim by the Mine Officials and Salaried Staff Association.

In 1957 the companies began to negotiate with the union for the removal of restrictive practices in the interests of economy, while the union put forward a demand for a 15 per cent general wage increase. After prolonged conciliation over the union's long-established lines of job demarcation the dispute led to a two-month strike in the autumn of 1958.

The strike renewed concern about the negotiating procedures in the industry, and representatives of the Government, led by the Governor himself, participated in its settlement. A condition included by the Government in the final agreement required the Chamber of Mines and the European union to meet to consider their negotiating procedure, and to take into account the Honeyman Commission's advice on compulsory arbitration.[1] Despite this the Government was now in a much less strong position to press the recommendation because of current changes in industrial relations practices in Britain. In October 1958 Ian Macleod, then Minister of Labour, announced that the system of compulsory arbitration in force with various modifications since 1940 would shortly be ended. It no longer had the support of both sides of British industry, for employers believed it gave an unfair advantage to the workers, who were not bound by an unfavourable award. A request from the mining companies and the European union that they should be allowed to revise the industry's negotiating machinery themselves was, under the circumstances, particularly well timed.[2] The Government agreed to the proposal, and early in 1959 an industrial relations expert, Sir Frederick Leggett, arrived from Britain to advise the companies and the union on alterations in the disputes clauses of their recognition agreement.[3]

Leggett was not in favour of adopting the Southern Rhodesian system of arbitration,[4] even although the Honeyman Commission had strongly recommended it in 1957 and the Colonial Office Labour Adviser, George Foggon, had suggested its use for job demarcation

[1] C.I.S.B., 70.29: Sir Arthur Benson, Governor of Northern Rhodesia to the Secretary of the Chamber of Mines, 10 Nov. 1958.

[2] C.I.S.B., 90.14.7, vol. i: Record of decisions of the Executive Committee of the Chamber of Mines, 19 Nov. 1958.

[3] Sir Frederick Leggett entered the Civil Service in 1904. Under-Secretary, Ministry of Labour, 1939; Chief Industrial Commissioner, 1940–2; British Government Member, Governing Body, International Labour Organization, 1932–44; Deputy Secretary, Ministry of Labour, 1942–5.

[4] C.I.S.B., 90.14.7, vol. i: Telegram from Chamber of Mines to RST and Anglo American Corporation, Salisbury, 17 Feb. 1959.

disputes after the 1958 strike.[1] Instead he helped to devise changes in existing voluntary procedures which were designed to shift the emphasis in the settlement of disputes from top level to shop floor participation. The role of shop stewards in presenting grievances became more important, and a series of three-day 'cooling off' periods was written into the disputes procedure so that grievances could not go straight to union executive level in a day, as had happened occasionally in the past. At the top level, joint consultation was to be established through a Mining Joint Industrial Council, on which the companies and the union were each to have six representatives.[2] George Honeyman had been doubtful if either the companies or the European union had the skilled personnel for a general shop floor application of the 'highly technical process' of joint consultation,[3] but Leggett felt that a high level Joint Industrial Council meeting at regular monthly intervals might help to restore good will and better management–worker communications in the industry.[4]

The great virtue of Sir Frederick Leggett's proposals was that they were negotiated within the industry, thus avoiding the quarrels which had plagued attempts to impose change on the European union in the past. The Mine Workers' Union hailed them as a 'revolutionary change' which marked 'the virtual death knell of the old system which experience has shown to be completely useless in settling industrial disputes'.[5] However the old system had merely been revised, not abandoned, and the 'revolutionary change' was applied only to a small minority of the labour force.

The Government's success in applying restrictive legislation to the European union's closed shop agreement and its effort to impose compulsory arbitration contrasted sharply with the treatment of the African Mineworkers' Union after the rolling strikes. Officials saw two different problems, that of political influence in African unions and that of irregular strikes by European ones: as long as the slow pace of African constitutional advancement set limits on permissible African trade-union activities a double standard of trade-union conduct was inevitable. The Government knew that African union leaders and politicians had compared the detentions of 1956 with the lenient treatment of European trade-unionists in similar

[1] C.I.S.B., 70.29: Secretary of Chamber to General Managers, 13 Nov. 1958.
[2] *Northern News*, 26 Mar. 1959; *Union News*, Special Edition, Apr. 1959.
[3] *Honeyman Report*, pp. 35–6,
[4] *Northern News*, 26 Mar. 1959.
[5] *Union News*, Special Edition, Apr. 1959.

circumstances the following year, but noted with relief that the African union was now powerless to follow the European union's bad example for some time.[1]

The African union had been in no position to resist the conditions the mining companies, with Government approval, wrote into the 1958 check-off agreement to bypass the rights of trade unions under territorial law to maintain political funds.[2] The application of the Leggett Agreement in 1959 was a further instance in which the treatment of the African union differed from that of European workers. Sir Frederick Leggett had intended his recommendations to apply to both unions, but the companies felt that his proposals were too advanced for the African union and that 'very serious repercussions . . . may stem from the appointment of immature and irresponsible Africans as shop stewards'.[3] The appointment of African shop stewards had been under consideration during the Branigan Commission hearings in 1956,[4] but was later dropped by the companies when the extent of the leadership crisis caused by the detentions became evident. Provision for African shop stewards and a second Joint Industrial Council was not made until 1963.

The wavering course of policy reflected an important aspect of the voluntary tradition of British trade-unionism. It provided no single authoritative solution for industrial relations problems to guide a colonial government in search of precedents. Individual judgements on Northern Rhodesia's problems varied, as the Government discovered when it sought advice. An economist, Claud Guillebaud, and a lawyer, Sir John Forster, both experts on British industrial relations, found the territory's trade union and conciliation laws satisfactory.[5] So did Sir Patrick Branigan, who had wide experience of industrial law locally and in other African territories.[6] George Honeyman, a member of Britain's National Arbitration and Industrial Disputes Tribunals, found the legislation inadequate, but Sir Frederick Leggett, who had had a long career in the Ministry of

---

[1] Information provided by D. C. Mulford from his research record of 1957 Secretariat files.

[2] See pp. 162–4; also C.I.S.B., 70.29, vol. i: Notes of a meeting between representatives of Government and the Copper Mining Companies, 18 Dec. 1957.

[3] C.I.S.B., 90.14.7, vol. i: Anglo American Corporation, Salisbury to Chamber of Mines, 19 Mar. 1959; RST, Salisbury to Chamber, 18 Mar. 1959; Chamber to RST and Anglo American Corporation, Salisbury, 24 Mar. 1959.

[4] *Branigan Report*, 1956, pp. 53–4.

[5] *Legislative Council Debates*, 83, 17 Nov. 1954, 175.

[6] *Branigan Report*, 1956, pp. 52–3.

Labour, disagreed with his solution and preferred to introduce reforms by agreement within the mining industry.[1] The experts tried to take into account both British experience and local circumstances. Similarly the Northern Rhodesian Government and the parties to industrial disputes in the territory were concerned about current developments in British industry and accepted advice from the Colonial Office, the Overseas Employers' Federation and British trade-unionists, despite their own arguments that local circumstances were different. The contacts and concerns of those who dealt with industrial relations were so wide, involving Britain, other African countries, and international trade-union circles, that no question could be isolated in a local context.

During the prolonged period of unrest at the copper-mines in the 1950s the Government developed no firm line of policy, but responded to events and to diverse pressures from those directly involved in disputes. A leading Labour Department official claimed at a later date that the mining industry had shown itself unable to solve its own problems and had welcomed the Government-sponsored advice of Honeyman and Leggett. But the Government also had reason to welcome these interventions. It had neither the expertise to give detailed advice to industry on industrial relations, nor any desire to alter the principles of labour relations generally accepted in Britain and her colonies, without some outside sanction.

[1] This difference of opinion reflected the bias of Honeyman's and Leggett's respective careers: George Honeyman had had wide experience of arbitration, but the Ministry of Labour tended to stress the role of mediation and conciliation in settling industrial disputes.

CHAPTER X

Federation

THE plan to create a Federation of Rhodesia and Nyasaland gave an unexpected impetus to African political development. After 1948 the growth of the African National Congress led by Harry Nkumbula was fuelled by opposition to closer relations with the south. Although this first burst of political activity collapsed temporarily when the Federation was established in 1953, two years later the Congress began to reassert its influence through a series of campaigns against the indignities imposed by the colour bar. Increasing boldness in the party's methods coincided with the growth of a more determined leadership, which made Harry Nkumbula seem like a moderate to the Government. The movement was torn apart by rival factions and in October 1958 Kenneth Kaunda and Simon Kapwepwe left the Congress to form a more radical organization, the Zambia African National Congress (Z.A.N.C.).

Z.A.N.C. made rapid progress and by March 1959 had at least eighty-five branches.[1] One of its major objectives was the boycott of elections to be held that year under a new constitution which, although providing direct representation for Africans in the Legislative Council for the first time, only gave them eight of the twenty-two elected seats. The boycott caused the Government considerable embarrassment and Z.A.N.C. was banned on 11 March 1959, just before the elections were held. Despite this set-back a new radical nationalist party, the United National Independence Party (U.N.I.P.), emerged later in the year, again under the leadership of Kenneth Kaunda. The organization soon developed a strong provincial political machine.

In response to growing African discontent, yet another constitution was introduced in 1962, with a complicated formula for increased African participation in elections. Under the new arrangements the number of Africans registered to vote, which had been scarcely a dozen before 1958, and 7,617 at the 1959 elections, rose to 129,093 out of a population of more than 3,000,000.[2] The constitution pro-

[1] Mulford, *Zambia*, p. 85.
[2] Mulford, *Zambia*, pp. 49, 84, 253. In 1963, when universal adult suffrage was introduced, 1,403,785 voters registered.

vided for a lower (predominantly African) and an upper (predominantly European) electoral roll with 15 seats each in the Legislative Council. In addition 15 seats were reserved for newly created national constituencies in which candidates had to secure 10 per cent of the votes cast by each race, a device intended to encourage multiracial political activity. In a closely fought campaign U.N.I.P. won 78 per cent of the votes on the lower electoral roll, which entitled it to 12 seats against the African National Congress's 3 seats. On the upper roll the United Federal Party had 70 per cent of the votes, entitling it to 13 seats, while U.N.I.P. had 1 seat. In the national constituencies 10 seats could not be filled because candidates failed to win the minimum percentage of votes. Two seats went to the United Federal Party, 2 to the African National Congress, and 1 to a U.N.I.P.-supported independent candidate. At later by-elections for the void national constituencies, 2 more A.N.C. candidates were elected. The Congress then held the balance between the 2 major parties, and although it had co-operated with the United Federal Party during the election campaign, Nkumbula decided to join a coalition with U.N.I.P. to form the country's first African government.

The political changes in Northern Rhodesia since the prospect of Federation had sparked off a nationalist response were tremendous: the changes to come were even more rapid and far-reaching. At the end of 1962 Nyasaland won the right to secede from the Federation. Having defeated the United Federal Party, the new African rulers in Northern Rhodesia demanded the same right. This was granted on 29 March 1963, and the Federation was dissolved at the end of the year. Meanwhile the African coalition government did not last long. Kaunda's party successfully pressed for universal suffrage, and in a fresh election in December 1963 it swept into power to form the government which received independence from Britain in October 1964.[1]

This sequence of events could scarcely have been imagined by the country's European population in 1953. The inauguration of the Federation seemed to be another step towards securing European political power and freedom from British control, perhaps through the attainment of Dominion status. In these first optimistic years the

---

[1] The detailed history of nationalism and the African political parties is found in D. C. Mulford, *Zambia*, and R. I. Rotberg, *The Rise of Nationalism in Central Africa*.

vulnerability of the new Federation to shifting opinion among British politicians was discounted by local Europeans, who were confident about the future course of progress.

The creation of the Federation presented two prospects for labour policy in Northern Rhodesia. One was the strengthening of the European electorate's influence on politics, and the other was the promise of partnership between the races. The past history of the movement for union between the northern and southern territories had shown that it might be difficult to reconcile these elements. In both countries European trade-unionists and artisans had combined to ensure that Africans were kept out of certain jobs which were recognized as a European field of employment. This field had been successfully defended by demands for equal pay for equal work, by the educational advantages enjoyed by Europeans, and by controlled restrictive entry into industrial training. The preservation of the European's place in industry did not preclude Africans from acquiring skills, but if they did so Europeans were expected to get further training to maintain their position at the top of the industrial ladder.[1] The need to preserve the European field of employment received an added impetus from the Federal Government's policy of encouraging European immigration. In the years 1955 to 1957 net European immigration to the Federation rose to 11,000, 17,800, and 14,300 from 5,900 and 5,100 in 1953 and 1954.[2]

Although the Federal Government's policy on advancement for Africans varied according to circumstances, it encompassed two general views. It supported European trade-unionists in their demand that Africans, if promoted into European work, should get equal pay; and it also supported the view that a fast pace of advancement should not be encouraged. Thus in August 1955 the Prime Minister, Sir Godfrey Huggins, condemned a motion in the Federal Assembly that Civil Service employment conditions should apply to all according to qualifications and regardless of race. He said that although the Constitution made no person ineligible on account of race, there was no provision that all Federal civil servants should be treated on the same basis. He then turned to his well-known description of junior and senior partners in the Federation.[3]

---

[1] *Report of Survey of Facilities for Technical Education in the Federation*, F. Bray (Salisbury, 1958), p. 11.

[2] P. Mason, *Year of Decision* (London, 1960), p. 269.

[3] *Federal Assembly Debates*, 4, 2 Aug. 1955, 1029–33.

'Partnership' was a useful slogan for the Federation, since it was open to varied interpretations. It proved to be a partnership in which the weight of Federal influence was used to protect the interests of Europeans permanently settled in the country, and to encourage others to take up residence there. The implications of this policy were most clearly illustrated in the case of Rhodesia Railways, the only industry directly under Federal rather than territorial control.[1] The Railways had become a statutory corporation in 1947, responsible to the governments of Northern and Southern Rhodesia and Bechuanaland. In 1954 the Federal Government became the guarantor of its debts and the following year the Federal Minister of Transport, Roy Welensky, took over responsibility from officers of the three territories for the general direction of railway policy. Before the Railways were incorporated in 1947 the Secretary of State for the Colonies announced that the new body would 'promote the welfare and advancement of the African employees'. At the same time Godfrey Huggins, the Prime Minister of Southern Rhodesia, wrote to the General Secretary of the Rhodesia Railway Workers' Union assuring him that existing conditions of employment would be continued.[2] This agreement was revealed to surprised Colonial Office and Northern Rhodesian officials during the negotiations on the Federal Constitution in London in 1953, when Southern Rhodesian representatives demanded that a similar guarantee for the Railways be written into it.[3]

Later, despite a serious shortage of semi-skilled staff, the Railways preferred to recruit men from Europe rather than promote or train Africans. In 1955 the mining companies, who were concerned about delays in the railway service, were told that two hundred recruits from Italy and Greece were expected shortly but 'their availability for immediate service depended upon the extent to which they were able

---

[1] Because of their responsibilities in Bechuanaland the Railways operated in an area wider than the Federation: the corporation's submission to the Monckton Commission, dated 29 April 1960, pointed out that 'Rhodesia Railways are therefore not strictly an instrument of Federal Government policy but naturally there is a close liaison between the Government and the Railways.' *Report of the Advisory Commission on the Review of the Federation of Rhodesia and Nyasaland, Appendix VIII, Evidence,* vol. iv (Cmnd. 1151–111), p. 423. (The *Monckton Commission Report.*)

[2] Ibid., pp. 422–4.

[3] *Conference on the Federation of Southern Rhodesia, Northern Rhodesia and Nyasaland* (London, January 1953), vol. xi: Minutes of the first and second meetings of the Working Party on Trade Unions, 13 and 16 Jan. 1953.

to speak English'.[1] African advancement on the railways in Northern and Southern Rhodesia made little progress until the life of the Federation was almost over, because of the management's wish to avoid friction with the two trade unions representing European employees, the Railway Workers' and the Amalgamated Engineering unions.[2]

INDUSTRIAL TRAINING

Federal policy not only provided strong reinforcement for European workers' advocacy of equal pay for equal work, but also helped to maintain barriers which kept Africans from access to equal industrial training. Such restrictions had first been given legislative approval in Northern Rhodesia ten years before the establishment of the Federation, in the Apprenticeship Ordinance of 1943. The law was introduced after a strong campaign by European trade-unionists who wanted apprenticeships limited in a proportion of one for every five qualified artisans.[3] Apprentices were to be not older than twenty-one years, to have completed the second class of secondary school (form II), and to be willing to accept a five-year contract for instruction in their chosen trade. The system was designed to protect the position of artisans by restricting the numbers of those entering trades, and to maintain high standards by prolonged training.

Africans were already receiving basic training in various trades at mission centres, government schools and in industry, but not at the level of a formal apprenticeship. Secondary education for Africans had only begun in 1939, and the generally backward state of African education at that time meant that industrial training could not be linked to conventional Western standards. The Government decided to exclude Africans from the apprenticeship bill, at the Chamber of Mines' request, because the pay rates, educational and age qualifications discriminated against them.[4] The Labour Commissioner pointed

[1] C.I.S.B., 10.27: Record of a meeting on coal supplies attended by Federal Government officials, representatives of Rhodesia Railways and members of the Northern Rhodesia Chamber of Mines, Salisbury, 30 Nov. 1955.

[2] *Monckton Commission Report, Evidence*, vol. iv, pp. 423–5.

[3] C.I.S.B., 70.17, vol. i: A. H. Brunsden, Secretary of Chamber of Mines to the General Managers of the mining companies, 16 June 1942.

[4] *Report of the Committee on Trade Testing and Apprenticeship for Africans* (Lusaka, 1957), p. 2; SEC/LAB/195, vol. i: Crown Counsel Edgar Unsworth to the Chief Secretary, George Beresford Stooke, 11 Nov. 1942.

out that exclusion would also discriminate against Africans, and that
the solution was to lower the education requirements, but his protests
were ignored.[1] At that time officials were not anxious to provoke
opposition from European trade-unionists which might affect the
war effort, and the Governor, Sir John Waddington, told the Secretary of State that it was 'politically desirable to proceed as early as
possible' with the Bill.[2]

After the war the Government decided to introduce a system of
'trade testing' for Africans, which was not intended as a substitute
for apprenticeship but which covered many of the same occupations.
The highest of the three grades of achievement in the tests was considerably lower than that reached in a full apprenticeship. When testing began in 1950 the system proved popular with African workmen,
and in the following year 2,152 men passed tests in such trades as
brick-laying, carpentry, painting, driving, welding, and woodwork.
During 1955, when the number of European youths in the thirty-five
trades with formal apprenticeship was 343, nearly 3,500 Africans
passed trade tests in eighteen fields of work.[3]

In the early years of the Federation entrance to apprenticeship
training became a public issue. For sharply different reasons African
workers and politicians, building industry employers, and European
trade-unionists in Northern Rhodesia all pressed for the extension of
the Apprenticeship Ordinance to Africans. The building trade wanted
a higher grade of work from able employees, for less pay than was
given to Europeans.[4] African trade-unionists wanted equal treatment
and advancement.[5] European workers, who had not objected to the
exclusion of Africans from the Ordinance in 1943, now thought that
the success of the trade testing scheme was allowing cheap labour to
undermine the position of fully-trained artisans.[6] Artisans accounted
for about a quarter of the daily-paid workers at the mines, and

[1] SEC/LAB/195, vol. i: Labour Commissioner Rowland S. Hudson to Chief
Secretary, 28 Nov. 1942, and same to same, 10 Apr. 1943.

[2] SEC/LAB/195, vol. i: Governor Sir John Waddington to Secretary of State,
20 Jan. 1943.

[3] *Report of the Committee on Trade Testing*, 1957, pp. 2–4; *Department of
Labour Annual Report 1956*, pp. 54–5.

[4] C.I.S.B., 70.17.3: Memorandum on African apprenticeship in the building
industry by D. W. Winchester-Gould, Master Builders and Allied Trades Association, 28 July 1954.

[5] *Northern News*, 23 Nov. 1955; C.I.S.B., Evidence to the Forster Commission,
1954, A.M.U. Memorandum.

[6] Zambia Expatriate Mineworkers' Association: Mufulira branch correspondence, B. J. Petersen to Labour Commissioner, 1 Nov. 1955.

jealously guarded their position against other European workers as well as Africans. If trade testing were to be abolished, as European artisans demanded, the requirements of two classes of secondary school would have barred almost all African workers from apprenticeship.

In 1956 the Government set up a committee to examine trade testing and apprenticeship for Africans, with representatives of employers and of European and African trade-unionists among its members. Their interests were so diverse that they could not reach a majority decision, but it was agreed that apprenticeship should be opened to Africans and that trade testing ought to be abolished.[1] The Labour Department persuaded the officials in the Government to accept its view that although apprenticeship ought to be opened quickly, trade testing should be ended gradually and its standards slowly lifted towards those of apprenticeship.[2]

When the Apprenticeship Ordinance was at last amended in 1958 to include Africans, complications arose for both the Government and the mining industry, in which more than half of the apprentices in the country were indentured. The companies faced the prospect that an African who had had a full apprenticeship would produce work equal to a European, and the mines would therefore be committed to providing equal pay under the terms of the 1955 advancement agreement with the European Union. Such a test case had not yet arisen. Further advancement talks were scheduled, and officials feared that a precedent would strengthen demands from the African Union that all African pay rates should be graded in relation to European wages. The companies felt that they should announce their support for African apprenticeship in principle, but try to defer its introduction until after the new advancement pay scales were settled.[3] The Government's difficulty lay in the fact that technical education, hitherto a European monopoly, had been assigned with other aspects of European education in 1953 to the Federal Government, while African education had been retained by the territorial authorities. The establishment of the Federation had reinforced European workers' claims to a permanent field of European employment in which their present status in relation to African workers

[1] *Report of the Committee on Trade Testing*, 1957, p. 6.
[2] *Legislative Council Debates*, 94, 25 Mar. 1958, 210, 235–6.
[3] C.I.S.B., 70.17.3: S. Taylor, Secretary of the Chamber of Mines, to the General Managers, 25 Jan. 1957; and memorandum 'Apprenticeship for Africans', dated 1 Feb. 1957.

would be preserved, and part of the price of the companies' settlement with the European Union in 1955 had been a promise to provide training to fit members for more advanced posts.[1] One result was the mining groups' endowment of a Copperbelt Technical Foundation for the further education of European youths, which took over the theoretical side of apprenticeship training on the Copperbelt early in 1957 at the request of the Federal Government.[2]

This development coincided with the growth of pressure to extend the Apprenticeship Ordinance to Africans, and produced unforeseen problems for both the companies and the territorial Government. The 1958 amendment to the Apprenticeship Ordinance was passed during a serious financial depression caused by falling copper prices. The Government felt that it could not afford a separate apprenticeship training scheme for Africans, and the Labour Department thought that the most economical course was to use the existing facilities.[3] The Chamber of Mines proved to be flexible about admitting Africans to the Foundation,[4] but the idea was opposed in the Legislative Council,[5] and by the Federal Minister of Education, who also refused to admit Africans to the technical colleges at Salisbury and Bulawayo. When the mining companies sought a grant from the Northern Rhodesian Government to offset the growing expenses of the Foundation, they were told help could only be given if they admitted Africans: the Federal Government refused permission, and then refused to take over the Foundation, because its costs were too high.[6]

The Government edged its way round the problem with customary caution. In 1960 a committee to examine technical education in the territory was set up, with the approval of the Federal Government and the mining companies, under Sir David Lindsay Keir, Chairman of the Council for Overseas Colleges of Arts, Science, and Technology.

[1] *Branigan Report*, p. 76: Agreement between the companies and the European Union, 30 July 1955, clause 17.

[2] C.I.S.B., 140.3: Minutes of first meeting, Copperbelt Technical Foundation committee of management, 14 Feb. 1956.

[3] C.I.S.B., 104.3: Record of a meeting called by the Federal Department of Education's Regional Director to discuss technical education, 17 Feb. 1956.

[4] C.I.S.B., 140.3: Record of decisions of the Executive Committee of the Chamber of Mines, 13 Mar. 1956.

[5] *Legislative Council Debates*, 94, 25 Mar. 1958, 233–4

[6] H. Franklin, 'The Technical Foundation Riddle still Unsolved', in the *Northern News*, 13 June 1960. The incidents are also reported in H. Franklin, *Unholy Wedlock* (London, 1963), pp. 185–6.

The Keir Committee recommended two grades of apprenticeship, and the opening of the Copperbelt Technical Foundation to students of all races who could meet the entrance requirements.[1] The Federal Government did not accept the report until the end of 1961.

The Copperbelt Technical Foundation was opened to all races in May 1962.[2] At that time the total number of African apprentices in the country, all indentured in Government departments, was four.[3] There was subsequently a rapid expansion in the number of African apprentices under the impetus of Independence, but in 1967 the number of Zambians who were indentured was still less than half of of the 586 apprentices in the country. The Acting Controller of Apprentices, Ambrose Muzuwa, who spoke from experience as one of the first Africans to complete an apprenticeship in motor mechanics, observed that low pay was a deterrent to competent Africans for whom better jobs had now opened in the civil service, commerce, and industry.[4]

The history of apprenticeship in the country, an unlikely object of political concern, had been a matter of long public controversy and one of missed opportunity. Apprenticeship is considered by some critics to be an old-fashioned and laborious form of preparation for work in modern industry. In the case of Africans who had been deprived of formal education by the backward state of the country's development, it might have been an appropriate means of instruction. The Labour Department supported industrial training for Africans to the limit of its own resources and of Government policy. It resisted the attempt of European trade-unionists to make the admission of Africans to apprenticeship a restrictive measure instead of a progressive one. It persistently fostered its programme of trade testing against strong opposition, and planned to use existing trade schools as a springboard to full African apprenticeship. But when it finally won the support of the Legislative Council, the complicated constitutional arrangements of the Federation permitted Federal authorities to put a brake on the implementation of apprenticeship for Africans until African political independence was almost a reality.

[1] *Annual Report of the Department of Labour 1961*, p. 7.
[2] C.I.S.B., 140.4, vol. iii: Minutes of the managing committee of the Copperbelt Technical Foundation, 4 Apr. 1962.
[3] C.I.S.B., 70.17.3: Ministry of Labour and Mines, memorandum on the law relating to apprenticeship for the Morison Commission, 22 May 1962.
[4] *Zambia Mail*, 18 Aug. 1967.

THE MINING GROUPS AND THE FEDERATION

It seems strange that the mining companies, with their growing commitment to African advancement, also supported the establishment of the Federation and later co-operated closely with the Federal Government; but if there was a conflict of interests, it was not emphasized at the time. The copper companies saw economic advantages in federation which would be of direct benefit to the mining industry. Since the end of the war the mines had been pressed by a shortage of coal from the Wankie colliery in Southern Rhodesia, and of wagons on the Rhodesia Railway system, which had its headquarters at Bulawayo. Many management officials, their political sympathies apart, felt that federation with Southern Rhodesia might ease the bottlenecks in planning, which by 1952 had become so bad that the mines were intermittently forced to reduce or shut operations because of the coal shortage.

The course of politics in South Africa had increased the interest of the Anglo American Group in a northern bloc of British territories. The victory of the Nationalists led by Dr. Daniel Malan in 1948 reinforced Sir Ernest Oppenheimer's support for a 'new Rhodesian Dominion'. He had predicted this development in the north early in the Second World War, and was impressed by Rhodesia's improved prospects for obtaining capital which had previously been routed through Johannesburg from the London financial market.[1] He was a strong advocate of federation, and revised his earlier opinion that European workers should not expect to play a permanent role in mining development in Central Africa.[2] Early in 1951 the registered offices of the Northern Rhodesian companies in the Anglo American Group were transferred from London to the Protectorate. The Rhodesian Selection Trust companies did not follow until 1953, although the change of domicile offered important tax advantages.[3] The companies of both Groups were incorporated in Northern Rhodesia in 1954.

Strangely enough, the economic prospects which were so attractive to supporters of the Federation were never explicitly analysed, although there was a general conviction that common services could

[1] Sir Theodore Gregory, *Ernest Oppenheimer*, p. 462; Gann, *History*, p. 409.
[2] 'The Advancement of Africans in Industry', Sir Ernest Oppenheimer, *Optima*, Sept. 1953, pp. 1–3; 'Sir Ernest Oppenheimer: A Portrait by his son', H. F. Oppenheimer, *Optima*, Sept. 1967, pp. 98–9.
[3] Gann, *History*, pp. 409–10.

be improved, bigger markets provided for secondary industry, and substantial foreign investments brought into the area. These prospects appear to have been greatly exaggerated, and the rate of investment in the Federation proved to be no greater than it had previously been in Central Africa.[1] The companies' susceptibility to the economic arguments arose from their need to develop their properties after the war, their difficulties with transport to the coast and with coal supplies, and probably from a lack of faith in Government development planning in Northern Rhodesia, which made a late start with the publication of a ten-year plan in 1947. The industry, expecting a post-war recession in copper, could not foresee the Korean War boom which was to make it the financial broker of Central Africa. The general trend of colonial rule had led the companies to expect that political development would be under white control for many years to come. The managements were aware that closer association with Southern Rhodesia might affect their advancement plans, but they believed that an accommodation was possible: given the political ambitions of Northern Rhodesia's white community, the Federation was no more unfavourable as a background to advancement than a Legislative Council dominated by European elected members would have been, and certainly more favourable than an independent Government dominated by European interests.

The Northern Rhodesian Government's policy on wages gave some justification for the companies' sanguine attitude. Although 'equal pay for equal work' was firmly upheld by the elected members who belonged to the United Federal Party, it was not applied to government employees. The principle of equal pay had been considered for African graduates qualified to enter the higher posts of the Civil Service while the problem was still a theoretical one, and it was decided that an African graduate should receive two-thirds of the equivalent European pay rate. This arbitrary proportion was justified on the grounds that European salaries included expatriation pay, and that account should be taken of ruling income levels in an officer's own community.[2] A unified Civil Service replaced the European and African Civil Services in November 1961, but the Govern-

---

[1] *African Integration and Disintegration*, ed. Arthur Hazlewood (London, 1967), p. 202.

[2] *Report of the Commission on the Civil Services of Northern Rhodesia and Nyasaland* (Lusaka, 1947), p. 7; *Report of the Commission appointed to review the salary structure . . . of the Civil Service of Northern Rhodesia* (Lusaka, 1952), Part II, pp. 19–20.

ment did not adopt the principle of a single basic wage for each post, with separate allowances for expatriate officers, until just before independence.

Under the Federal Constitution labour policy was one of the subjects reserved for territorial governments. This arrangement was necessary because labour law in the northern territories embodied a fundamental difference from that in Southern Rhodesia. African trade unions were legally recognized in Nyasaland and Northern Rhodesia, but were excluded from registration under Southern Rhodesia's Industrial Conciliation Act.[1] The attitude of European workers in Southern Rhodesia to African encroachments on their skills and jobs was uncompromisingly hostile, and enjoyed the support of both the territorial and Federal Governments. But in 1954 in Northern Rhodesia the Government endorsed the Moffat Resolutions, which included the promise that every lawful inhabitant of the country had the right to progess 'according to his character, qualifications, training, ability and industry, without distinction of race, colour or creed'.[2]

These points were advantageous to the companies. On the debit side was the fact that Government officials found it difficult to come out clearly in favour of immediate progress for Africans while three United Federal Party members were prominent in the Executive Council. Because of the 1948 agreement by which the Governor did not normally overrule the unanimous advice of the elected members, the Executive Council was said to operate 'virtually as a Federal Party Government. If the three elected members stand firm on any issue they are almost certain to carry the day.' By 1957 the Governor's position, according to a historian of the period, had become 'impossibly difficult' in face of the Federal Party's militancy.[3]

Despite acknowledged support for the Federation, the mining companies claimed in later years that it had been an unfavourable time in which to tackle the problems of advancement on the Copperbelt.[4] This was true, even although the Federal Government had no direct control over labour policy in Northern Rhodesia, and the Northern Rhodesia Government's official pronouncements

[1] *Central African Territories: Comparative Survey of Native Policy* (Cmd. 8235), p. 22.
[2] *Legislative Council Debates*, 82, 29 July 1954, 616–17.
[3] Mulford, *Zambia*, p. 50.
[4] *Report of the Commission of Inquiry into the Mining Industry*, 1966, p. 92. (The *Brown Commission Report*.)

supported advancement. The leader of the United Federal Party in Northern Rhodesia, John Roberts, became the country's first Minister of Labour in 1959; and the general Federal aim of maintaining equal pay went against the trend of the companies' plans. After the Forster Commission had rejected the principle of equal pay in 1954 and recommended that African advancement should be based on the fragmentation of European jobs, the companies were forced into a compromise by their European workers. The European union allowed the boundaries of its closed shop to be altered slightly, but equal pay applied to all remaining 'European' jobs. Under heavy pressure from the mining companies, low-calibre jobs were removed from the union's sphere of representation in two stages, twenty-four of them in 1955 and thirty-eight in 1960. The 1955 agreement was recognized as an interim measure until a survey of European work by independent industrial consultants helped to pinpoint other low-content jobs. The time needed for a detailed survey, together with unrelated disputes between the companies and the union, caused a four-year delay in the negotiations. After a further year of talks, agreement was reached in 1960 on the second group of jobs to be released by the union. The companies planned to fragment these jobs and to add to them another twenty categories of new work, providing ninety new types of job for African employees. Africans who advanced into jobs represented by the European union would be entitled to equal pay and membership of the union.

The plan was publicized to European workers as a 'final solution', in the sense that the European union would not be asked to surrender any more jobs and that further advancement would be on the basis of equal pay. African trade-unionists feared it was the last effort to provide for advancement in the industry.[1] The European union had not given up its belief in equal pay, but had drawn the line at which it was to apply higher up the wage scale. European leadership in the industry was not endangered. Nevertheless, the settlements in 1955 and 1960 represented an important effort by the companies to lessen restrictions which had been imposed by European workers since the beginning of the Second World War. By promoting African advancement and at the same time reducing the area in which 'equal pay for

---

[1] *African Advancement Proposals in the sphere of the Northern Rhodesia Mine Workers' Union, evolved by the Mining Joint Industrial Council . . . 4 Oct. 1960; Report of the Commission Appointed to Inquire into the Mining Industry in Northern Rhodesia*, 1962, pp. 5–7, 11. (The *Morison Commission Report*.)

equal work' applied, the two agreements were a considerable
embarrassment to the Federal Government.[1]

[1] Interview with Sir Roy Welensky, London, 16 Nov. 1970.

CHAPTER XI

The Price of Advancement

THE mining companies' position on African wages was simply that they were not willing to pay much more than any other employer in the country for their labour. The industry could have afforded to pay higher wages, and rarely countered a wage demand with a claim that it could not be met. Instead company representatives pointed out that their pay rates were the best in the country. They felt bound to employ local labour at rates above, but not far above, prevailing local wage levels, as it was generally assumed by other employers that sharp increases at the mines would have repercussions on wages not only in Northern Rhodesia, but all over Central Africa.[1] The copper industry's general wage policy was summarized in 1956 by Sir Ronald Prain, chairman of the RST Group, as follows:

... current wage-rates have evolved by the normal processes of supply and demand tempered by collective bargaining and by the Companies' social conscience and general wish to pay not only well but better than other employers. The Companies have declined to increase wages merely because their African employees are acquiring the habit of buying European clothes and other consumer goods. In the absence of any reliable yardstick for computing a 'correct' wage for an African employed in industry in his own country it is difficult to know what other course could be adopted; but it would be rash to assert that ... this policy is necessarily right. ... The arguments we have so far worked on are that in fixing our wages we must have regard to the present economy and standards of the African community as a whole. ... Accordingly, the reward paid to the African mineworker should be related to, although constantly in advance of, the standard of living he enjoys at home. Secondly, it is assumed that our wages should not be outrageously incompatible with what other industries, including farming, are paying.[2]

The companies felt that the guide-lines by which general wage increases should be judged were rises in the cost of living; the availability of labour to the industry; and a comparison with wages paid

[1] C.I.S.B., 100.20.9A, vol. i: Memorandum of the Associated Chambers of Commerce and Industry for the Guillebaud Tribunal, 21 Jan. 1953.

[2] R. Prain, 'Stabilization of Labour on the Rhodesian Copperbelt', *H.R.H. The Duke of Edinburgh's Study Conference*, 1956, vol. ii, pp. 55–6.

in other industries in the country and in mining concerns in other developing countries.[1] During the first series of advancement negotions in 1954–5 they tried to relate wages for Africans in senior positions to those of the African labour force in general, holding that

the diminution of the gap between African and European pay-rates must be related to an improvement, first in the productivity and thereafter (and as a consequence) in the standard of living and civilization of the African community *as a whole*. Any attempt to apply at once full European pay-rates and conditions of service to a section of African labour would have a disastrous effect on the individual, on the African community and on the economy of the Territory.[2]

This policy was soon modified, and the following year the advancement plan published by the RST Group related senior African pay rates to European wages, with the promise that pay for advancement candidates would eventually approach European levels or even equal them as individual productivity improved.[3] By the time the 1960 negotiations began, this had not yet happened, but nearly 2,000 African workers had wages above the highest level for ticket-paid employees at the time of the first advancement plan.[4]

The companies now began to give closer consideration to the problem of how to splice their African and European wage scales together. The two scales had been determined by historical developments and justified by different methods of job evaluation. It was difficult to assign common values to the jobs on either side of the proposed joining point. A study of job content in the highest African and lowest European jobs indicated that the European wages should be reduced to effect the splice, but not surprisingly the European union refused to co-operate.[5] The companies therefore left a gap of 13*s*. 8*d*. between the highest African wage, 50*s*. 4*d*., and the lowest European daily rate, 64*s*.[6]

AFRICAN WAGE DEMANDS

Compared with the rest of the African labour force, mine-workers were in a favourable position. In 1954 annual average wages in the

[1] *Morison Commission Report*, p. 18.
[2] *Forster Commission Report*, 1954, Appendix 4, p. 46.
[3] *Northern News*, 4 Feb. 1955. See pp. 127–8.
[4] *Morison Commission Report*, p. 13.
[5] C.I.S.B., Evidence submitted to the Morison Commission, Memorandum on job evaluation from the companies, p. 19.
[6] *Morison Commission Report*, p. 12.

industry were £131, much higher than in any other type of employ-ment. Northern Rhodesian wages in general were considered by the Colonial Office to be more satisfactory than those in East Africa, especially in Kenya, where rates were still based on the needs of a single man and took no account at all of family requirements. Within six years the mines' average African earnings had been pushed up to £255.[1] African workers in other industries also received increases but as their basic rates were lower, the gap between African mine wages and those in other industries increased (see Table 5).

TABLE 5
Average Annual Earnings of Africans employed in Northern Rhodesia[2]

	1954 £	1960 £
Mining and quarrying	131	255
Building and construction	59	99
Government administration	73	121
Manufacturing	61	95
Transport and communications	87	148
Domestic service	55	80
Agriculture	42	62

By 1960 average African wages in the copper industry were 37 per cent above those in mining in the Congo and 56 per cent above those in South African mining.[3] The increases had been achieved through the consolidation of efficiency awards and cost of living allowances into basic pay in 1957, and by wage increases negotiated by the African union in 1958 and 1960.[4]

The situation of African mine-workers could be presented in its most favourable light if total earnings were contrasted with basic wages. The basic wage on the mines was supplemented by free housing, rations (until 1956), a cost of living allowance and a variable annual bonus related to the level of the industry's profit. By including the cost of living allowance and bonus payments in their calculation of earnings at the Harragin arbitration proceedings in 1957, the mining companies were able to show that African real earnings had risen by an average of 53 per cent between 1950 and 1956. In that period the total earnings of the lowest-paid Africans, adjusted to take rises in the cost of living into account, had increased by

[1] Average European earnings at the mines in 1960 were £2,260.
[2] C.I.S.B., Companies' statement of case to the Morison Commission, Appen-dix 4, Table D.
[3] Ibid., Appendix 19.
[4] Ibid., Appendix 5, Table 2.

59 per cent.[1] The mines' lowest earnings for thirty days' work, 202*s*. 6*d*., compared with 157*s*. 6*d*. on Rhodesia Railways, 67*s*. 6*d*. at the Chilanga Cement Works, and 90*s*. for casual labour employed by the Government.[2]

At this point, however, the mine labour force was profoundly discontented with its conditions of employment. In view of these workers' progressive advances in earnings, and their position as wage-leaders in the territory, the causes of their disillusionment were of considerable importance. African trade-unionists at the mines were not impressed by the rise in their total income or their favourable position in relation to other industries. Their attention was fixed on two things, the gap in wages between African and European employees, and the wide spread of wages among African workers. The gap between the lowest-paid European handyman and the highest-paid African boss boy had narrowed as the 1955 advancement plan was implemented. In 1954 their basic monthly wages stood at £63. 9*s*. 8*d*. and £16. 14*s*. 6*d*. respectively. In October 1956 these monthly rates had changed to £69. 11*s*. 0*d*. and £40. 15*s*. 0*d*.: the different systems used to calculate European and African bonuses, which were very favourable to European workers, resulted in total earnings of £115. 11*s*. 2*d*. against £50. 15*s*. 0*d*.[3] Although the wage gap was somewhat narrower than before, the integrated wage scale envisaged in RST's first advancement plan early in 1955 did not materialize.[4]

African trade-unionists had learned from bitter experience in 1955 that the majority of advancement jobs would probably be given to the Mines African Staff Association in future negotiations. Although they supported the principle of closing the wage gap between Africans and Europeans, if this was done by the 'ladder' plan their own members would gain nothing. The difference between the wages of unskilled African workers and the highest-paid Africans was just as great as the gap between African and European wages: in 1956 the range of African basic wages ran from £8. 15*s*. 0*d*. per ticket of thirty working days to £40. 15*s*. 0*d*. for monthly paid workers.[5] This gap

---

[1] C.I.S.B., Companies' statement of case to the Harragin arbitration tribunal, Jan. 1957, 'Changes in the real wage rates of ticket-paid African employees between July 1950 and October 1956', p. 5.

[2] Ibid., Appendix 28.

[3] Ibid., note on wage 'gap', dated 22 Jan. 1956.   [4] See pp. 127–8.

[5] C.I.S.B., Companies' case to the Morison Commission, 1962, Appendix 5; and companies' case to the Harragin Arbitration Tribunal, 1957, note on wage 'gap'.

attracted the attention of African trade-union leaders as much as the difference in African and European pay, and they could not tolerate the extended wage scale the companies seemed to have in mind.

Another source of discontent was the companies' treatment of some of the advancement jobs assigned to the union in 1955 which had previously been 'ragged edge' work done by Africans at one mine and Europeans at another. The pay for these jobs surrendered by the European union was reduced to the rate received by Africans already doing the work, resulting in a drop from 63s. a shift to 9s. in some cases.[1] The companies pointed out that the European rate represented the premium for scarce labour paid in the earliest days of the mines when Africans were not available to do the work. Basically the jobs were low grade and did not merit even the salaries recently paid to other Africans in staff or supervisory jobs. This explanation was accepted by the Morison Commission of Inquiry, but the African union could not acquiesce.[2]

The discontent that existed among African workers before any measures of advancement were introduced was accentuated by the partial accomplishment of advancement in 1955. Pressure continued among the most skilled African workers for promotion, while it also mounted among the lower groups of workers for cash compensation to recognize the fact that they wanted a higher standard of living and would not benefit directly from advancement.[3] The division of workers into two employees' organizations emphasized this separation of interests, from which the more militant of the two bodies seemed likely to benefit least. By 1962 the maximum basic rate union members could earn was 25s. 9d. a shift, compared with a maximum of 50s. 4d. for Staff Association jobs, and a minimum rate on the European union's pay scale of 64s.[4]

The African union could not prove that the productivity of unskilled labour had increased, so it based its claims on the workers' right to a higher standard of living.[5] In the special circumstances of the Copperbelt there was an irresistible appetite for material acquisitions as urban workers acquired needs beyond those of subsistence

---

[1] Evidence to the Morison Commission of Eric Bromwich, Chief of Study at Roan Antelope Division, RST, 18 May 1962, pp. 57–60.

[2] *Morison Commission Report*, 1962, p. 11.

[3] Evidence to the Forster Commission of Lawrence Katilungu, 13 Sept. 1954.

[4] *Morison Commission Report*, p. 12.

[5] Companies' case to the Harragin Arbitration 1957, Appendix 6, annexures B and C (minutes of meetings with A.M.U. 5 Oct. and 20 Nov. 1954).

living, with the example of a privileged European élite always before them. The mines' labour force was loosening its ties with rural life, and a decisive change took place in the second half of the 1950s when labour turnover sharply decreased. As late as 1953 the companies still maintained that their policy was one of limited stabilization, and that their workers kept regular contact with their country homes through periodic leaves.[1] At the Roan Antelope mine, where there had always been support for a more settled labour force, 25 per cent of the workers had served for more than five years.[2] In the next few years improvements in the wages and housing of Copperbelt workers hastened the trend towards stability. In 1953 the Guillebaud arbitration award almost doubled the lowest mine wages, and in later wage adjustments they were increased still further. The lowest basic wage had been 30s. in 1948. It was 45s. in 1952, 80s. after the arbitration award, and 175s. in 1956 after an allowance for rations had been incorporated in wages.[3] In this period the mines began to improve their workers' housing, and later, between 1956 and 1964, they built almost 17,500 houses at a cost of £11 million, compared with 25,000 houses completed by Government and municipal authorities in the rest of the country at a cost of £8 million.[4] The annual turnover of African labour dropped dramatically, and by 1956 had already reached a level which the companies considered comparable with British industry. In 1959 the average length of service in the mines was over five years (see Table 6).[5]

Despite this rapid progress towards a stable labour force, few Africans looked on the towns as their permanent homes. The reason lay in the insecurity of urban residence. Housing was generally unsuitable for large families. Pensions for long-service employees were not designed to meet urban rents and the rising cost of living in town. There was no system of state social security, and the extent of government protection for employees was a workmen's compensation law. If a man lost his job he had nowhere to turn except to his relatives.

[1] C.I.S.B., 100.20.9A, vol. ii: Speech made by Sir Hartley Shawcross, presenting the companies' case, at the Guillebaud arbitration proceedings, 23 Jan. 1953.

[2] Epstein, *Politics*, p. 13; also J. C. Mitchell, *African Urbanization in Ndola and Luanshya*, Rhodes–Livingstone Communication No. 6 (Lusaka, 1954), p. 17 and Table XVII.

[3] Companies' statement of case to the Morison Commission, 1962, Appendix 5, Table 2, African Wage Structure, 1948–61.

[4] *Brown Commission Report*, p. 57.

[5] Companies statement of case to the Morison Commission 1962, Appendix 16.

TABLE 6
Annual Labour Turnover, all Copperbelt Mines, 1952–64*

Year	Local employees Annual turnover per cent	Expatriate employees Annual turnover per cent
1952	60·1	16·5
1954	47·6	17·3
1956	27·6	13·1
1958	42·7	36·0
1960	30·2	17·4
1962	17·7	15·2
1964	8·3	25·5

* Source: *Brown Commission Report*, 1966, Appendix XVI, p. 160. Both the African and European figures were abnormally inflated in 1958, the year of a lengthy European strike which shut the mines.

African workers provided for their families and their future by maintaining their rural connections, and children were often sent back to the country to be brought up there.[1] The link with the villages was not only a matter of necessity: many Africans retained a sentimental attachment to their home areas and preferred to retire there. This led to a strange dualism in the African family's position in town. Social changes were taking place which undermined the force of traditional tribalism in the urban areas where, at least in times of crisis, common interests arising from the industrial or urban situation seemed to outweigh tribal divisions. At the same time men kept their options open in the villages as far as possible, and usually expected to return there when their period of employment ended. Within this framework urbanization appeared to be an ambiguous process, but also one in which standards of living had changed rapidly in the past and were likely to continue to do so.

UNEMPLOYMENT

As wages rose in the 1950s, and the mines committed themselves to establishing a more stable African labour force, concern abou unemployment on the Copperbelt increased. The companies felt that higher wages were attracting job-seekers to the area, and that unemployment could be exploited for political agitation.[2] The Government

[1] Baldwin, *Economic Development and Export Growth*, p. 113; J. Van Velsen, 'Labour Migration as a Positive Factor in the Continuity of Tonga Tribal Society', in *Social Change in Modern Africa* (London, 1961), ed. Aidan Southall, pp. 230 ff.

[2] C.I.S.B., 100.51, vol. i: S. Taylor, Secretary to the Chamber of Mines, to the Chief Secretary to the Government, 29 Oct. 1953, and Note on African labour, urbanization and stabilization, by D. Symington, Director of the Chamber of Mines, 4 Mar. 1955.

thought that the problem was partly the companies' own fault: it recommended rural recruiting instead of recruitment at the mine gates, and a faster rate of stabilization of the labour force.[1] It also considered establishing a mesh of rural and urban labour exchanges to control the flow of labour to the towns.[2] The scheme was elaborate and expensive, and on detailed examination it had to be modified. To fit the budget of the 1959 four-year plan, the Labour Department was limited to a programme which covered only a few parts of the country.[3] The mining companies were critical of this reduced version, for they had become increasingly worried by the prospect of political unrest and, situated at the Katanga border, were aware of the rising level of unemployment in Congo towns and its contribution to unrest there.[4] The Chamber of Mines even re-examined the possibility of getting labour from the rural areas as a solution, but finally rejected it because of the cost.[5] Instead the mine managements began to hold their periodic local recruiting parades on the same day, to prevent unemployed men from circulating from mine to mine. An average of 2,000 men had appeared monthly at Rhokana for 400 vacancies, the same number weekly at Mufulira for seventy jobs, and well over 1,000 weekly at Roan Antelope for the thirty jobs available. The African Personnel Manager at Nchanga reported 'well over one thousand (increasing daily) chasing 20–30 jobs (the majority hungry, frustrated and penniless) with a slender hope of obtaining any form of employment'.[6]

Heavy unemployment was a characteristic of the Copperbelt towns' growth. In Northern Rhodesia many young men would have flocked

[1] C.I.S.B., 100.51, vol. i: Record of decisions of the Executive Committee of the Chamber of Mines, 22 Nov. 1955, and minutes of a meeting between the Governor, representatives of the Government and of the mining companies, 30 May 1956.

[2] C.I.S.B., 100.51, vol. i: telegram from Chamber of Mines to RST and Anglo American Corporation, Salisbury, 25 June 1958.

[3] C.I.S.B., 100.51, vol. ii: Memorandum . . . on control of influx of African labour into urban areas by means of urban and rural labour exchanges, 4 Mar. 1959.

[4] C.I.S.B., 100.51, vol. ii: N. R. K. Davis for Secretary of Chamber of Mines to the General Managers of the mining companies, 4 Mar. 1959; Notes of fourth meeting of working committee on movement of labour; and O. B. Bennett, General Manager of Rhokana to Secretary of Chamber, 16 Nov. 1959.

[5] C.I.S.B., 100.51, vol. iii: Record of decisions of the Executive Committee of the Chamber of Mines, 4 Aug. 1960.

[6] C.I.S.B., 100.51, vol. ii: Notes of fifth meeting of working committee on movement of labour, 9 July 1959; Secretary of Chamber to General Managers, with enclosure, 11 Sept. 1959; Nchanga African Personnel Manager, R. Gabbitas, to General Manager of Nchanga, 8 Mar. 1960.

to the new towns regardless of the impetus of taxation. The desire for money to buy European goods grew quickly, and sometimes a journey to town and a period of work there became almost a rite of initiation.[1] But the general course of Government and employers' policies encouraged the trend. Even African trade-unionists, by pressing for higher wages, reinforced it. Employers correctly predicted that higher wages would increase the flow of labour to the towns, while encouraging industry to make a more economic use of labour. At the mines the substantial Guillebaud wages award in 1953 led to a sharp reduction in the number of Africans employed in relation to total production. One economist has speculated that the labour force of about 35,000 men would have almost doubled if the rationalization plan had not been introduced.[2] Continued pressure from the African Mineworkers' Union carried with it a threat of mechanization and new reductions in the size of the labour force, a prospect illustrated by the development of open-pit mining at Nchanga with scoops and conveyor belts which required few operators.[3] In the construction and manufacturing industries, where wages accounted for 40 per cent of operating costs compared with 18 per cent on the mines, the danger of a reduction in the size of the labour force after a wage increase was even greater.[4] Pay rises tended to cut employment opportunities in terms of numbers, while increasing them in terms of the actual work performed.

THE 1960 ADVANCEMENT PLAN

The African union, despite its deeply-felt grievances over wages, was not in a position to force its demands on the companies. About three-quarters of the workers eligible for membership were unskilled labourers in the four lowest job groups.[5] The union had no closed shop, and the presence of a large pool of unemployed men on the Copperbelt constantly undermined pressure for higher wages. In the 1955 strike the companies had been able to discharge the strikers and recruit thousands of new labourers on the spot. After the loss of its leaders in the 1956 detentions the union was in an even weaker posi-

---

[1] W. Watson, *Tribal Cohesion in a Money Economy* (Manchester, 1958), pp. 43–4.
[2] Baldwin, *Economic Development*, p. 99.
[3] *Morison Commission Report*, p. 19.
[4] Baldwin, *Economic Development*, p. 107.
[5] *Morison Commission Report*, p. 12.

tion, and in 1957 membership dropped to 6,500, about one-sixth of those eligible. In the next two years there were no major disputes with the companies and membership recovered to between 14,000 and 15,000 men.[1]

Just as the companies prepared to transfer advancement negotiations from their European workers to representatives of African employees, the leadership of the African union changed hands. Lawrence Katilungu, the president of the union since its formation in 1949, was dismissed by its Supreme Council at the end of 1960. Members thought that he was neglecting union affairs for his growing interest in the African National Congress. Supporters of the newer political party, the United National Independence Party, challenged his leadership through the Trade Union Congress, of which he was also president. Personal rivalries entered into it, and the Luanshya branch leaders in particular had maintained a steady hostility to him for many years.[2] Katilungu might have ridden out these troubles had he not accepted a place on the Monckton Commission which examined the Federal Constitution in 1960. Many Africans associated it with the continuation of the Federation, since its terms of reference did not include secession, and mine-workers thought Katilungu's presence on it was proof that he was not attending to union affairs.[3] He was replaced as president of the union by John Chisata, a second-generation mine-worker who was then aged about thirty. Chisata had been elected chairman of the Mufulira branch and Vice-President of the union in 1960. The other officers, who included several old union stalwarts, remained unchanged.[4]

Katilungu's dismissal reflected a renewed controversy over the role of trade unions in politics, sparked by the bitter rivalry between the old African National Congress and the more dynamic United National Independence Party which had been formed in August 1959. The Copperbelt was seething with political propaganda, but the African Mineworkers' Union had not yet aligned with either side and leading officials still seemed disposed to maintain the union's

[1] Information from the Registrar of Trade Unions, Lusaka, 2 Oct. 1967.

[2] Mulford, *Zambia*, pp. 170–4; Bates, *Unions*, pp. 101–2; C.I.S.B., 100.20, vol. xx: telegram from the Chamber of Mines to the Anglo American Corporation, Salisbury, 3 Jan. 1960; C.I.S.B., file 100.60 on the African Trade Union Congress from Apr. 1960 to July 1962.

[3] Bates, p. 145.

[4] Among them were James Namitengo and George Bentley Chima, officers of the union since its foundation, and Gabriel Mushikwa, who became General Secretary after the 1956 detentions.

political independence. They were subject to pressure from U.N.I.P. supporters in other unions, who were powerful in the new United Trades Union Congress.[1] Katilungu himself posed a threat to their independence, for after his dismissal he was free to indulge his interest in politics. When the Congress leader Harry Nkumbula received a prison sentence for a driving offence Katilungu became acting president of the A.N.C. and set about reviving its flagging organization and finances, with some success. Before his death in a car accident in November 1961 he had threatened to form a pro-Congress trade union based on his loyal clique of supporters at Mufulira.[2]

In addition to political problems the African Mineworkers' Union had run into administrative difficulties. Its leaders had persuaded the companies that because of a drop in income, presumably caused by a drop in membership, it was necessary to increase the check-off from $1s.$ to $1s. 9d.$ The increase was not welcomed by the members, and out of some 35,000 eligible workers and an official membership of nearly 17,000, only about 5,000 men agreed to pay the higher subscription when it was first introduced.[3] Chisata and his colleagues entered the negotiations on the new advancement plan against a background of growing troubles in the union after the period of enforced calm which had followed the detentions of 1956.

After securing the release of new job categories from the European union in 1960 the companies opened negotiations with the African union and the Mines African Staff Association about pay and representation in April 1961. In a rare display of co-operation the union and the Staff Association formed a Liaison Committee to present their views to the companies. The talks made little progress and in June the companies tried to implement their plans for ninety-two new job categories without the African organizations' consent. The attempt was soon dropped, and in further talks between August and November agreement was reached about representation for the new jobs. M.A.S.A. was to have sixty-one of them, and the African union

[1] Mulford, *Zambia*, p. 174; C.I.S.B., 100.60 (especially information officer to General Manager, Rhokana Corporation, 20 July 1961); C.I.S.B. 100.20, vol. xx: telegram, Chamber of Mines to Anglo American Corporation, Salisbury, 23 June 1961.

[2] C.I.S.B., 100.20, vol. xxi: telegram, Chamber to Anglo American Corporation Salisbury, 3 Nov. 1961.

[3] C.I.S.B., 100.20.14B: paper, 'Northern Rhodesia African Mineworkers' Trade Union subscription'.

thirty-one. In the process of negotiating this division of interests the Liaison Committee disintegrated. In January 1962 M.A.S.A. agreed to the companies' pay proposals for the new jobs it was to represent, with a 10 per cent increase over the rates originally offered.[1]

Meanwhile the African Mineworkers' Union began to show signs of rejecting the whole advancement plan. Grievances welled up, some specifically related to the plan and others carefully harboured from previous crises. It became obvious that many of these issues had been left in suspension during past conflicts, and that past settlements had not resolved them. In particular the union had not reconciled itself to the existence of M.A.S.A. and was still anxious to revoke the recognition of the Association which it considered had been forced on it after the rolling strikes of 1956 and in the check-off agreement of 1958. After the Liaison Committee disintegrated in 1961 the union put forward various demands for the abolition of M.A.S.A. or the reduction of its field of representation, and refused to recognize the Association's role in the company's advancement plan.[2] Ignoring M.A.S.A. pay rates which bridged the gap between union rates and European pay, it asked that the large gap between the highest-paid union member and the lowest-paid European should be closed, and that Africans should get equal pay when they took over Europeans' work.[3]

The union could not justify higher wages in terms of the rising cost of living, for the companies could show that since 1956 actual earnings had increased on average by 66 per cent, while the real increase, adjusted to take the rise in the cost of living index into account, was still 52 per cent.[4] This time the union used an elaborate argument which focused on the two different systems used by the companies to analyse European and African jobs respectively. The companies' advancement proposals linked the two systems together, but did not seek to re-evaluate either one of them according to the principles used to judge job content on the other wage scale. The lower levels of African pay would in general be undisturbed. The African union tried to overturn this aspect of the advancement proposals by demanding a unified wage scale 'in which the various wage levels are inter-related and [which] has as its sole criterion the

---

[1] *Morison Commission Report*, p. 17.

[2] Ibid., p. 9 and evidence of John Chisata to the Morison Commission, 21 May 1962.

[3] *Morison Commission Report*, p. 17.

[4] Ibid., p. 18.

comparative value of the jobs performed'.[1] Union leaders wanted the range of wages on the mines reduced from 90·8 per cent of the highest daily paid European wages to only 25 per cent, the existing wage spread on Canadian copper-mines.[2] This compression of the wage scale would raise the basic minimum pay of an African labourer from 8s. 1d. to 65s. 5d. a shift, making it roughly equal to the wages of the lowest-paid European.[3] The union also wanted shift differentials (the compensation paid for the inconvenience of working an afternoon or night shift) raised from 1s. to 11s. 6d. a shift.

After turning the negotiations over rates for senior jobs into a general pay demand, the union then unexpectedly also put forward a lesser wage claim. Realizing that the first claim was unlikely to be met at once, the union asked for a general increase of 8s. 2d. a shift, which would double the lowest rates of pay, as an interim measure.[4] The wage claim seems to have corrected the decline in its membership, for when the companies refused to take the claim to arbitration, the union held a strike ballot in which more than 21,000 members voted.[5] Shortly before the ballot the Governor, Sir Evelyn Hone,[6] noting 'the improbability of the parties ever reaching agreement', appointed a Commission of Inquiry into the dispute.[7]

The Governor was forced to appoint the Commission because the mining companies refused to go to arbitration on the union's assorted demands. The scope of the inquiry was limited, as its chairman, Sir Ronald Morison, Q.C.,[8] felt it would be inappropriate to make a precise wage recommendation as an arbitration tribunal might do. He considered that the union's 8s. 2d. demand was too high to be granted at any one time, but suggested that an unspecified general increase should be made throughout the whole African wage scale, which at its highest level would help to close the gap between African and

[1] *Morison Commission Report*, p. 8.　　　　[2] Loc. cit.

[3] Evidence to the Morison Commission by F. B. Canning-Cooke, manager of the Chamber of Mines, 15 May 1962.

[4] *Morison Commission Report*, p. 10.

[5] Evidence of John Chisata to the Morison Commission, 21 May 1962.

[6] Sir Evelyn Hone, b. 1911. Colonial Service, 1935. Chief Secretary, Aden, 1953–7; Northern Rhodesia, 1957–9; Governor, Northern Rhodesia, 1959–64.

[7] *Morison Commission Report*, p. 10.

[8] The other members of the Commission were A. R. I. Mellor, a former chairman of the Overseas Employers' Federation, representing the employers' interests; W. J. Tudor of the Transport and General Workers' Union, representing the interests of labour; Professor E. H. Phelps-Brown, Professor of Economics of Labour at London University, as economic adviser; and R. C. Pargeter, an independent mining consultant, as mining adviser.

European wages. A fresh start to collective bargaining on these lines would, he hoped, provide an opportunity for the companies and the union to try to improve their understanding of the other's point of view. To this end he also asked for the introduction of permanent machinery for joint consultation between management and workers, and for the establishment of a Joint Industrial Council parallel to the one in which the European union negotiated with the companies.[1]

The Commission provided a breathing space in the dispute rather than a solution for it. New negotiations ground to a halt and the union's leaders, John Chisata and Matthew Nkoloma, seemed to have decided on strike action again.[2] The impasse was resolved with help from an unexpected quarter. The United National Independence Party decided to fight the 1962 General Election, which was to be held under new constitutional arrangements. The forty-five seats in the new Legislative Council included fifteen for national constituencies in which candidates had to show multi-racial support by securing at least 10 per cent of both the European and the African votes.[3] U.N.I.P. leaders felt that a strike by African mine-workers during the election campaign would alienate European voters. The party appealed to the union not to strike. The union then accepted a company offer well below its demands; but its grievances had once again been shelved, to be revived on a future occasion.

The course of African advancement on the Copperbelt had changed rapidly in the period of the Federation. In 1953 the problem seemed to be one of securing an outlet, in inauspicious political circumstances, for the ambitions of senior African employees capable of undertaking more responsible work. Ten years later this had been accomplished, but it had spun off a second problem of satisfying the lower grades of workers who wanted greatly increased pay for the work they were currently doing.

The scale of the companies' advancement plans had been unique in industry in the Federation, yet the implementation of them in 1955–6 and 1961–2 had caused serious unrest among African workers. The companies' view of advancement as a matter affecting senior Africans

[1] *Morison Commission Report*, pp. 19–20, 22.

[2] Matthew Nkoloma, the former General Secretary of the A.M.U. detained for his part in the 1956 rolling strikes, was re-elected to his former post in March 1962 and was subsequently allowed by the companies to take part in negotiations and to enter the mine townships.

[3] See pp. 188–9.

did not correspond to the union's wider view of it which, by existing standards in the country, involved a revolutionary approach to African wages. The differences between the companies and the union over the representation of workers were closely related to the wages problem, since the higher pay of members of the Staff Association served to underline for union members their own unsatisfactory position.

The companies had no incentive to overthrow the conventions of the dual wage scale during the Federal period, as it was the accepted basis of economic development, but their plans were increasingly out of sympathy with African feelings. The interminable delays over advancement built up pressure within the industry and created an ever more demanding set of circumstances. Discussions opened so late in the history of African discontent that even if African labour had not been divided into rival organizations it is doubtful if advancement for a few would have headed off related wage demands by the many unaffected workers. Some aspects of advancement even caused discontent among the workers who benefited by it. The reassignment of work which had a recognized high wage rate when done by Europeans to lower (sometimes much lower) rates was bound to be extremely provocative to African trade-unionists. The companies were unimaginative in feeling that the impact of change would be greater on European leaders than on Africans, but their attitude reflected the European union's strong position politically and industrially, and the relatively weak one of the African union.

The African union leaders were in a vice, aware of their own weakness in negotiations, but forced to adopt extreme positions to win personal support or draw together a flagging membership. A pattern developed in which they began with an extravagant demand, and were eventually forced to accept a much lower offer from the companies. It is difficult to distinguish whether the high demands were always aimed at equivalence with European pay, or whether sometimes the demands for equivalence were simply a means of expressing a traditional trade-union aim, open to negotiation, which can be summed up as 'more'. Both aims were present, in varying proportions at different times, and they were not incompatible.

The prospects for the union's wage demands under Federation were poor. Under an African government many disadvantages were expected to disappear. Independence brought hopes of new and rapid initiatives in Africanization in all aspects of government and industry, and of corresponding increases in wages. The legacy of Federation and colonial rule was one of high aspirations, a disunited Copperbelt labour movement, and a major problem of wages policy which overshadowed future development planning by the government and the companies alike.

CHAPTER XII

Independence

WHEN Independence was granted in October 1964, the labour policies of the colonial government left the new African rulers with a difficult choice. Urban workers and civil servants expected to see long-cherished demands for higher wages fulfilled at last. These workers took their standards from the white men for whom they had worked, and did not relate their demands to the traditional African way of life. In contrast to these 'haves' were the 'have nots', thousands of unemployed men who had flocked to the towns, and rural villagers, four-fifths of the population, who lived in remote poverty beyond the line of rail. If these people were to have the fruits of Independence, money ought to be diverted from the towns to the country in a massive programme of rural aid, and urban wages kept low to encourage the expansion of job opportunities.

A rural-oriented policy would bring benefits to the great majority of the people. Unfortunately it also carried with it one of the least popular traits of colonial economic theory: the use of African traditional society to justify low wages in the urban sector of the economy. The new Government found itself unable to face this problem in its first years of power. It tried to promote rural development, increase the level of urban employment, *and* have a high wage policy, without declaring priorities.

To Zambia's leaders a wages policy was not at first a matter of urgency. Many other aspects of government demanded attention and the mechanics of the changeover to African rule absorbed much effort. In any case, the results of current wage trends were not apparent for some time. The Government naturally supported higher wages in reaction to the dual wage system which had held African wages down and was so closely connected with colonialism. Higher wages seemed to urban workers to be a legitimate reward of self-government, and political leaders could scarcely deny this in the heady years after Independence.

An early warning of the difficulties which might arise was given in a United Nations report published in 1964 on the prospects for the

Zambian economy. It pointed out that substantial wage increases would narrow the options of economic planning open to the Government:

> There is no question of the country being able to afford to pay everyone the £22 a month claimed by some union officials as a basic living wage; desirable though this would be in itself, it would wreck the economy and lead eventually to far lower living standards. There is really a choice for Zambia: in the next 5 years it can have big increases in wages or big increases in employment, *not both*.
>
> The dilemma is in fact even more serious than this. For if wage increases were substantial the Government would be forced to slow down the programme of development; it would be compelled, for example, to postpone the day when all Zambian children would have at least some schooling.[1]

As the report mentioned elsewhere, big wage increases were not in themselves disastrous to the country, and they would bring prosperity to certain sections of the community; but they represented an allocation of resources which could otherwise be used for basic development needs.

The reasons for the Government's damaging indecision could be found on the Copperbelt. Mine-workers hoped that Independence would bring an end to many of their grievances, including their long fight for higher pay. Unemployment was high, and men out of work also had a claim to social justice. Both discontented employees and the unemployed posed a political threat. In 1963, when the first African Government faced disturbances and widespread unrest on the Copperbelt, unemployment was an important contributory factor. Between 30,000 and 50,000 men were thought to be jobless, compared with a work force of about 91,000 in the Copperbelt towns.[2]

African mine-workers were a demanding section of the urban population. Unfortunately, their expectations were not fulfilled by the changes which took place in the mining industry at Independence. White workers, on whom the companies depended for skilled and technical jobs, had to accept that their positions were no longer permanent and would in due course be 'Zambianized'. The Mine Workers' Union was still a well organized and militant body, and

[1] *Report of the UN/ECA/FAO Economic Survey Mission on the Economic Development of Zambia* (Ndola, 1964), pp. 32–3.

[2] *Report of the Commission of Inquiry into the Unrest on the Copperbelt, July–August, 1963* (Lusaka, 1963), p. 5.

the companies' interest in avoiding the embarrassment of a white workers' strike at the time political power changed hands gave the union a useful bargaining position. By comparison the badly-organized African union may well have appeared less powerful or even less important to company officials. On the eve of Independence, in a serious misjudgement, they decided to base their plans for Zambianization on a dual wage scale of separate rates for Africans and Europeans, abandoning the principle of equal pay which had been conceded in 1960.

This decision was naturally unpopular with African workers, but at the time the companies thought it was justified because most white miners could no longer look forward to a long-term career in the country, and required compensation related to world market pressures rather than local ones to induce them to stay for the transition period. By 1966 the annual turnover rate for expatriates rose for a short period to $42\frac{1}{2}$ per cent, lending substance to the companies' view.[1] A similar problem in the Civil Service had been handled in a different manner. The Hadow Commission appointed in October 1963 had recommended that a common basic salary scale should be adopted for all civil servants. Expatriates would be given additional allowances as part of their contract terms. The mining companies rejected this solution partly because they feared that to place local and expatriate salaries on the same basic scale would invite pressure for all-round wage increases when circumstances only justified a rise for one or other section of the labour force.[2] Their decision to reject the Hadow formula may have been unwise, but at the time mine officials seemed to feel that the retention of a dual wage scale gave them more flexibility to deal with the European workers' representatives, who were temporarily capable of causing more trouble than the African unions.

The transition from Federation to African Independence made new arrangements with the Mine Workers' Union necessary: the traditional barriers to African advancement—the 'closed shop', job demarcation, and the rate for the job—all had to go, preferably without a strike among key workers at a politically delicate moment. Talks began in June 1963, and in February 1964 agreement was reached on these points in return for the transfer of all members of the Mine Workers' Union to staff status, with greatly increased benefits. The

[1] *Brown Commission Report*, p. 35.
[2] Ibid., pp. 15–16.

union then changed its name to the Mine Workers' Society (M.W.S.). A second round of negotiations which opened in August 1964 dismantled the guarantees of employment given in the past to European workers as a basic part of the various advancement settlements. Agreement was reached on this in October 1964 in return for compensation for displacement. Further difficulties over the terms led to an increase in expatriate allowances the following year.

The companies linked African wage negotiations at Independence to plans for a progressive new manning structure in the industry which would enable many more men to take over semi-skilled work. The separate wage scale envisaged for African workers was a reversal of the principle which had been established in the 1960 advancement agreement, when the wages of the most senior Africans were related to those of European workers, with those who reached 'Schedule A' receiving full European rates. The new local wage scales were based on an analysis of the job content of these senior positions, which were then regraded in relation to existing lower-level African jobs and assigned a lower wage than before. Africans already receiving wages based entirely or partly on European rates were given compensation. Only a small number of men, 105 in all, were affected but the effect on general morale was considerable.[1]

The representatives of the African Mineworkers' Union accepted the new manning structure and local wage scales in return for a general wage increase, at a time when their own position was insecure. The union's leadership had been challenged by Ditton Mwiinga, General Secretary of the Mines African Staff Association since 1959, who had ambitions to establish one politically active African labour organization for the whole mining industry. He induced the Association to change its name to the United Mineworkers' Union, adopt a strike clause and widen its membership rules, causing the companies to withdraw their recognition. In October 1963 Mwiinga began a campaign to persuade A.M.U. members to cancel their union subscription orders. By the end of June 1964 he had secured more than two thousand cancellations, mainly at the Rhokana and Roan Antelope mines.[2] One consequence of the bitter struggle for support was the willingness of A.M.U. leaders to reduce

[1] *Brown Commission Report*, pp. 21–2.

[2] C.I.S.B. 100.47, vol. viii: N. R. K. Davis to the General Managers, 30 Aug. 1963, and same to same, 4 Mar. 1964; vol. ix: Chamber of Mines to RST and Anglo American Corporation, Salisbury, 22 July 1964. See also Bates, *Unions, Parties and Political Development*, pp. 146–53.

their demands sharply during the important negotiations over wages and the new manning structure, in order to reach a quick settlement and have results of some sort to show their members. In talks with the companies between February and June 1964 the union accepted the terms for manning and local wage scales, while reducing its demand for a general wage increase from 4s. 6d. a shift to 3s. 1d., 2s. 11d., 2s. 8d., 2s., 1s. 6d., and finally to 1s. 3d., which the companies agreed to pay. The struggle with the rival United Mineworkers' Union lasted until the end of the year. In January 1965 the U.M.U. changed its name to the Mines Local Staff Association and as part of its recognition agreement accepted the local wage scales.[1]

The mining companies were later criticized for negotiating these far-reaching changes in the context of wage and recognition agreements when the leadership of the A.M.U. and the new Staff Association was under extreme pressure.[2] The companies were hardly responsible for the internal problems of the two bodies, and were under some pressure themselves to make arrangements for Zambianization as quickly as possible, but in these circumstances the union leaders did not have the full support of their members, while the companies acted ahead of the development of government policy.

A crisis broke in 1965 over a dispute concerning new rates for senior jobs represented by the union, which had changed its name to the Zambia Mineworkers' Union (Z.M.U.) at the beginning of the year. During the negotiations the union asked for a revision of the 1964 agreement on the local wage scales and demanded a substantial general wage increase which seemed to be related to European pay rates. The union was apparently having second thoughts about the separate wage scale it had accepted the year before. Sporadic talks continued into 1966 when, in circumstances bearing some similarity to the signing of the 1964 agreement, the union's leaders hastily signed an agreement for wage increases averaging 8 to 9 per cent to bolster their position in union elections. Soon after they were re-elected they discovered that the settlement was unacceptable to their members. A spontaneous strike began at Nchanga on 21 March and quickly spread to the other mines. By 4 April the whole industry was affected, with 23,000 men out of a black labour force of 42,000 on strike. A Commission of Inquiry under the chairmanship of Roland Brown, Attorney-General of Tanzania, was appointed by President Kaunda the following day.

[1] *Brown Commission Report*, pp. 25–7.   [2] Ibid., p. 26.

The Brown Commission found that the companies' decision to revert to separate wage scales at Independence had been a serious psychological error. Independence was expected to bring rewards, not regression, and the common wage scale had been an important symbol of progress for African workers, although few of them had reached its higher levels. Its existence was also a support to the general urge for all-round wage increases, which still motivated a large section of the labour force. If the companies were aware of the advantages of separate scales in wage negotiations, their African workers appreciated the disadvantages it brought to their position.

The Commission recommended the adoption of the Hadow principle of a common wage scale plus expatriate allowances. As the basis for the new unified wage scale it suggested raising all local wage rates by about 22 per cent, an arbitrary amount chosen after examination of the African and expatriate rates for shift bosses, which were £110 and £181. 16s. 0d. respectively. The companies granted the wage increase, but because of problems in grading expatriate allowances to compensate for reduced wages the unified wage scale was not incorporated into expatriate contracts until January 1970, when it was applied to new employees, but not to existing ones.

The Commission's wage recommendations were by no means extravagant, compared with settlements that have been won by trade unions in more developed countries. Although the increase for senior Zambian workers was quite substantial—shift bosses earning £110 a month received an additional £23. 18s. 8d.—the majority of the workers were on much lower scales. For those near the mines' minimum monthly wage rate of £22. 7s. 6d. the 22 per cent increase involved a less dramatic sum.[1] However, the effect of the Brown Commission's report was not confined to the mining industry, in which the £22. 7s. 6d. minimum wage compared favourably with the country's statutory minimum wage of £10. 8s. 0d.[2] The mineworkers' success set an example for others, and within eight months about 125,000 workers in various industries had secured wage increases. In many cases the increases for the lowest-paid workers were 22 per cent or more above previous rates.[3]

The Brown Commission stressed that it did not challenge the earlier United Nations report's recommendation on wage restraint, but that

---

[1] *Brown Commission Report*, pp. 45–6.   [2] Ibid., p. 33.
[3] J. B. Knight, 'Wages and Zambia's Economic Development' in *Constraints on Zambia's Economic Development*, ed. C. Elliot (Nairobi, 1971), pp. 101–2.

it had had to weigh this against the need to restore industrial peace in the country's most important industry. The Commissioners felt that there was now an urgent need for the Government to guide the movement of wages in the mining industry and the rest of the country with an official wages, incomes and profits policy.

A measure of wage restraint will not be achieved by economists writing about it in their reports; still less because it is enthusiastically espoused by the mining companies as their own policy. In some respects what is good for the mining companies may be good for Zambia, but the workers in the industry are not likely to accept this simply because their employers say so.[1]

The Government had supported the mine-workers' demands for greatly increased wages at the Brown Commission's hearings. In fact Aaron Milner, a Minister of State and Deputy National Chairman of the United National Independence Party, gave evidence on the Party's behalf that the minimum monthly wage in the mining industry should be £35 instead of £22. 7s. 6d. He was confident that the Government could cope with economic problems which might arise from the increase, including inflationary pressures and a ripple effect on wages in other industries, and suggested counteracting it with a compulsory savings scheme. According to Milner the dual wage structure made a Zambian 'feel that he is a second rate citizen, makes him feel that he is still not independent, he is still not governing himself and I think this is the source of all the problems'.[2]

The Government was slow to take up the challenge of formulating a wages policy, for the 1966 wage increases could be considered as politically necessary to demonstrate the reality of Independence. Their effect in narrowing economic choices was not fully appreciated until three years later, when the progress of the First National Plan running from 1966 to 1970 was assessed. By 1969 it was plain that little improvement had been achieved in the rural sector, which supported four-fifths of the population.

At this time the prospect of another round of sharp general wage increases arose. In 1969 skilled mine employees demanded big wage rises to close the gap with expatriate workers; the Zambian Mine-workers' Union wanted to reduce the gap between low-paid workers and skilled men; the railwaymen's union claimed a 30 per cent increase for lower grades, justifying it by a comparison with mine-

[1] *Brown Commission Report*, p. 48.
[2] C.I.S.B., Evidence to the Brown Commission, Aaron Milner, 14 June 1966.

workers' pay; and lower-paid Government workers also prepared a wage claim.

This situation at last forced the Government to give urgent attention to a wages policy. In a speech to U.N.I.P.'s National Council on 11 August 1969 President Kaunda coupled a surprise announcement that the State would take a 51 per cent shareholding in the copper-mines with a tough line on wage increases, including a temporary wage freeze and a ban on strikes as a bargaining weapon. The wage freeze was justified by the need to curb inflation, halt price increases in the rural areas, and create more jobs in the towns. The real tensions caused by Zambia's industrial development, according to the President, were not so much between employers and labour as between urban and rural life. Since the State had taken a majority holding in the country's biggest enterprises, including the mines, a system of industrial relations with unions on one side and employers on the other was, 'to say the least, absurd . . . [The State] holds industrial investments, not for its own good, not merely for the good of those directly employed in the State enterprises, but for the benefit of Zambians everywhere. Thus, for a union to push a claim against the State is to push a claim against the people.'[1]

A few months after these measures were announced the Government received a report it had requested from the International Labour Office on incomes, prices, and wages in Zambia. The report, prepared by Professor H. A. Turner of Cambridge University, underlined the President's comments about the growing rift between urban and rural society. Between 1963 and 1968, when the price index for lower incomes rose by 46 per cent, average money wages increased by 143 per cent; but the total increase in the incomes of peasant farmers between 1964 and 1968 was possibly as little as 3 per cent.[2] Professor Turner calculated that the average earnings of a peasant farmer in subsistence production and cash were worth about Kwacha 145 in 1968, compared with Kwacha 1,300 for an African mine-worker and Kwacha 640 for an African wage-earner outside the mines.[3]

The report's conclusions on the productivity of the urban labour

[1] *Africa Contemporary Record 1969–70*, eds. C. Legum and J. Drysdale (Exeter, 1970), p. B238.

[2] H. A. Turner, *Report to the Government of Zambia on Incomes, Wages and Prices in Zambia: Policy and Machinery* (International Labour Office, Geneva, 1969), pp. 10–11.

[3] *Turner Report*, p. 11. One Kwacha, the currency unit adopted in Jan. 1968, was worth 11*s*. 8*d*.

force since Independence were also disconcerting. If productivity had risen in proportion to wage increases, some justification could be made for current wage trends. But labour efficiency had fallen by about 20 per cent in 1965–6, and had not yet recovered to former levels: 'The reason for this fall in labour efficiency seems to be basically that the colonial system of labour discipline has broken down and nothing has yet developed in its place.'[1]

The Turner report found a dangerous pattern of rising wages, falling output, soaring labour costs and a declining level of employment. The economy had withstood these strains because of the continued prosperity of the copper industry, which had enjoyed exceptionally high prices for part of the post-Independence period; but this prosperity rested on volatile world market trends.[2] Rising costs had also placed Zambia in an unfavourable position to apply for membership of the East African Common Market. According to President Kaunda, by 1967 average wages in Zambia were 85 per cent more than wages in Tanzania, and 45 per cent above those in Kenya.

By the end of the year the Government had prepared the outline of a new interim policy on prices and wages to meet immediate needs until the next National Development Plan was initiated in 1972. Underlying the new policy was a change of emphasis from urban to rural development. Dr. Kaunda justified this by referring to the country's adherence to 'humanism' and to the distribution of benefits for the greatest good of all citizens. In the past, urban workers had enjoyed more than their fair share of privileges, while the rural population was neglected.

On 12 December 1969 President Kaunda announced details of the new approach to productivity, prices, wages, and industrial relations at the Second National Convention in Kitwe.[3] Wages would be controlled through a new Industrial Court, to which trade disputes could be referred by the Minister of Labour. Wage agreements would have to be registered with the Ministry of Labour and would require its approval before taking effect. They could be referred to the Industrial Court for revision. The Court's awards, which would be binding on all of the parties concerned, would be kept within guide-lines which

---

[1] *Turner Report*, p. 18. See also Bates, *Unions*, pp. 58–61.
[2] The danger was brought home by a sharp drop in copper prices in 1970.
[3] Dr. Kaunda's Address at the opening of the Second National Convention, Kitwe, 12 Dec. 1969.

the Government would set with the assistance of a new Productivity, Wages and Prices Council.

These proposed measures promised to be the strongest effort yet made to control industrial relations and trade-union activities in Zambia. The President tried to sweeten the pill by placing his new policy within the context of the officially accepted doctrine of 'humanism', and of the new situation created by the State's recent entry into industry as a majority share-holder in various enterprises, including the copper-mines. He pointed out that the State had a duty to protect the interests of both workers and peasants, and to cultivate workers' co-operation by giving them a more important role in industry, both in ownership and management functions. This would be done through workers' representatives on Boards of Directors, and through Works Councils which would participate in management decisions. Workers were urged to bring a new attitude to industrial relations, to accept the necessary restrictions on traditional trade-union rights, and to 'remember that in all wage-bargaining there is a third party, the community, whose interests are paramount'.

Despite the new measures and the accompanying appeal to idealism and high principles it will be difficult to secure the co-operation of urban workers. The dilemma facing the Government has echoes of the situation in the 1930s, when colonial authorities first tried to encourage the spread of money earned at industrial centres into deprived rural areas. This time the Government can call on an organized national political party with a powerful propaganda machine. It has the wherewithal to pay for expert economic advice. But the problem of balancing urban and rural interests remains, and even a small redistribution of the resources now concentrated in the towns will demand an enormous effort.

Conclusion

IN some respects the economic problems now facing the Zambian Government have remained unchanged since the colonial period. African leaders have had to accept a view held by their colonial predecessors, which caused great controversy and unrest, that it is desirable to hold back urban wage levels to reduce unemployment and encourage development in the poverty-stricken rural areas where the majority of the people live. The labour history of the Copperbelt developed around this theory, which was a justification for the dual wage system. It was supported not only by the mining companies and the Government, but by many independent authorities: the Dalgleish Commission in 1948, the Guillebaud wage tribunal in 1953, and the Forster Commission in 1954, all found separate wage scales for Africans and Europeans suitable to the country's needs. Theories of development were bolstered by reality. Widespread poverty and unemployment provided a pool of workers willing to take jobs at rates lower than those paid to whites.

In the face of many difficulties Copperbelt mine-workers broke the low-wage pattern, so that the present problem, unlike that of the colonial period, is the control of high wages. Given the impetus of the dual wage structure and the nature of the Zambian people's struggle for Independence, this development was inevitable. If the white field of employment had been clearly confined to managerial and supervisory functions and to certain skilled operations, wage differentials might have been accepted. Instead, the different pay rates given to each race for similar work in 'ragged edge' jobs, and the barriers to Africans acquiring skills, produced intolerable pressures. Although dual wage scales could be justified in conventional economic terms, they were irrevocably linked to the colonial system, with its overtones of racialism and political bias. An African population moving towards independence could not accept their continuance.

The hostility of urban workers to the system was encouraged by the Colonial Office's miscalculation in thinking it possible to build up a trade-union movement, supposedly on a British pattern, in which workers of different colour would accept different wages for similar work. Yet although the authorities did not intend to encourage conflict, the introduction of industrial relations machinery responsive to the local pressures on the Copperbelt provided a substitute for a political solution to the advancement problem. Its importance in providing an outlet for African aspirations can hardly be over-estimated. In South Africa the industrial relations system had become a bulwark protecting the rights of white trade-unionists. In Northern Rhodesia its flexible and permissive character gave African workers a powerful voice in industrial affairs.

If this machinery was valuable as an outlet for discontent among African labour, it also had a major weakness in its peculiar place in the political structure of the territory. African labour leaders' complete control of the strike weapon soon outweighed their less secure grasp of other aspects of trade-union organization, and their activities contrasted strangely with the limited participation of Africans in the central political system. The contrast was particularly marked in view of the fact that one of the industries in which the growth of trade-unionism was encouraged provided the territory's main source of revenue.

Colonial Office and Government officials felt that the system could work if African trade-unionists stayed aloof from politics. This was a difficult condition to impose. The proper political interests of a trade union were not clearly defined. The unacceptability of African nationalism to the European political community placed African trade-unionists at a disadvantage in pursuing any form of affiliation with it. They were placed at a further disadvantage because the interests of African trade unionism and African nationalism over-lapped, and the European population was unable to distinguish clearly between them. The situation which led to the proclamation of a State of Emergency in 1956 was almost inevitable: the introduction of African trade-unionism in circumstances where the Government supported low African wage rates, competition with European workers was discouraged, and African political activity had few outlets, might even be thought to indicate a certain lack of co-ordination in Colonial Office policy.

The Colonial Office was unable to find a direct political solution to the problem presented by the conflict of interests between black and white workers. Indeed, such a solution seemed to be ruled out by its methods of operation. Labour policy in Northern Rhodesia reflected the dilemmas of constitutional development in territories with large settler communities. The Colonial Office stood firmly by the principle

of segregation in Central African political development, and expected
it to last for many generations. Indirect Rule encouraged a com-
pulsive dualism in political arrangements. Officials were lulled into
thinking that theirs was the deciding power which held the balance
between the interests of the African community and the settlers. The
convenience of this arrangement delayed consideration of further
political goals, as Sir Cecil Bottomley, Assistant Under-Secretary of
State at the Colonial Office, noted in 1934.

> Since the date of Mr. Churchill's pronouncement in 1922 (in regard to
> Kenya) in favour of 'equal rights for all civilized men' down to the Report
> of the Joint Select Committee in 1931, there has been a constantly growing
> reluctance to form any opinion as to the ultimate destiny of black and
> white in East Africa, and I very much doubt whether we should allow the
> special difficulties of Southern Rhodesia to force us into an enunciation of
> any theory while we retain the practical safeguard of the official majority in
> the parts of Africa with which we deal.[1]

After the Second World War constitutional changes gave the
European electorate a greater share in the direction of policy. In
particular the convention accepted in 1948 by which the unofficial
members of Northern Rhodesia's Executive Council could impose
their views on the official majority was a striking advance. An expert
on constitutional law considered that the arrangements 'probably
gave more power to the unofficials than in any other territory under
Colonial Office rule'.[2]

The increased participation of the European community in political
affairs had an obvious bearing on the ability of the Colonial Office
and the officials of the Northern Rhodesian Government to shape
policy for the territory. In the main issues which faced the Government in the Copperbelt—the stabilization of African labour, the
colour bar in industry, and the question of equal pay for Europeans
and Africans—the options open to the Government were limited by
political considerations. The colour bar could not easily be removed
by legislation when the elected members in the Legislative and
Executive Councils were sympathetic to the European workers'
position.

Under such circumstances progress in social policy could not
follow the lines laid down in Britain by members of the Conservative
and Labour parties during the war. The Conservative Secretary of

[1] C.O. 795/72/25659: Minute by Sir W. Cecil Bottomley, 18 Sept. 1934.
[2] H. V. Wiseman, *The Cabinet in the Commonwealth* (London, 1958), p. 92.

State had told the House of Commons in 1941 that 'the Colonial Office and the Government do not stand for the colour bar either in this country or in any of the Colonies'.[1] The Labour Party announced that it was 'absolutely opposed to the colour bar operating in political or economic spheres'.[2] But the Colonial Office's approval of the successive political advances of the European population minimized its ability to put these principles into action.

The Colonial Office and the Northern Rhodesian Government forced the mining companies to tackle controversial issues which might properly have been made matters of public policy. It was by no means unusual for private enterprise to be used to solve imperial difficulties in Africa, at high or low levels: Northern Rhodesia itself had come under British protection in such a case, through the activities of the British South Africa Company at a time when official intervention was impossible. The Northern Rhodesian Government evaded the political pressures which hampered its own freedom of action by passing the problem of African advancement in industry to the most important employers in the country. But the mining companies were subject to similar pressures from their white employees, and were equally restricted in the opportunities for action open to them. They inevitably felt that the job of finding a solution belonged to the Government. There was some justification for their attitude in view of the official regulation of the industry during the Second World War, and of the lesser controls which lasted until 1953.

The companies were responsible for their conduct of operations to their shareholders abroad, to the Government of Northern Rhodesia and to the British Government, especially during the Second World War and the period following it. The managements had a strong sense of responsibility towards their employees, black and white, but in view of the conflicting claims of different interests—commercial, national, strategic, and industrial—it is not surprising that their labour policies sometimes seemed indecisive. The companies were never able to pursue these policies as local issues isolated from wider considerations. Changes in policy which carried the risk of labour unrest involved not only the possibility of damaging profits, but of reducing national revenues from taxation of the industry and, for a long time, of depriving the United Kingdom of strategic supplies.

[1] *Hansard*, 5th series, vol. 369, 12 Mar. 1941, 1260.
[2] *The Colonies: The Labour Party's Post-War Policy* (1943), p. 7, cited in J. W. Davidson, *The Northern Rhodesian Legislative Council*, p. 125, f.n. 3.

These limitations were important, but the companies were not always forced to compromise to avoid labour unrest. They held firm convictions about the rights and duties of management, which were reflected in their unwillingness to send to arbitration issues other than those involving wage claims. In pursuing their advancement plans they ran the risk of provoking a European strike in 1955, and forceful policies led to African strikes in 1955, 1956, and 1962. Company officials may have felt on some of these occasions that it was not unfair to involve the Government in what they considered to be issues of national importance.

Under existing circumstances in Central Africa it was difficult for the mining companies to break out of the conventional economic system, yet to some extent they did so with their advancement plans. This achievement deserves to be weighed against the imperfections of their efforts. Unlike employers in less-organized industries, they were subject to pressures which were not yet general in the country. Their African employees expressed forceful opposition to inequality before workers in other forms of employment, in protests which began earlier than political expressions of nationalism. The mine managements were sensitive to the current, and although they were restricted by the powerful position of their European workers, they moved slowly away from the traditional arrangements in Central Africa by widening the scope of employment for Africans and offering pay rates higher than elsewhere.

After their long conflict with the African union over wages, they may appreciate the irony of the fact that the Zambian Government has now, in its own interests, issued warnings which they gave many years ago in theirs: that the never-ending upward spiral of Copperbelt wages presents difficult problems for the general development of the country's predominantly rural economy. African advancement has in the end proved easier to deal with than the related question of wage levels, to which there is no satisfactory answer.

Appendix A

'Ragged edge' jobs performed by Africans in 1948 or earlier, at one or more of the mines, but carried out by Europeans at other mines.[1]

1. Main level lashing (clearing mined ore underground).
2. Grizzley operating and tramming (blasting mined rock into pieces small enough to fall through a safety grill underground to a lower level, from which it was trammed by locomotive to a collection point).
3. Underground storeman.
4. Fuse capping.
5. Tripper operating (at the discharge point from a conveyer belt into collection bins).
6. Routine cleaning up.
7. Routine slag dumping.
8. Operating a reverberatory furnace.
9. Casting and operating holding furnaces (casting copper cakes).
10. Rehandling of 'reverts' (return of scrap from various machines to the smelter).
11. Cutting steel scrap (cutting scrap into pieces small enough for the furnace).
12. Weighing, and weighbridge attendants (weighing copper at the smelter and at the weighbridge before transport to the railway).
13. Inspecting blister copper.
14. Crane chasing in the convertor aisle (signalling directions to the crane driver).
15. Bricklaying (simple work of all types).
16. Carpentry, simple work only.
17. Operating a machine saw.
18. Operating a screw machine.
19. Operating a crosscut timber-saw.
20. Simple low-pressure pipe fitting, surface and underground.
21. Driving winding engines, when the cage had a rope speed of less than 500 ft. per minute and carried a maximum of five people.
22. Driving overhead cranes, except in the smelter convertor aisle.
23. Driving electric and diesel locomotives.
24. Shunting and coupling.
25. Stripping operations at the refinery.
26. Assistant ganger to European plate-layers, and laying light tracks without supervision.
27. Boiler attendants (small boilers, up to 100 lb. pressures).

[1] *Report of the Commission Appointed to Enquire into the Advancement of Africans in Industry* (Lusaka, 1948), pp. 9–15. (*Dalgleish Commission Report.*)

The Commission recommended that main level lashing, grizzley operating and tramming should be done under European supervision, while routine cleaning up and slag dumping, the operation of reverberatory furnaces and the rehandling of 'reverts' could be done with Africans in charge.

Appendix B

Advancement jobs for Africans recommended by the Dalgleish Commission, 1948:[1]

1. Sub-level lashing (cleaning out excavated rock underground).
2. Stope scraping and drift scraping (removal of ore from the mining areas).
3. Attending endless rope haulages.
4. Crusher operating in the concentrator department (operating machinery to break down the ore into fine pieces).
5. Simple routine repair work on concentrator pumps.
6. Flux handling and concentrator handling.
7. Anode casting.
8. Operating take-off cranes for lifting the anodes.
9. Assistants to European inspectors in the tank house.
10. Operating drilling machines (simple work) in the engineering department.
11. Operating small air compressors.

Jobs which could be taken over after suitable advanced training:

1. Skipmen at shaft loading boxes.
2. Cage tenders and banksmen (workers on the cages and cage-stops underground).
3. Pipe fitting, more advanced work.
4. Timbering, more advanced work (on timber supports in underground workings).
5. Supervizing sanitation gangs.
6. Track-laying (but not major work).
7. Assistant at the concentrator ball mill (process of crushing the ore).
8. Handyman's work in the mine townships.
9. Driving steam locomotives.
10. Drilling and rock-breaking in small drives (tunnels along the ore body).
11. Riveter's work, after apprenticeship.
12. Jack hammer repairs.
13. Electrical work (wiring).
14. Fitting ventilation pipes.
15. Rock drill repairs, after apprenticeship.
16. Sample preparation in the concentrator.

[1] *Dalgleish Commission Report* (1948), pp. 39–41.

Appendix C

1954

5 Feb.–24 July Four-party talks on African advancement.

Mar. M.A.S.A. registered as a trade union, under Government regulations.

1–13 Sept. Forster Board of Inquiry.

1955

Jan.–Mar. Nine week Copperbelt African strike (10s. 8d. per shift wage demand).

22 Mar. African Personnel Managers met African Mineworkers' Union to discuss amendment of Recognition Agreement and subsequent recognition of Mines African Staff Association.

22 Mar. Chamber of Mines informed M.A.S.A. that the companies were now prepared to consider recognition of the Association.

Apr. African Mineworkers' Union presented new wage demand (6s. 8d. per shift plus other benefits, which totalled 10s. 8d. per shift).

13 Apr. M.A.S.A. requested introduction of monthly pay for African staff.

12 May Companies gave six months' notice of termination of 1949 Agreement with the African Mineworkers' Union.

26 May Chamber informed African Union of introduction of monthly pay on an optional basis for certain grades of workers, as from 1 June 1955.

5 July Agreement reached between companies and the African union on the subsidiary benefits claimed with the April wage demand, resulting in a general wage increase. The wage demand itself went to arbitration.

27 Sept. African advancement agreement signed between the companies and the European Mine Workers' Union, which

[1] Derived from Chronological List of Main Events, submitted by the mining companies to the Branigan Commission, 1956. (C.I.S.B., 100.20.20.)

surrendered the representation of twenty-four categories of work.

11 Oct.	African Union signed revized agreement surrendering representation of staff categories of work.
9 Nov.	Schedule of advancement jobs sent by the Chamber of Mines to the African Union and to M.A.S.A.
3 Dec.	M.A.S.A. formally recognized by the companies.

1956

23–4 May	Token strike at Nchanga about shortage of advancement jobs for union members.
18 June	Strike at Nkana because of alleged management pressure on boss boys to accept the monthly pay option.
22–5 June	Sympathy strikes at Roan, Mufulira, and Nchanga.
21 June	Companies informed of union's intention to hold sympathy strikes at other mines. Companies gave notice to terminate the monthly pay option and made monthly pay compulsory for staff employees from 1 July.
26–7 June	Strike at Nchanga as a protest against wearing of legguards by African workers underground.
2–7 July	Strike by some of the Nkana boss boys, over withdrawal of monthly pay option.
3–5 July	Strike at Mufulira, over withdrawal of monthly pay option.
30 July–23 Aug.	The 'rolling strikes' at Bancroft, Roan Antelope, Rhokana, Broken Hill, Mufulira, Chibuluma, and Nchanga mines.
1 Aug.	Companies declared a dispute and asked for the appointment of a Board of Inquiry.
11 Aug.	Government announced the appointment of a Commission of Inquiry.
28 Aug.	Ban on overtime by the African Union.
1–5 Sept.	Protest strike at Roan Antelope mine.
3 Sept.	Ban by the African Union on Sunday work, on wearing protective leggings, and on posting identity discs when going underground.
11 Sept.	Acting Governor proclaimed a State of Emergency in the Western Province.

Appendix D

Average yearly copper price (London Metal Exchange); Northern Rhodesian copper production in long tons (2,240 lb. per ton); gross value of copper sales; and average numbers of Africans and Europeans employed in the industry.

	L.M.E. average yearly price (electrolytic)	1,000 long tons copper (electrolytic and blister)	Gross value copper sales £m.	African employees	European employees
1932	26	68		5,572	893
1933	32	104		7,190	1,026
1934	39	138		13,808	1,729
1935	40	144		13,224	1,758
1936	44	142		11,957	1,575
1937	61	148		17,926	(2,037)
1938	46	213	8·9	20,358	(2,296)
1939	51	212	9·5	20,924	2,609
1940	64	263	12·7	24,382	2,971
1941	62	228	10·5	27,270	3,098
1942	62	247	11·3	30,425	3,306
1943	62	251	11·6	32,805	3,566
1944	62	221	10·3	30,470	3,445
1945	62	194	11·2	28,304	3,272
1946	77	183	12·3	27,832	3,426
1947	131	192	20·4	29,166	3,681
1948	134	213	25·8	30,932	3,958
1949	133	259	31·2	33,061	4,293
1950	179	277	43·4	34,814	4,604
1951	221	309	62·2	35,432	5,184
1952	260	313	72·4	36,668	5,504
1953	256	363	90·0	36,147	5,879
1954	249	378	91·2	37,193	6,294
1955	352	343	114·2	35,190	6,566
1956	329	383	116·2	37,533	7,065
1957	219	417	89·4	38,763	7,304
1958	198	375	75·3	32,824	6,739
1959	238	417	115·4	35,014	7,259
1960	246	559	132·6	36,806	7,528
1961	230	560	119·4	39,036	7,641

	L.M.E. average yearly price (electrolytic)	1,000 long tons copper (electrolytic and blister)	Gross value copper sales £m.	African employees	European employees
1962	234	539	119·4	37,681	7,780
1963	234	568	127·8	36,948	7,676
1964	352	633	164·3	38,097	7,455

Sources: Column 1—L. H. Gann, *A History of Northern Rhodesia*, p. 329 (1932–40); *The Economist* (1941–5); *Northern Rhodesia Chamber of Mines Year Book 1956*, p. 60 and *Copperbelt of Zambia Mining Industry Year Book 1964*, p. 44 (1945–64).

Column 2—W. J. Barber, *The Economy of British Central Africa*, p. 127 (1932–58); *Mines Department Reports*, 1959–64.

Column 3—*Northern Rhodesia Economic and Statistical Bulletins*, 1939–54; *Northern Rhodesia Chamber of Mines Year Books*, 1956–63; *Copperbelt of Zambia Mining Industry Year Book*, 1964. Figures for the value of copper exports in S. H. Frankel, *Capital Investment in Africa* (p. 254) give an indication of the rate of expansion in the 1930s. The value of exports in 1932, a year after production began, was over £2 million, and had risen to almost £4 million in 1936.

Columns 4 and 5—Paper prepared by the Chamber of Mines for submission to the Forster Board of Enquiry, 6 September 1954 (1932–40); *Branigan Commission Report*, 1956, p. 5 (1941–55); *Brown Commission Report*, 1966, p. 160 (1956–64). Figures for European employees in 1936 and 1937 are estimates.

Bibliography

MANUSCRIPT SOURCES

(1) *Library of the Copper Industry Service Bureau, Kitwe* (formerly the Chamber of Mines of Northern Rhodesia)

African advancement, general files (100.46).

African Mineworkers' Union, general files (100.20).

Minutes of meetings between the African Mineworkers' Union and the Executive Committee of the Chamber of Mines, and between the Union and the African Personnel Managers' Committee (100.20.1).

African Mineworkers' Union, local disputes (100.20.4).

African Copperbelt Strikes, 1952–5 (100.20.5).

Forster and Dalgleish Commissions (100.15, vol. i).

African advancement, 1948–54 (100.15, vol. ii).

Guillebaud Arbitration, 1952–3 (100.20.9).

Minutes of meetings of the Executive Committee of the Chamber of Mines, 1955 (10.27, vol. x).

Minutes of meetings of the African Personnel Managers' Committee, 1952–4 (40.4, vol. i).

African Mineworkers' Union 6s. 8d. wage demand, 1955 (100.20.11).

1956 unrest and the Branigan Commission (100.20.20).

Branigan Commission of Inquiry, working papers for companies' statement of case (100.20.20.B6).

Morison Commission of Inquiry, working papers for companies' statement of case (100.20.14B).

Detentions after the 1956 strike (100.20.25).

Mines African Staff Association (100.47).

African labour, politics, 1952–61 (100.41).

African labour, urbanisation and stabilisation, 1953–64 (100.51).

African Trade Union Congress, 1960–4 (100.60).

Trade Unions and Trade Disputes Ordinance (70.7).

Compulsory Arbitration (70.29).

Complete copies of the companies' statement of case, in unnumbered files, are held for the following commissions, boards, and tribunals:

> Guillebaud Arbitration Tribunal, 1953.
> Forster Board of Inquiry, 1954.
> Branigan Commission of Inquiry, 1956.
> Harragin Arbitration Tribunal, 1956.
> Honeyman Commission of Inquiry, 1957.
> Hoffman Arbitration Tribunal, 1959.
> Morison Commission of Inquiry, 1962.
> Brown Commission of Inquiry, 1966.

(2) *National Archives of Zambia, Lusaka*

Departmental and Provincial Administration, organisation, 1935–41, SEC/NAT/4.

Provincial Administration, mining area, 1935, SEC/NAT/5.

Re-organisation of Copperbelt staff, 1938–9, SEC/NAT/16.

Native policy, 1939–40, SEC/NAT/92.

New stations in mining areas, 1930–40, SEC/NAT/339.

International Labour Organization convention on recruiting, SEC/LAB/5.

Migrant labour agreement with Tanganyika and Nyasaland, 1938–42, SEC/LAB/9.

Migrant labour agreement with Southern Rhodesia, 1939–41, SEC/LAB/11.

Investigation of labour conditions, by province, 1936–7, SEC/LAB/17–22.

Stabilisation of native labour, SEC/LAB/27.

Native Industrial Labour Advisory Board, 1935–47, SEC/LAB/33–4.

Proposed Labour Department, 1929–39, SEC/LAB/35.

Labour Department organisation, 1939–41, SEC/LAB/36.

Labour Commissioner's reports, 1941–7, SEC/LAB/41–7.

Repatriation of children in industrial areas, 1937–45, SEC/LAB/56.

Labour conditions on mines, 1939, SEC/LAB/68.

African strike on the Copperbelt, 1940, SEC/LAB/78–9.

Report on Copperbelt strike by Secretary for Native Affairs, 1940, SEC/LAB/104.

Tribunal for settlement of wartime trade disputes, SEC/LAB/106–7.

Trade unions, general, 1930–47, SEC/LAB/110.

Trade Unions and Trade Disputes Ordinance, 1938–42, SEC/LAB/111.

Trade union legislation and industrial relations, SEC/LAB/112.

African strike on the Copperbelt, 1940, reports, SEC/LAB/136–9.

African strike at the Zambesi Sawmills, 1943, SEC/LAB/142.

Memorandum by the Anti-Slavery and Aborigines Protection Society, 1941, on the Report of the Copperbelt Commission, SEC/LAB/163.

Dilution of labour, 1941, SEC/LAB/191.

Bledisloe Commission, ZP/2 and SEC/EA/5, 9–14.

Russell Commission, 1935, ZP/10.

Forster Commission, 1940, ZP/12.

(3) *Evidence to Commissions and Boards of Inquiry*

Copies of the evidence given by witnesses before the Russell (1935) and Bledisloe (1938–9) Commissions of Inquiry are deposited at the Commonwealth Office Library, London. The evidence to the Forster Commission (1940) was consulted at the National Archives of Zambia, Lusaka. Verbatim reports of the evidence given before the following Inquiries are held in the library of the Copper Industry Service Bureau, Kitwe:

> Dalgleish Commission of Inquiry, 1948.
>
> Forster Board of Inquiry, 1954.
>
> Branigan Commission of Inquiry, 1956 (incomplete).

Honeyman Commission of Inquiry, 1957.
Morison Commission of Inquiry, 1962.
Brown Commission of Inquiry, 1966.

(4) *Miscellaneous sources*
(*a*) Colonial Office files, Public Record Office.
(*b*) Fabian Colonial Bureau records, and papers of Arthur Creech Jones
    and G. St. J. Orde Browne, in the Colonial Records Project collection,
    Rhodes House, Oxford.
(*c*) Minutes of the Colonial Office Advisory Committee on Education in
    the Colonies, J. Merle Davis Papers, and records of the United Missions
    in the Copperbelt, at the World Council of Churches, Edinburgh House,
    London.
(*d*) Records of the Northern Rhodesia (European) Mine Workers' Union,
    Zambia Expatriate Mineworkers' Association, Kitwe.
(*e*) Records of the Northern Rhodesia Associated Chamber of Commerce,
    National Archives, Lusaka.
(*f*) Philpott Papers. Collected speeches given by members of the Depart-
    ment of Labour, in the possession of R. Philpott, Kitwe.
(*g*) Mulford Papers. Material on the recent history of political development
    in Zambia collected by D. C. Mulford, St. Antony's College, Oxford.
(*h*) Harries Jones Papers. Material on labour history in Zambia collected
    by Peter Harries Jones, Nuffield College, Oxford, and University of
    Swansea.

(5) *Theses*
E. J. BERG, 'Recruitment of a Labour Force in Sub-Saharan Africa'
    (Harvard University Ph.D. thesis 1960).
W. H. FRIEDLAND, 'Institutional Change: A Study of Trade Union
    Development in Tanganyika' (University of California Ph.D. thesis
    1963).
P. GIFFORD, 'The framework for a nation, an economic and social history
    of Northern Rhodesia from 1914 to 1939' (Yale University Ph.D. thesis
    1964).

(6) *Unpublished reports and articles*
AMAX, 'The Corporate Structure of Rhodesian Copperbelt Mining Enter-
    prise', 31 Aug. 1962.
Anglo American Corporation, 'Joint Memorandum on the Companies
    Operating in Northern Rhodesia of the Anglo American Corporation
    and Rhodesian Selection Trust', 11 July 1963.
E. C. BROMWICH, 'African Advancement', 5 Feb. 1962 (RST).
N. S. WALDSTEIN, 'The Struggle for African Advancement Within the
    Copper Industry of Northern Rhodesia' (M.I.T. Center for International
    Studies).

BIBLIOGRAPHY
PRINTED MATERIAL

PRIMARY SOURCES

(1) *Annual series*
Northern Rhodesia Legislative Council Debates.
Annual Reports of the Department of Labour of Northern Rhodesia.
Annual Reports of the Department of Mines of Northern Rhodesia.
Annual Reports by the Accountant-General of Northern Rhodesia.
Northern Rhodesia Chamber of Mines Year Books, Kitwe, 1956–63.

(2) *Official reports*
NORTHERN RHODESIA
Report of the Finance Commission. Livingstone, 1932.
Chairman's Report of Meetings of the Native Industrial Labour Advisory Board held at Ndola on November 7th and 8th and December 16th and 17th, 1935. Lusaka, 1936.
Report of the Sub-Committee of the Native Industrial Labour Advisory Board, Administrative Control of Industrial Population. Lusaka, 1936.
Northern Rhodesian Copper Mines Wages Arbitration July, 1940. (Arbitrator, R. McIlwaine.)
Report of the Commission appointed to inquire into the disturbances in the Copperbelt of Northern Rhodesia. (Chairman, Sir John Forster.) Lusaka 1941.
Statement by the Government of Northern Rhodesia on the recommendations of the report of the Copperbelt Commission, 1940. Lusaka, 1941.
A Report on some aspects of African Living Conditions on the Copper Belt of Northern Rhodesia. A. Lynn Saffery, Lusaka, 1943.
Report on the Development of Secondary Industries in Northern Rhodesia, W. J. Busschau, Lusaka, 1945.
Report of the Commission on the Civil Service of Northern Rhodesia and Nyasaland. Lusaka, 1947.
First, Second and Third Reports of the Advisory Committee on Industrial Development, 1946–48. Lusaka, 1949.
Report of the Commission appointed to enquire into the Advancement of Africans in Industry. (Chairman, A. Dalgleish.) Lusaka, 1948.
Report of the Commission appointed to review the Salary Structure . . . of the Civil Service of Northern Rhodesia. Lusaka, 1952.
Report and Award of the Arbitrator C. W. Guillebaud, January, 1953.
Report of the Board of Inquiry appointed to inquire into the Advancement of Africans in the Copper Mining Industry in Northern Rhodesia. (Chairman, Sir John Forster.) Lusaka, 1954.
Report of the Commission Appointed to Inquire into the Unrest in the Mining Industry in Northern Rhodesia in recent months. (Chairman, Sir Patrick Branigan.) Lusaka, 1956.
Report of the Committee on Trade Testing and Apprenticeship for Africans. Lusaka, 1957.

Report of the Commission appointed to inquire into the Stoppage in the Mining Industry in Northern Rhodesia in July, 1957, and to make Recommendations for the Avoidance and Quick Settlement of Disputes in the Industry. (Chairman, G. G. Honeyman.) Lusaka, 1957.

Report of the Commission Appointed to Inquire into the Mining Industry in Northern Rhodesia. (Chairman, Sir Ronald Morison.) Lusaka, 1962.

Report of the Commission of Inquiry into Unrest on the Copperbelt, July–August, 1963. (Chairman, F. J. Whelan.) Lusaka, 1963.

Preliminary Report of the May/June 1963 Census of Africans in Northern Rhodesia. Lusaka, 1964.

Report of the Commission Appointed to Review the Salaries and Conditions of Service of the Northern Rhodesia Public and Teaching Services . . . Part 1. (Chairman, Gordon Hadow.) Lusaka, 1964.

Report of the Commission of Inquiry into the Mining Industry. (Chairman, Roland Brown.) Lusaka, 1966.

UNITED KINGDOM

Conference of Colonial Governors and Officials. Colonial Office, London, 1930.

Report of the Commission appointed to enquire into the Disturbances in the Copperbelt, Northern Rhodesia, 1935. Cmd. 5009 of 1935.

Report of the Commission Appointed to Enquire into the Financial and Economic Position of Northern Rhodesia. (Chairman, Sir Alan Pim.) Colonial No. 145 of 1938.

Labour Conditions in Northern Rhodesia. Report by Major G. St. J. Orde Browne, O.B.E. Colonial No. 150 of 1938.

Rhodesia–Nyasaland Royal Commission Report. (Chairman, Lord Bledisloe.) Cmd. 5949 of 1939.

Central African Territories: Report of Conference on Closer Association. Cmd. 8233 of 1951.

Central African Territories: Comparative Survey of Native Policy. Cmd. 8235 of 1951.

Conference on the Federation of Southern Rhodesia, Northern Rhodesia and Nyasaland, vol. 2. London, 1953.

MISCELLANEOUS REPORTS

Report of the Committee appointed . . . to enquire into Emigrant Labour, 1935. Zomba, 1936.

Report of Survey of Facilities for Technical Education in the Federation. F. Bray, Salisbury, 1958.

Report of the UN/ECA/FAO Economic Survey Mission on the Economic Development of Zambia. Ndola, 1964.

Report to the Government of Zambia on Incomes, Wages and Prices in Zambia: Policy and Machinery. H. A. Turner, International Labour Office, Geneva, 1969.

SECONDARY SOURCES

(3) *Books*
General History
ALLAN, WILLIAM. *The African Husbandman.* Edinburgh, 1965.
ALLIGHAN, G. *The Welensky Story.* Cape Town, 1962.
ANSTEY, R. *King Leopold's Legacy.* London, 1966.
BARBER, J. *Rhodesia: The Road to Rebellion.* London, 1967.
BULL, THEODORE, ed. *Rhodesian Perspective.* London, 1967.
BUSTIN, E. 'The Congo', in *Five African States,* ed. G. Carter. Ithaca, 1963.
COHEN, SIR ANDREW. *British Policy in Changing Africa.* London, 1959.
DAVIDSON, J. W. *The Northern Rhodesian Legislative Council.* London, 1948.
EPSTEIN, A. L. *The Administration of Justice and the Urban African.* London, 1953.
FRANKLIN, H. *Unholy Wedlock.* London, 1963.
GANN, L. H. *The Birth of a Plural Society: The Development of Northern Rhodesia under the British South Africa Company.* Manchester, 1958.
———. *A History of Northern Rhodesia, Early Days to 1953.* London, 1964.
GELFAND, M. *Northern Rhodesia in the Days of the Charter.* Oxford, 1961.
GRAY, R. *The Two Nations: Aspects of the Development of Race Relations in the Rhodesias and Nyasaland.* London, 1960.
HAILEY, LORD. *Native Administration in the British African Territories, Part II.* London, 1950.
———. *An African Survey, revised 1956.* London, 1957.
HALL, R. *Zambia.* London, 1965.
HEPPLE, A. *South Africa.* London, 1966.
KAY, G. *A Social Geography of Zambia.* London, 1967.
KUCZYNSKI, R. R. *Demographic Survey of the British Colonial Empire.* London, 1942.
LEE, J. M. *Colonial Development and Good Government.* Oxford, 1967.
LEMARCHAND, R. *Political Awakening in the Belgian Congo.* Berkeley, 1964.
LEYS, C. *European Politics in Southern Rhodesia.* Oxford, 1959.
LEYS, C. and PRATT, C. *A New Deal in Central Africa.* London, 1960.
MASON, P. *Year of Decision.* London, 1960.
MULFORD, D. C. *Zambia, The Politics of Independence.* London, 1967.
RICHARDS, A. *Land, Labour and Diet in Northern Rhodesia.* London, 1939.
ROBINSON, R. and GALLAGHER, J. *Africa and the Victorians.* London, 1961.
ROTBERG, R. I. *The Rise of Nationalism in Central Africa.* Cambridge, Mass., 1966.
SEGAL, R. *Political Africa.* London, 1961.

TAYLOR, J. V. and LEHMANN, D. *Christians of the Copperbelt*. London, 1961.

WELENSKY, SIR ROY. *Welensky's 4000 Days*. London, 1964.

WISEMAN, H. V. *The Cabinet in the Commonwealth*. London, 1958.

Economic history

BALDWIN, R. E. *Economic Development and Export Growth: A Study of Northern Rhodesia, 1920–60*. Berkeley, 1966.

BARBER, W. J. *The Economy of British Central Africa*. London, 1961.

DEAN, E. *The Supply Responses of African Farmers*. Amsterdam, 1966.

DEANE, P. *Colonial Social Accounting*. Cambridge, 1953.

FRANKEL, S. H. *Capital Investment in Africa*. London, 1938.

HAZLEWOOD, A. 'The Economics of Federation and Dissolution in Central Africa', in *African Integration and Disintegration*, ed. A. Hazlewood. London, 1967.

HORWITZ, R. *The Political Economy of South Africa*. London, 1967.

KNIGHT, J. B. 'Wages and Zambia's Economic Development', in *Constraints on the Economic Development of Zambia*, ed. C. Elliot, Nairobi, 1971.

REYNOLDS, C. W. 'Development Problems of an Export Economy', in *Essays on the Chilean Economy*, eds. M. Mamalakis and C. W. Reynolds. Homewood, 1965.

VAN DER HORST, S. T. *Native Labour in South Africa*. London, 1942.

The copper-mining industry

BANCROFT, J. A. *Mining in Northern Rhodesia*, prepared by T. D. Guernsey. London, 1961.

BOHM, P. *Pricing of Copper in International Trade*. Stockholm, 1968.

BRADLEY, K. G. *Copper Venture*. London, 1952.

COLEMAN, F. L. *The Northern Rhodesian Copperbelt 1899–1962, Technological Development up to the End of the Central African Federation*, Manchester, 1971.

GREGORY, SIR THEODORE. *Ernest Oppenheimer and the Economic Development of Southern Africa*. Cape Town, 1962.

HERFINDAHL, O. C. *Copper Costs and Prices: 1870–1957*. Baltimore, 1959.

HURSTFIELD, J. *History of the Second World War: The Control of Raw Materials*. London, 1953.

MINING JOINT INDUSTRIAL COUNCIL. *African Advancement Proposals 1960*.

PRAIN, SIR RONALD. *Selected Papers 1953–7*. London, 1958.

——. *Selected Papers 1958–60*. London, 1961.

——. *Selected Papers 1961–64*. London, 1964.

RHODESIAN ANGLO AMERICAN. *Mining Developments in Northern Rhodesia*. Johannesburg, 1929.

WILLIAMS, H. M. *The Mining Law of Northern Rhodesia*. London, 1963.

Trade unions

BATES, R. H. *Unions, Parties and Political Development, a Study of Mineworkers in Zambia*, New Haven, 1971.

BERG, E. and BUTLER, J. 'Trade Unions', in *Political Parties and National Integration in Tropical Africa*, ed. J. Coleman and C. Rosberg. Los Angeles, 1964.

DAVIES, I. *African Trade Unions*. Harmondsworth, 1966.

MEYNAUD, J. and SALAH-BEH, A. *Le Syndicalisme Africain*. Paris, 1963.

MINERS' INTERNATIONAL FEDERATION. *Report of Proceedings of Thirty-Sixth International Congress*. Dortmund, 2–6 August 1954.

——. *Report of Proceedings of Thirty-Seventh International Congress*, London, 17–22 June 1957.

——. *Report of Proceedings of Thirty-Eighth International Congress*, Stockholm, 1–5 August 1960.

ROBERTS, B. C. *Labour in the Tropical Territories of the Commonwealth*. London, 1964.

SCOTT, R. *The Development of Trade Unions in Uganda*. Nairobi, 1966.

TRADE UNION CONGRESS, *Annual Report of Proceedings*, 1944, 1945.

WARMINGTON, W. A. *A West African Trade Union*. London, 1960.

WODDIS, J. *Africa, The Lion Awakes*. London, 1961.

Industrial relations

CITRINE, N. A. *Trade Union Law*. London, 1960.

FLANDERS, A. *Industrial Relations: What Is Wrong with the System?* London, 1965.

KAHN-FREUND, O. 'Legal Framework', in *The System of Industrial Relations in Great Britain*, ed. A. Flanders and H. A. Clegg. Oxford, 1964

KERR, C. and SIEGAL, A. 'The Interindustry Propensity to Strike—An International Comparison', in *Industrial Conflict*, ed. Kornhauser, Dubin and Ross. New York, 1954.

MCCARTHY, W. E. J. 'Compulsory Arbitration in Britain: The Work of the Industrial Disputes Tribunal', *Three Studies in Collective Bargaining*, Royal Commission on Trade Unions and Employers' Associations Research Papers, No. 8, 1968.

WEDDERBURN, K. W. *The Worker and The Law*. Harmondsworth, 1965.

Industrialization and social change

DAVIS, J. MERLE, ed. *Modern Industry and the African*. London, 1933.

EPSTEIN, A. L. *Politics in an Urban African Community*. Manchester, 1958.

FORDE, D., ed. *Social Implications of Industrialisation and Urbanization in Africa South of the Sahara*. Unesco, Paris, 1956.

HUNTER, G., ed. *Industrialisation and Race Relations*. London, 1965.

LEWIN, J. *The Colour Bar in the Copper Belt*. Johannesburg, 1941.

MINER, H., ed. *The City in Modern Africa*. New York, 1967.

MITCHELL, J. C. *African Urbanization in Ndola and Luanshya*. Rhodes–Livingstone Communication No. 6. Lusaka, 1954.

——. *The Kalela Dance*. Rhodes–Livingstone Paper No. 27. Manchester, 1956.

MOTTOULLE, L. *Contribution a l'étude du déterminisme fonctionnel de l'industrie dans l'éducation de l'indigène congolais*. Institut Royal Colonial Belge, Section des Sciences Morales et Politiques, III, 3, Brussels, 1934.

——. *Politique sociale de l'Union Minière du Haut-Katanga pour sa main-d'œuvre indigène* . . . Institut Royal Colonial Belge, Section des Sciences Morales et Politiques, XIV, 3, Brussels, 1946.

ORDE BROWNE, G. ST. J. *The African Labourer*. London, 1933.

RHODES–LIVINGSTONE INSTITUTE, 11th Conference Proceedings, *Present Interrelations in Central African Rural and Urban Life*, ed. R. J. Apthorpe, 1958.

——. 12th Conference Proceedings, *Social Relations in Central African Industry*, ed. R. J. Apthorpe and D. Matthews, 1958.

SOUTHALL, A., ed. *Social Change in Modern Africa*. London, 1961.

WATSON, W. Tribal Cohesion in a Money Economy. Manchester, 1958.

WILSON, G. *An Essay on the Economics of Detribalisation*. Livingstone, 1941–2.

(4) *Articles in periodicals*

BETTISON, D. 'The Poverty Datum Line in Central Africa', in *Rhodes–Livingstone Journal*, no. 27, June 1960.

——. 'Factors in the Determination of Wage Rates in Central Africa', in *Rhodes–Livingstone Journal*, no. 28, December 1960.

——. 'Reply to Thomson and Kay', in *Rhodes–Livingstone Journal*, no. 30, December 1961.

CLAUSEN, L. 'On Attitudes Towards Industrial Conflict in Zambian Industry', *African Social Research*, 2 December, 1966.

COOMBE, T. 'The Origins of Secondary Education in Zambia', *African Social Research*, 3–5, 1967–8.

GANN, L. H. 'The Northern Rhodesia Copper Industry and the World of Copper: 1923–52', *Rhodes–Livingstone Journal*, no. 18, 1955.

GORE-BROWNE, S. 'Legislative Council in Northern Rhodesia Twenty Years Ago', *Northern Rhodesia Journal*, vol. ii, no. 4, 1954.

HOCHSCHILD, H. K. 'Labour Relations in Northern Rhodesia', *Annals of the American Academy of Political and Social Science*, ccvi, July 1956.

HOOKER, J. R. 'The African Worker in Southern Rhodesia: Black Aspirations in a White Economy 1927–36', *Race*: vol. vi, no. 2, October 1964.

——. 'The Role of the Labour Department in the Birth of African Trade Unionism in Northern Rhodesia', *International Review of Social History*, vol. x, 1, 1965.

MAXWELL, SIR JAMES C. 'Some Aspects of Native Policy in Northern Rhodesia', *Journal of the African Society*, vol. xxix, no. CXVII, October 1930.

MENZIES, I. R. 'Tribalism in an Industrial Community', 16th Conference, Proceedings of the Rhodes–Livingstone Institute, *The Multitribal Society*, Lusaka, 1962.

MITCHELL, J. C. 'The Distribution of African Labour by Area of Origin on the Copper Mines of Northern Rhodesia', *Rhodes–Livingstone Journal*, no. 14, 1954.

MOORE, R. J. B. 'Native Wages and the Standard of Living in Northern Rhodesia', *African Studies*, vol. i, no. 2, June 1942.

OPPENHEIMER, SIR ERNEST. 'The Advancement of Africans in Industry', *Optima*, vol. iii, no. 3, 1953.

OPPENHEIMER, H. 'Sir Ernest Oppenheimer: A Portrait by his son' *Optima*, vol. ii, no. 3, September 1967.

PERLMAN, R. 'The Great Copper Killing', *Management To-day*, September 1966.

ROTBERG, R. I. 'Race Relations and Politics in Colonial Zambia: The Elwell Incident', *Race*, vol. vii, no. 7, July 1965.

SANDERSON, F. E. 'Labour Migration from Nyasaland', *The Journal of African History*, vol. ii, no. 2, 1962.

SPEARPOINT, F. 'The African Native and the Rhodesia Copper Mines', supplement to the *Journal of the Royal African Society*, vol. xxxvi, no. CXLIV, July 1937.

Index